TICKET
TO
EVERYWHERE

The Best of **Detours** Travel Column

As seen in the *Chicago Sun-Times*

Dave Hoekstra

First Edition

LAKE CLAREMONT PRESS

4650 North Rockwell Street • Chicago, Illinois 60625
www.lakeclaremont.com

**Ticket to Everywhere: The Best of *Detours* Travel Column
by Dave Hoekstra**

Published November, 2000 by:

4650 N. Rockwell St.
Chicago, IL 60625
773/583-7800; lcp@lakeclaremont.com
www.lakeclaremont.com

Publisher's Cataloging-in-Publication
(Provided by Quality Books, Inc.)

Hoekstra, Dave.
 Ticket to everywhere : the best of Detours travel
column / by Dave Hoekstra. — 1st ed.
 p. cm.
 Includes index.
 LCCN: 00-107839
 ISBN: 1-893121-11-9

 1. Middle West—History—20th century. 2. Middle
West—Description and travel. 3. United States Highway
66—Description and travel.   I. Title

F351.H64 2000   977.033
                       QBI00-839

**Printed in the United States of America by United Graphics,
an employee-owned company based in Mattoon, Illinois.**

04 03 02 01 00   10 9 8 7 6 5 4 3 2 1

There are endearing remembrances of a personal odyssey, a journalist growing up. In 1938 and 1939 I joined the WPA writers' project. I wrote radio scripts, state travel guides and histories. Although I didn't get into writing until the 1950s, this was what I called *guerrilla* journalism. That's what this is. *Guerrilla* journalism. Enjoy!

—STUDS TERKEL

Studs Terkel worked on the American Guide Series, hailed as the nation's first "self-portrait," including the legendary WPA Guide to Illinois in 1939.

PUBLISHER'S CREDITS

Cover design by Timothy Kocher. Artwork "Vehicle" by and courtesy of Tony Fitzpatrick. Interior design by Sharon Woodhouse and Ken Woodhouse. Layout by Sharon Woodhouse and Ken Woodhouse. Input by Ken Woodhouse and Amy Formanski. Proofreading by Karen Formanski, Sharon Woodhouse, Dave Hoekstra, Gabriel Robinson, and Ken Woodhouse. Photos by Lisa Day, Dave Hoekstra, and others as listed. Maps by Lisa Day. Index by Karen Formanski. The text of *Ticket to Everywhere* was set in Toure with heads in DomCasual and Edifice.

NOTE

Contents

5. Indiana

6. Ohio

7. Wisconsin

8. Iowa/Minnesota

9. Route 66

10. Drive South

Acknowledgments

There are many people to thank for the spirit behind this book. Deep appreciation to Andrea Hanis, Margaret Maples, Nigel Wade, Mary Cameron Frey, Lon Grahnke and Marily Hollman for their encouragement, and the *Chicago Sun-Times* library staff of Herb Ballard, Virginia Davis, Terri Golembiewski, Judith Halper, Dale McCullough, Ron Theel, Zig Ulmanis and Ted White—all of whom assisted with invaluable research over the years.

Also thanks to Maureen Geoghegan and Annice Tatken for road inspirations, publisher Sharon Woodhouse, Tony Fitzpatrick for the art and title, Angelo Varias for his friendship and Mom, Dad and Doug for the first road trips across U.S. 40. Deep appreciation also goes out to my 1997 Pontiac Sunfire that got me through most of these essays.

And loving gratitude to Lisa, who has taught me many lessons along the road. As we learn to separate past from present, we can better see objectivity.

A good road trip is about a sense of place.

After all the maps, mileage and mayhem have been cast aside, it's the discovery of a moment that will stay with you. Rolling trips down Route 66 and stops in forgotten Midwestern inns and diners aren't always about nostalgia. They're about understanding your place in the world.

It happened to me many times in the essays that appear in this book. I felt confidence to face the future while casting pennies in a Wishing Well motel; I was humbled by the love between the couple who run the Kitch-Inn restaurant in Mendota, Ill.; and I rediscovered a childlike innocence while walking into a Polynesian restaurant-Tiki bar in Columbus, Ohio. That wacky Kahiki was still bigger than life—just as it was the first time I walked in when I was a kid.

As you write your own ticket to everywhere, remain modest. Move softly. Turn down the Steve Earle and Jimmy LaFave cassettes and listen to all that is around you. Don't be afraid to go left when the sign says right. Rendezvous with old friends to see them in a new light.

And consider the words of Arthur Frommer, the big kahuna of travel writers, who wrote, "Travel is a chance to bring your provincial habits and prejudices and rub them up against the real world. . . . Travel means the free movement of people across boundaries. It is the essence of peace."

Somewhere along the way, these themes will slowly begin to connect in a landscape shaped by fast lanes and white lines. And at that particular moment in time you will know you have arrived.

—DAVE HOEKSTRA
AUGUST, 2000

ROAD
ESSAYS

ż·p.   V E H I C L E   TF 99

Photo by Dave Hoekstra.

Just north of Gardner, Illinois, on Route 66.

Burma-Shave jingles embark on comeback

Chatty Charley bought a phone
for his car
He didn't go far
While juggling java
It slipped down his arm
He bought the farm
Burma-Shave

The Burma-Shave sign painters would have been in a lather about all of today's technological bumps in the road. Between 1925 and 1963 more than 600 warm and fuzzy rhymes were planted on rural highways across America.

There was nothing fancy about the lines on the pine signs.

Like roadside graffiti, the Burma-Shave couplet was written on five sequential signs. A sixth sign said "Burma-Shave," plugging the brushless shaving cream made at Burma-Vita Co. in Minneapolis.

Burma-Shave signs were strategically placed along farmers' property lines. Participating farmers even received a "Burma Shavings" newsletter and farmers who maintained the signs were placed on an honor roll.

Cincinnati filmmaker Jim Delaney wrote and produced a comprehensive 53-minute entertainment documentary "Signs & Rhymes of Burma-Shave," ($29.95; write to Sentimental Productions, Box 14716, Cincinnati, Ohio, 45250).

"I remembered the signs," said Delaney, a 50-year-old former police reporter and city editor of the Cincinnati Enquirer newspaper. "One of the most intriguing things to me was the size of the company. Here's a company that had only 35 employees and eight trucks. Yet, they got into the consciousness of America. Almost everybody remembers the jingles."

The Odell family of Minneapolis originated the foamy stuff based on a mysterious liniment that grandfather Clinton Odell brewed from ingredients a company chemist supposedly picked up in Burma.

But the company was at a dead end until Odell's sons, Leonard and Allan, signed on. Allan installed the first signs in Minnesota along U.S. 61 near Red Wing and Route 65 near Lakeville.

Allan wrote most of the signs until the 1930s, when the company began a popular contest soliciting roadside prose came from across America. Allan helped choose contest winners. A $100 cash prize was awarded for each of the top 25 jingles. Leonard died in 1991 at the age of 83. Allen died in 1994 at the age of 90. Delaney's 1991 video was played at a reception following Allan's funeral. He had interviewed Allan six months before his death. "I was attracted to the story because this was a family-run company," Delaney said. "And through all the production the Odells were true to that."

Allan was married for 66 years to Grace, 91, who still lives in suburban Minneapolis. She said Allan would get some of his best ideas in the middle of the night. "I had to have a flashlight and a piece of paper by the bed," Grace recalled recently by phone. "He'd wake me up and have me write down his little rhymes. I knew he was that witty when I met him [at a summer resort in Wisconsin]."

In the "Signs & Rhymes" video, Leonard admitted the Odell family was bucking three elements of bad luck in trying to get Burma-Shave started. His father, a former Minneapolis attorney and insurance man, was broke. Serial advertising signs had never been done before. And no one had heard of brushless shaving cream.

During their peak popularity in the 1950s, 7,000 sets of Burma-Shave signs were in 45 continental states.

"Allan had to drive to all the states . . . to get permission to put the signs up," Grace recalled. "We had great fun on our road trips."

The Burma-Vita Co. was sold to Phillip Morris Inc. in 1963. In Delaney's video, Leonard recounts that as company president he fought with Phillip Morris for six months to keep the signs alive. But big business won out.

"In retrospect, the family would agree that the creation of the interstate highways in the early 1960s changed driving habits so much the idea wouldn't have worked as well as it did with two-lane roads," Delaney said. "It wasn't so much a company takeover."

Burma-Shave existed until 1967 as a Phillip Morris spinoff

under the American Safety Razor Co. umbrella. The razor company took the product name when it became a separate entity in the 1970s.

Last year the American Safety Razor Co. launched an encore version of the Burma-Shave product, erecting replica signs along highways in more than a dozen states as well as minor league baseball parks. The Staunton, Va., based company also created television commercials that aired on CNN and ESPN.

But a set of Allan Odell's original favorite Burma-Shave signs stand in the Smithsonian Institution. It's a verse he wrote in 1933:

> *Within this vale*
> *Of toil*
> *And sin*
> *Your head grows bald*
> *But not your chin.*
> *Burma-Shave.*

May 17, 1998

Auto bingo:
A faithful friend on the road

One of the most rewarding moments of going on the road is when you recognize a sign of the times. Good times. You can be motoring along a country two-laner and suddenly see a polished Royal Blue 1948 Plymouth your grandfather might have driven. Or, standing in a distant field there will be a full-service gas station—with bells ringing at every gallon.

That's what Auto Bingo means to me.

Auto Bingo is as basic as it sounds. Five squares across, five squares down, one free square in the middle on a cardboard magenta card. Each square is devoted to a roadside attraction: Barn. Bus. Pig. Wheelbarrow. Each square features a plastic sliding door that is to be shut when a sleepy passenger notices the appropriate attraction. "Silo." Yes! High-five.

Auto Bingo was invented in 1960 by Regal Games Mfg., at Irving Park and North Elston. Auto Bingo is so cool because it seems so outdated in a world of Game Boys and other computer toys. I always keep a couple of Auto Bingo cards in my glove compartment.

"We've had our ups and downs," said Kurt Geringer, president of Regal Games, founded in 1945. Geringer, 56, has worked at Regal since 1956. "When those computer games first came out in the 1980s, it took us for a loop," he said. "But it always comes back. We took a nose dive last year because Milton Bradley and Parker Brothers started putting out games like Travel Monopoly, Travel Yahtzee, miniaturized games. At one time there was no competition in the travel category; there's 45 items now. But this year we've had a large rebound."

Auto Bingo is a hands-on project. Only 10 people work at the Regal Games plant. Geringer designs the graphics and updates the concept himself. "For instance, a couple years ago I redid Auto Bingo," Geringer explained. "I took the pig off. Another one had a chicken on it. I took that off. You don't find the family farm along the side of the road as much anymore. So I substituted other items, like a public telephone and a satellite dish."

A two-card package of Auto Bingo retails between $2.95 and $3.95, depending on the outlet. I've found Auto Bingo in high-class truck stops. Most Osco drugstores and Stuckey's sell Auto

Bingo. And because of a loyal distribution deal, Regal road games can be found in almost every National Park in America.

"Auto Bingo started because we made fingertip bingo cards by using the same little windows," Geringer said. "In 1960 our former president [now retired] Erich Spitznerwe came up with the Auto Bingo concept. It's been a mainstay ever since. I came up with some of the ones that followed it."

Those would be Find-a-Car Bingo, where a passenger is one the lookout for different car models; Traffic Safety Bingo, which features only traffic signs; and Interstate Highway Bingo, which is the same idea as Auto Bingo, except there are more state troopers.

Geringer did not mention Trucker's Angst Bingo.

He did reminisce about playing car bingo as he drove his light blue 1965 Bonneville Pontiac north during summer jaunts to the Wisconsin Dells. Geringer and his wife, May, have two sons, Kurt, 33, and Michael, 30.

"Our glove compartment was full of all the games," he said. "The boys would keep themselves occupied for hours. They were very competitive. Sometimes items like power lines did get pretty easy to spot. That's why we came out with the Interstate Highway edition. There's items on Auto Bingo you won't find on I-40 or I-80, like [the interstate] perpetual road repair sign.

"But Auto Bingo has become an item where we find second- and third-generation buyers out there. Moms and pops played it as kids. They want their kids to play it, too."

On a recent trip to the New Orleans Jazz & Heritage Festival, local club owner Bill FitzGerald and I were talking about Auto Bingo and the Hall of Fame of Road Games. FitzGerald's wife, Kate, loves Auto Bingo.

"She remembered it from when she was a kid," said FitzGerald, who has four children between the ages of 3 and 13. "We bought it for our kids. Then, of course, there's the alphabet game."

Of course.

"That's a competition where you're driving along and you have to find the correct letters [in alphabetical order]," FitzGerald explained. "You always have trouble with 'Q' and 'X,' but now 'X' is easy [because of Exit]. Whoever gets 'Z' wins.

"It's an honor system, you basically have to shout out your letter. Kids are looking at license plates. It's a vision test as far as

Courtesy of Regal Games Mfg. Co., Inc. of Chicago.

staying alert. It's kind of exciting. If someone is lazy, they'll lose out."

Bill, it's just a game.

Here are some other Fourth of July road game memories from

folks who have spent some quality—and not so quality—time on the road.

"We used to play 'Who Am I?,'" said Jon Langford of the Mekons. "You could 'be' any person and people would have 20 'no's.' There would be 10 of us in a horrible van with no air conditioning and the cassette machine would be broken. Once you got someone up to 20 'no's,' you've won.

"Sally [Timms, Mekon vocalist] is always Hitler or Flipper. Another good one is [to be] someone who is in the van. Or your manager. Then we broadened the game to where you could be colors, abstract concepts or corporations. The best one then was Aer Lingus, the Irish airlines."

Brian Henneman is guitarist-lead vocalist for the road-weary Bottle Rockets. "We have two road games," Henneman said. "We buy Country Weekly magazine, and we guess the hits from five years ago.

"But our big game is to pick a subject from A to Z. For example, you could pick [country singer] 'Mindy McCready.' The four of us go around and somebody gets 'A' and they go 'awful.' Then 'B' would be 'beautiful.' Whoever gets 'X' gives the standard answer—'xylophonic.' That game really passes the time well."

June 28, 1998

The original road-foodie

Duncan Hines first made his name by eating his way across America

A good road trip was icing on the cake for Duncan Hines.

Hines was America's first nationally known independent food critic. His *Adventures in Good Eating* paperback books were kept in most of the country's automobile glove compartments from 1935 until his death in 1959.

These days, Duncan Hines is better known as a cake mix.

A native of Bowling Green, Ky., Hines drove around the country in the early 1930s designing and writing corporate brochures. During his travels he jotted down notes on his favorite restaurants. He would share these tips with friends.

Hines' humble treasures were so popular that he printed a booklet listing 167 favorite dining spots in 30 states and mailed 1,000 copies out as a Christmas card in 1935. The following year Hines published his first *Adventures in Good Eating*. He also wrote spinoff books such as *Lodging for a Night* and the cutting-edge *The Art of Carving in the Home*.

Hines had an acquired taste for the simple life.

The first thing the rotund road scholar did when he walked into a restaurant was sniff, according to a 1986 national historic tour sponsored by the Duncan Hines Co. One of Hines' favorite mottos was, "Good Food Smells Good." Hines would usually ask to see the kitchen. If his request was denied, he left without eating. Chicago investigative reporter/kitchen krusader Pam Zekman would love this guy.

Hines was a champion of regional cuisine, a trend that has resurfaced in the 1990s. Since transportation and refrigeration systems were erratic in the 1930s and 1940s, Hines reasoned that locally grown foods were bound to be the freshest.

Here's a snippet from a 1956 interview of Hines in the old Chicago American newspaper: ". . . He and his wife are inseparable. Their day—always on the road—goes like this: Up at 6, first breakfast by 7, then rolling down the highway in an air-conditioned Cadillac. A second breakfast. A nice lunch.

"Then, said Hines: 'At 4 in the afternoon we stop. We shower, nap a couple of hours, enjoy a leisurely dinner. A light supper and into bed by 10.' On the road they eat lightly, though often. Both have good digestion. Hines said, 'My last snack, before bedtime, like my first breakfast, is corn flakes and vanilla ice cream. Try it. Sleep like a rock.' "

I'd sleep like a rock, too, with a life like that.

Over the years Hines had offices in Ithaca, N.Y., and Bowling Green, Ky. He employed a skeleton staff of eight people, three for clerical duties and five "traveling representatives" who would do sanitation checks on restaurants and roadside rest stops that had the "Duncan Hines Recommends" sign outside blowing in the wind.

Hines relied on a "volunteer" network of more than 300 foodies across the country who would find places to be included in *Adventures in Good Eating*, which shook down as a mid-1900s Zagat Survey.

Between 1905 and 1931 Hines lived in Chicago. His favorite restaurants included the Golden Ox, 1578 N. Clybourn, the old Red Star Inn and Wrigley Building Restaurant. In his 1955 autobiography, *Duncan Hines Food Odyssey,* he wrote about the pizzazz of the Pump Room, "You'd do well, if this is your first visit, to order something that comes off a flaming sword."

Interest in convenience foods heated up after World War II, and in 1948 Hines was approached by the director of a farmer's cooperative who was entering the food marketing business. The cooperative's first product was a cake mix that called for fresh eggs instead of the dehydrated eggs usually included in box mixes. Hines lent his name to the product. *Presto!* Duncan Hines, the company, was born.

The Procter & Gamble Co. purchased the cake maker in 1956. Just last year Procter & Gamble sold it to Aurora Foods of San Francisco. Ian Wilson is chairman of the board and CEO of Aurora Foods. A native of South Africa who has lived on every continent but South America, he is more aware of Duncan Hines as a cake mix than a roaming restaurant critic.

"But we base all our marketing on nostalgia to a degree," Wilson said last week in a phone interview. "Our brands average 70 years old, so Duncan Hines is one of the youngest. When brands have a heritage that long, they have a huge reservoir of brand equity. We've got Aunt Jemima, Log Cabin Syrup, which is over 100 years old, Mrs. Butterworth, Mrs. Paul's Seafood, Mama Celeste Pizza. So Duncan Hines is the only man in our stable."

January 24, 1999

POSTSCRIPT:

Several years ago, Hines' widow, Clara, donated Duncan's cookbooks, scrapbooks, promotional material, recipes and newspaper clippings to the Division of Rare and Manuscript Collections at Cornell University. For more information on the life of Duncan Hines, write the Cornell University Kroch Library, Ithaca, N.Y. 14853.

Soulmates in love, work
Building an inn and a marriage

Interior decorating.

Now that's a way to test any romance. But Alex and Phyllis Madonna have fixed up 110 different hotel rooms at their Madonna Inn in San Luis Obispo, Calif. And they've been happily married for 48 years.

The one-of-a-kind hotel is just off Highway 1, halfway between Los Angeles and San Francisco. The Madonna Inn has no religious significance, and the singer of the same name never has stayed there. But Barbra Streisand is a regular customer. As is Dom DeLuise. President Reagan slept here once.

The Madonna Inn is my favorite romantic getaway.

Let met count the ways: "The Caveman Room," the hotel's most requested room, features solid rock floors, walls and ceilings, as well as a rock shower, and sinks that are recast as waterfalls. A small couch is finished in leopard-pattern upholstery. And a custom hand-crafted stained-glass window welcomes natural light into "The Caveman Room." Me Tarzan, you Jane.

Photo by Phyllis Madonna. Courtesy of the Madonna Inn.

The Madonna Inn's rock-studded Caveman Room.

Of course, the Madonnas have decorated a small room called "Romance," a split-level semi-suite painted in baby blues and an opal-glittered ceiling. "Romance" is accented with hand-carved beams and furnished with a king-sized bed.

Each room is as different as the Hatfields and McCoys.

"We've never had a disagreement," Phyllis says, with Alex listening on a phone extension. "Alex gets the ideas and I follow through." Alex adds, "Most of our rooms run in sequence, four or five in a group. Like the 'Swiss Room' is followed by the 'Edelweiss,' 'Matterhorn,' 'Carin' [cah-reen, the Swiss term for endearment] and 'Swiss Belle.' With each room being different, you can't make the same mistake twice."

Phyllis says, "You make more people happy by having a bigger variety. We always discuss back and forth how we wanted to do this. We love everything we see. So we decided to do everything. Fortunately, we enjoy the same things. I've heard so many people say they have problems, if they redo one room. We've worked closely together all our lives."

The Madonna Inn's 110 rooms are in three separate buildings that rest on 2,200 acres at the base of Mount Serro San Luis on the California Central Coast.

You don't even have to get a room to enjoy the Madonna Inn. Tourists just passing by can relax in one of the pink leather heartshaped booths in the outrageous Gold Rush Dining Room or have a drink in the "Let's Eat and Forever Be Happy" bar, peppered with copperwork, German wood carvings and red leather stools and booths.

Then there's the wine cellar men's room. The Madonna Inn postcards (all photographs by Phyllis Madonna) call it "the most talked about men's room in the world."

And where else can you buy a postcard of a men's room?

The urinal is a rock waterfall accented by huge clamshell sinks. As you step up to the urinal, an electric eye is triggered. Water cascades down the rocks, which creates a waterfall flush. Every time I've been to the Madonna Inn, I've seen women sneaking in the men's room for a peek at the bathroom, which looks like something out of a Flinstonian Sybaris.

"He was trying to outdo me, if you want to know the truth," Phyllis says. Alex says, "That's true. She did a heck of a job on the ladies' room." That room has gold tassels dangling from an overhead canopy. "The doors going to the ladies' stalls are hand-

Photo by Phyllis Madonna. Courtesy of the Madonna Inn.

The pink leather booths of the Madonna Inn's steakhouse.

crafted in red leather and velvet. The floor and walls are made out of pink marble," Alex says.

Even the registration desk is done in pink marble with pink carpets on the office floor.

Alex, 78, is a native of San Luis Obispo. A contractor by trade, he built and paved 148 miles of Highway 1 between San Luis Obispo and Monterey.

He planned and built the Madonna Inn himself. "I went to several architects and didn't get anywhere." So he built it the way he saw it.

The first 12 rooms were completed by Christmas Eve, 1958. Through the heat of passion, a bunch of lovebirds inadvertently helped burn down the original rooms in 1960.

"We had baseboard heat," Alex says. "Not knowing enough about the business, we didn't do some things right. That was one of them. We had seven honeymooners. One of them threw the blankets down against the heater, and when it caught fire the whole thing went up in no time."

The Madonnas live in a house on the north side of San Luis Obispo. They have four children between the ages of 29 and 44.

Alex met Phyllis when he returned to California from a stint in the Air Corps Engineers. He was working on a highway in Orchid, about 40 miles south of San Luis Obispo. He took a break at a diner called Elmer's.

"I went there for lunch, and she was giving a birthday cake to a friend of hers working in Union Oil's main office," Alex recalls. "I saw her a couple times later. We just clicked.

Phyllis says, "It only took one date. And I was hooked. We've always had a lot in common."

Alex says, "She says 'Frog,' and I jump."

Phyllis says, "You know what he's saying? *I'm* the one that jumps. But I love him, you know. And then you do."

The Madonna Inn is at 100 Madonna Rd., San Luis Obispo, Calif. 93405. Rooms for two people range from $127 to $230 per night. (800) 543-9666.

May 3, 1998

POSTSCRIPT:

Alex and Phyllis Madonna celebrated their 50th wedding anniversary on Dec. 28, 1999. Friends and family gathered at the Madonna Inn for barbecued chicken, lobster, steaks and big band dancing. Guests dined on a three-tiered pink and gold wedding cake adorned with dozens of miniature gold cherubs. Time takes care of everything. The Madonnas never had a formal wedding reception when they were married in Las Vegas, Nev.

ILLINOIS

VEHICLE

a.p.

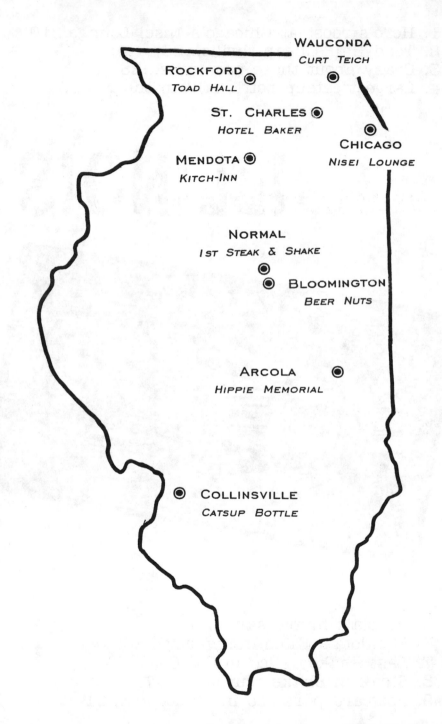

WAUCONDA
Curt Teich

ROCKFORD
Toad Hall

ST. CHARLES
Hotel Baker

CHICAGO
Nisei Lounge

MENDOTA
Kitch-Inn

NORMAL
1st Steak & Shake

BLOOMINGTON
Beer Nuts

ARCOLA
Hippie Memorial

COLLINSVILLE
Catsup Bottle

Map by Lisa Day.

Hero's roost
Nisei Lounge started as a haven

CHICAGO, Ill.—Sometimes the glories of travel can be found at home.

Just about every night Kenny Kuzuharu, a regular, wanders into the Nisei Lounge, 3439 N. Sheffield Chicago. The Nisei are second-generation American-born children of Japanese immigrants. (The Gosei are fifth-generation Japanese-Americans.)

This 76-year-old Nisei will always sit on the same barstool. He will always order a dollar draught of Hamm's beer. Once in a while he looks across the bar into a mirror and cracks himself up. Kuzuharu has an enchanting toothless grin, punctuated by a thin white Confucius goatee. He's known as one of the last great wanderers in the Wrigley Field neighborhood, bringing to mind the J. R. R. Tolkien travel line:

Not all those who wander are lost.

During World War I, Kuzuharu was a member (field artillery) of the all-Japanese 100th Infantry Battalion/442nd Regimental Combat Team, the most decorated unit in American military history. In 1998 Hasbro Inc. even introduced a Nisei G.I. Joe in commemoration of the 442nd.

Japan's bombing of Pearl Harbor marked the United States' entry into World War II. The Japanese-American community felt shame for the actions of their ancestral home. As a display of patriotism, the community complied with government orders removing them from their homes on the West Coast and thousands of young men volunteered for service in the armed forces.

Kuzuharu was one of a few hundred who returned home.

He fought in a war while his family was interned behind barbed-wire fences in Colorado.

"He's decorated from here," says Nisei Lounge co-owner Scott Martin as he points to his collarbone, "to there," and he moves his hand to his belt. Down the bar, Kuzuharu is chain-smoking under the warmth of a dark green ski cap. He mumbles aloud. The world spins around him.

And the Wrigley Field neighborhood has turned a tad more Japanese after the Cubs' historic trip to Tokyo last month. When the lounge opened in its current location in 1958, Chicago was home to more than 150,000 Japanese-Americans, about 30,000 of whom had been interned in camps during World War I. Lake View was home to many Japanese-Americans who since have moved to the suburbs.

"That's how this bar came to be," says Martin, 39. "After the war ended they were back with their families. Having lost all their property by going in the camps, they came to the Midwest to find work. They'd go into a bar after work and the white guys would tell 'em, 'Get the heck out of here.' "

So Kaunch Hirabayashi opened the original Nisei Lounge in 1950 at Clark and Division. "It was a place for Niseis to go and be with themselves," Martin said. Kuzuharu's longtime pal Jimmy Isuha had been a Nisei Lounge bartender for a quarter-century and he purchased the bar in the mid-1970s. The Hawaii native has no role in the business today, outside of dropping in every Friday night to say hello.

In 1993 Dave Jemilo of Green Mill jazz club fame bought the Nisei and brought in Martin as a partner. The pair had worked together for 10 years at Jemilo's old Vu tavern on North Lincoln Avenue. In 1997 Jemilo sold his portion of the Nisei to Mike Flammang, a former manager at the Sports Center.

No one ever considered changing the bar's name to accommodate the changing upscale neighborhood. (See Hi-Tops, Fuel, etc.) "People always ask what the name means," Martin explains. "We tell them, they look around the room and say, 'Well, there's nothing Japanese here.' That's the point. They were Americans. They were walking in with construction boots, drinking Schlitz and smoking cigarettes.

"We had a friend who brought in an original sign that said 'All Japanese citizens must report and bring a list of property . . . ' It was a cool piece of history. I asked Kenny if we should put it up, and he got angry."

At one time Kuzuharu was a teacher, but he is best-known as the longtime dishwasher at the defunct Chester's (now "The Hamburger King") just south of the Nisei Lounge. He remembers a time when there was more than one Japanese tavern in Lake View. "Bento," Kuzuharu mumbles in reference to the former Japanese-American bar that is now the Texas Star Fajita Bar, 3365 N. Clark.

With last year's closing of the beloved Wrigleyville Tap, 3724 N. Clark, the Nisei Lounge is one of a handful of neighborhood bars that remain around the ballpark. As a lost semi-regular from Wrigleyville Tap, I'm auditioning places for my post-game pout. The worldly Nisei Lounge will fit the bill.

The place is warm and fuzzy funky, adorned with a couple of pool tables that date back to 1958 and a CD jukebox that includes "The Best of Dean Martin," Buddy Guy's "Feels Like Rain" and Johnny Cash's "Live at Folsom Prison and San Quentin." There are four television sets spaced around the room, and a couple of crooked framed Japanese ideograms hang behind the bar.

During the 1980s Los Angeles Dodgers manager Tommy Lasorda and coach Joe Amalfitano would hit the Nisei Lounge after a game, and longtime Cubs equipment manager Yosh Kawano has been known to stop in for a visit.

"It's always frustrated me that bars take advantage of the ballpark in that their beers go up to $4.75 to match the price at Wrigley Field," Martin says. "I couldn't look anybody in the eye and charge $4.75 for a bottle of beer. Maybe I'm dumb."

The Nisei Lounge offers 14 different beers that range between $2.50 and $3.50 a bottle. (Huber beer is always $1.50 a bottle.) The Japanese beer menu consists of Sapporo, Asahi and Kirin (brewed in the states by Anheuser-Busch), all $3.50 a bottle.

And, of course, there's a limited menu of cold and warm sake at $3 a shot. I'd recommend the cool Momokawa Pearl, a roughly filtered uncut cold sake with a 20 percent alcohol content. It is the only nagori ginshu sake available in the United States. Its cloudiness is reminiscent of sakes of the past.

It is better—and safer—on the rocks.

Martin is also the sole owner of the popular Simon's Tavern, 5210 N. Clark in Andersonville. "That's the only Swedish bar left in that neighborhood," says Martin, who is half-Swede. "And I have the only Japanese bar in this neighborhood." Martin is not half-Japanese.

He was born and reared in Andersonville. His father, Thomas, is a retired vice president of the Chicago & North Western Ry. budget department. His mother, Delores, was a secretary at Ebenezer Lutheran Church, 1650 W. Foster.

While standing in the heart of a neighborhood that is shaped for heroes, Martin tells Kuzuharu he is his idol. Then, as Martin walks away he whispers, "When I first bought the bar, the first three people I threw out of here were people who were not treating Kenny right. And to this day, if anyone messes with him, they have to leave."

An artist's warm rendering of Kuzuharu is on the back of the Nisei Lounge blue souvenir baseball jerseys. At $30 each, they make great road garb. And the spirit behind the shirt is sure to move you.

April 16, 2000

Heap thrills
Toad Hall has mania for collecting

ROCKFORD, Ill.—From a distance, time seems to have passed Rockford by.

Last summer the Rockford Cubbies Class A baseball team left town for greener pastures in Dayton, Ohio. And in late November, Mayor Daley pilfered the Rockford Time Museum. He formed a committee to raise $25 million in private funds to acquire the collection of 1,500 timepieces. It is destined for the Museum of Science and Industry.

But one thing in Rockford keeps on ticking.

That's the Toad Hall Books and Records store, 2106 Broadway.

For a road trip with ample time passages, check out this place. Toad Hall has more than 235,000 33s, 45s and 78s from 1895 to the present. The 10-room complex also stocks 60,000 books and 20,000 pieces of sheet music.

Toad Hall's growing popularity denotes the academic shift toward nostalgia. Back in the 20th century, someone would walk into a place like Toad Hall and dismiss it as a junk shop filled with obsessive characters.

Photo by Lisa Day.

But a Dec. 31 Wall Street Journal article noted that the spiraling value of once overlooked flea market items such as cookbooks can be attributed to the fact that academics are looking at these objects as source documents. They show how people lived day-to-day instead of focusing on major events and political movements.

"It's certainly a developing area," said Bernard Beck, associate professor of sociology at Northwestern University. "Historians are more and more interested in telling the story of the lives of ordinary people, very often discovering things other than documents.

"Ordinary people don't write as much. So if historians want to find out about people who don't write about certain aspects of their lives, they have to find other ways of doing it—what they're reading, what they're using, the music they were listening to."

Presto!

I knew if I lived long enough there would be justification for past Toad Hall purchases of a vintage 1950 edition of Duncan Hines' *Adventures in Good Eating (Good Eating Places Along the Highways of America)* and a mint "Houston" LP by Dean Martin (with orchestra conducted by Bill Justis and produced by Jimmy Bowen, who went on to discover Garth Brooks).

Toad Hall owners Beverly and Larry Mason appropriately picked the store's name from *The Wind in the Willows* children's book. "Whenever Mr. Toad got an interest in something, it immediately became a mania," Beverly says, surrounded by LPs like Lorne Greene's "Welcome to the Ponderosa" and early 1940s pulp magazines such as "The Shadow."

"That's the way it is here. Larry had a passing interest in 78s. Now we have maybe 150,000 78s. I'm the same way with books. Comic books? We started out with 150 from my own collection. Within a few years we had 60,000. Pulp magazines are another one of my passions. My favorite is "The Spider." The body count is higher. We don't do anything by halves."

The Smithsonian Institution has purchased Duke Ellington material from Toad Hall for its collection. And the Chicago Public Library bought a stack of vintage 1960s WLS-AM Silver Dollar Surveys.

The Masons were married in 1970. Beverly, 63, met Larry, 57, in a Rockford bookstore. Beverly was reared in the small village of Norway, some 65 miles west of Chicago. She was an art major at Malcolm X College.

Larry hails from Minnesota. In the late 1980s the former Chicago public high school teacher was one of the highest rated speed chess players in northern Illinois.

In 1996 Larry suffered a serious stroke that shut down the right side of his body. But he still makes the daily trek to Toad Hall with his wife. His memory is as sharp as a tack, especially when it comes to inventory.

Among the clutter, he finds sanctity.

I mention the renewed interest in cookbooks to the Masons. Not surprisingly, Beverly says, "I collect cookbooks, too. We have between 1,200 and 1,500 cookbooks—more if you count cooking pamphlets.

"My earliest cookbook dates from the 1820s. I sold the chef at Cafe Patou [Rockford's best dining spot, a country French restaurant at 3929 Broadway, 815-227-4100] my two best cookbooks."

Chef Philippe Forcioli bought *Lemery on Foods and Drinkables*, an English cookbook from 1745, and *Culina Famulatrix Medicinae*, an American cookbook from 1806. He paid between $600 and $800 for the pair. "But he got a bargain," she says, "because he's a friend."

Forcioli formerly worked on the Orient Express and at Harry's Ciprani, 59th Street and 5th Avenue in Manhattan. The original Harry's was in Venice, Italy, a favorite subject in Ernest Hemingway's books. The *Harry's Bar Cookbook* is available for $40 at Cafe Patou.

"You could spend days in Toad Hall," chortles Forcioli, a 37-year-old native of Marseille, France. "It's like going inside your grandpa's attic. You feel as if you're in a treasure chest."

Cafe Patou is down the street from Toad Hall on the southeast side of town. The main building that houses Toad Hall was built in 1929 as a pharmacy for what was then a Swedish neighborhood. The Masons bought the building in 1987. Toad Hall opened at 8th and Broadway in 1972. Moving day? Forget it.

It took Beverly two and a half years to restock the shelves in the new digs. Today, the Toad Hall compound has sprawled to an annex across the street at 2019 Broadway and The Bait Shop at 2017 Broadway, so named because it was formerly a bait and tackle store.

The annex houses more than 25,000 45s, reel-to-reel tapes and Edison cylinders for 1890s record players. Just when you think you won't run into anyone you know on a foggy Sunday in Rockford, along comes Andy Cirzan, vice president and senior talent buyer for Chicago's Jam Productions.

He's dropping $100 for obscure Christmas 45s such as Bette Champel's "You Trim My Christmas Tree." Cirzan has a beady-eyed look about him. He's either been in the dimly lit annex too long, or he's excited about his friends. The records are indeed chestnuts roasting on an open market.

"We never regret what we sell," Beverly says. "I bought a set of 1931 lobby cards from the movie 'Dracula.' I sold them in the early 1990s in the $7,000 range. The man I sold them to sold them for $10,000. And the man he sold them to sold them at Christie's, and they went for $60,000. That was all in a two-year span, but I don't have any complaints. I made a very good profit. And it was fun to have them for a while."

A few years ago an Austrian couple in their early 30s flew in to O'Hare Airport, rented a car and drove to Rockford. "They got a motel room and spent a week here going through 78s," Beverly says. "We put between 400 and 500 78s in boxes and contracted a shipping company. They never saw Lake Michigan."

But they saw the Rock River.

Toad Hall has been a constant in an economically volatile city. In 1993 and 1996 Money Magazine ranked Rockford (pop. 143,000) last among 300 "Best Places To Live in America." Last year Sundstrand Corp.—Rockford's largest single employer—was purchased by United Technologies of Hartford, Conn. Sundstrand, which had been in Rockford for 94 years, moved its corporate headquarters out of town. The 3,400 jobs at their aerospace technology facility remained in Rockford.

And it can be tough to promote a city that is the largest screw product (fasteners, nuts and bolts) producer in America. Naturally, that earned Rockford the title of "Screw Capital of America."

"Rockford is a good town to buy in," Beverly says, "because you have a stable population. People lived in the same houses for two, three generations. And there was money here. People don't understand that. This was an industrial city with a strong base. We went through a hard time [in the 1980s], as did everyone else in the Rust Belt. But right now the economy is good."

The Masons do not have children. They are unsure what will happen to Toad Hall down the road. What will become of nuggets like the 1993 Marv Albert biography *I'd Love To, But I Have a Game (27 Years Without a Life)*? To whom will these presents be bequeathed?

"We've been talking about this," Beverly says as a tape of Larry's beloved King Oliver plays 1920s jazz in the background. "We had hoped to groom one of my nephews for the business, but he couldn't handle the stress. The place is just too big. We've thought about selling it, but who would be crazy enough to buy it?"

Someone who realizes the past is part of the present.

To get to Toad Hall, take Interstate 90 west to Business 20 south. The first light will be Bell School Road. Take a left and head toward Newburg Road. Turn right on Newburg—it becomes Broadway. Call Toad Hall at (815) 226-1259. Toad Hall is open six days a week, closed Tuesday except by appointment.

January 16, 2000

Crazy about those Beer Nuts
All-American snack makes town proud

BLOOMINGTON, Ill.—Several years ago a friend and I got lost driving around the Northwest Side. We stopped at a corner bar to ask directions. The tavern's ambiance was appetizing. Men were drooped over the bar like old branches weighed down by a winter storm. Ray Price sang "City Lights" on the jukebox.

My friend ordered a beer.

I asked the bartender, "Do you have any Beer Nuts?"

The bartender nodded to the tired men sitting in front of him and said, "Son, I got a bar full of 'em."

I've always been crazy about Beer Nuts. I probably began munching on the sweet and salty glazed peanut that's made with the red skin intact in the mid-1970s. Each time I emptied the small quarter bag, I'd flatten it out on the bar like a new map. The small print said that Beer Nuts were made in Bloomington, Ill. That was like sipping from a glass of Baron Rothschild and thinking about Paris. Bloomington seemed so far away.

★   ★   ★

The Beer Nuts plant and outlet shoppe is nestled among the tall trees and old homes of a residential neighborhood on the east side of Bloomington, 140 miles south of Chicago. An abandoned, weedy Illinois, Central & Gulf train line abuts the back of the quaint red brick factory. On a sunny autumn day, a few of the 80 Beer Nut employees lunch at a small picnic table across the street in a sandlot that workers affectionately call "Peanut Park."

Sometimes things are just as you imagined them.

Beer Nuts celebrate their 60th anniversary this year. Beer Nuts have always been a family business, started in The Caramel Crisp Shop, a downtown Bloomington candy store run by the Edward Shirk family. In 1937 the nuts were called Redskins because they were prepared with their red skins intact. The family was already skilled at coating caramel apples and popcorn balls. So they began glazing the nuts.

The nuts were processed by hand in the store's back room and sold over the counter by the scoop. Orange drinks were served on the side. The name was changed to Beer Nuts in 1953 after the

Shirks began packaging the nuts for the National Liquors store in Bloomington. With Edward's son Russell on production and Ellie Brewster as traveling salesman, the nuts sold like hotcakes in taverns.

"I don't know about you," says Jim Shirk, 53-year-old grandson of Beer Nuts founder Edward, "But they taste outstanding with a frosty beer. Sometimes I can't wait to sit down with a beer and Beer Nuts. They're OK with a Coke and lemonade. But to me and for Brewster, who was calling on taverns and liquor stores in McLean County—and who was a big beer drinker—it was a natural."

And, no, there's no beer in the nuts.

During a plant tour, Jim Tipton, manager of Beer Nuts marketing and communication, says, "In this day of focus groups who specialize in naming things, these guys [Russell Shirk and Brewster] just said, 'Let's call them "Beer Nuts" because they were so popular in bars.' It wasn't any big thing."

But Beer Nuts are a big thing in the Bloomington-Normal area. (Bloomington's population is 57,707; Normal's is 42,749). Beer Nuts are the region's second best-known company, next to State Farm Insurance. Every year when the local Kiwanis group hits the streets to raise money for local charities, they don't give away candy in return for a donation. They use Beer Nuts as incentives.

All Beer Nuts employees come from Bloomington and nearby rural towns like Heyworth and Leroy. And many of them represent the Midwestern ethic of loyalty. "Oddly enough, we have a lot of sons and daughters of employees who worked here," Tipton says. "Not by design, it just happens that way."

Everyone from Drew Carey to David Letterman has exalted the beauty of Beer Nuts. And Tipton has heard every nutty joke. "We hear all of them at trade shows," Tipton says. "The one I hear over and over is . . . " Well, you can imagine.

★　★　★

Beer Nuts have been produced in their current 100,000-square-foot plant—a couple of progressions from the candy store—since 1973. The main production item is peanuts, with cashews and almonds making up the other 20 percent of the product. Tipton said Beer Nuts are popular in the Midwest and, for some unknown reason, they also do well in California.

The peanuts used in Beer Nuts are grated and cleaned as they arrive from Alabama, Georgia and the Carolinas. (Almonds are shipped in from California, and cashews are imported from India and Mozambique.

The 110-pound sacks of peanuts are kept in cold storage, where they await their rebirth as Beer Nuts. By the thousands, the peanuts are dumped into six corrugated steel bins. The nuts slide through spiral chutes into a destoner machine, which catches foreign objects. The slide is necessary to keep peanut skins on as much as possible. If the peanuts were dropped, the skins would fall off.

"Since peanuts are dug up from underground [almonds and cashews grow on trees], you'll have rocks and sandstones that look like peanuts," Tipton explains. "So we have to pick them out." The peanuts pass through a cushion of air so objects heavier than peanuts fall to the bottom of the machine.

For the final look, three or four women sit before a conveyor belt, picking out the 10 percent of the stuff the machine misses. When the belt starts picking up its pace, the scene resembles the madcap Lucy and Ethel chocolate bon-bon assembly line scene from the "I Love Lucy" show.

"I've stood in here," Tipton says. "I don't know how they do it. You look at the belt, it's moving fast, you look up and the whole room is spinning around. It drives them nuts." No pun intended.

Once all the peanuts have checked out, they move to the kitchen, where they're glazed with the family's 60-year-old "secret" process. Then it's a shot through the final taste test, into packaging and out to the corner bar.

★   ★   ★

Although Beer Nuts provide opportunity for barroom jokes, they are a source of pride in Bloomington. The outlet shoppe, full of gift baskets, Beer Nut ball caps and t-shirts, shot glasses and even fishing lures, is standing room only in November and December (for mail order, call 1-800-BEER-NUT).

"A couple of months ago there was a little girl in town who, through the Make-a-Wish Foundation, wanted to see 'The Rosie O'Donnell Show,'" Tipton Says. "She brought Beer Nuts as a gift to Rosie. And very proudly Rosie set the nuts up on her desk. She simply loved it."

November 9, 1997

Nearly 50 years in the red
World's Largest Catsup Bottle
prepares to mark anniversary

COLLINSVILLE, Ill.—Let me be the first to drop this on you. Or drip it on you. Next year marks the 50th anniversary of the World's Largest Catsup Bottle, located in a resplendent ravine off Route 159, just south of downtown Collinsville.

The 170-foot-tall water tower was built in 1949 by W. E. Caldwell Co. for the G. S. Suppiger "Brooks Tangy Old Original Catsup" bottling plant. The water tower was needed to supply water to a new fire protection system.

The ketchup factory was Collinsville's biggest employer. The tangy smell of ketchup used to float through the community, located on the scenic hills off Interstate 55, about 12 miles northeast of St. Louis.

"In 1962 they quit bottling the ketchup here," said Judy DeMoisy, manager for Downtown Collinsville, during a conversation in her office. "They moved to Mount Summit, Ind., but left the warehouse and bottle here."

The property operated as a Brooks warehouse until 1993, when Curtice-Burns, the parent company of Brooks Foods, sold the property to local businessmen Larry and Jim Eckert. They used the site to expand their warehousing business.

But what about the bottle?

The Eckert brothers were all shook up. They commissioned an engineering study to get bids for restoration of the ketchup bottle. DeMoisy organized a Catsup Bottle Preservation Group and they raised more than $77,000 to restore the classic piece of roadside architecture to its original state.

Most of the money was raised by selling commemorative ketchup bottle T-shirts and sweatshirts. The bottle boutique has since been expanded to include a cool royal blue architectural bottle blueprint T-shirt ($16.95), 50th Anniversary World's Largest Catsup Bottle refrigerator magnets (95 cents) and a swell red, white and blue ketchup bottle baseball cap ($7.95). (For information, write the Catsup Bottle Preservation Group and International Fan Club, P.O. Box 1108, Collinsville, Ill. 62234.)

DeMoisy now calls the bottle Collinsville's Eiffel Tower. But

Photo courtesy of Judy DeMoisy and the town of Collinsville.

then, DeMoisy and her husband, Chuck, have a 14-year-old daughter named Brook—"just like on the bottle," she said—and Beth, 9.

Collinsville resident Tim Forneris retrieved Mark McGwire's record-breaking 62nd home-run ball at Busch Stadium in St. Louis. When Forneris appeared on "The Late Show," David Letterman asked him where he was from. Forneris answered, "Collinsville, Ill., International Horseradish Capital of the World—and we also have this really large ketchup bottle!" The generally cynical New York crowd went bonkers.

It was a great condiment. Er, compliment.

"The rebirth of the landmark parallels beautifully with the rebirth of the community," DeMoisy said. "When you look at communities that have two or three decades of ambivalence and decay, you have to do something drastic. The ketchup bottle was dormant for 25 years. No one did anything to it. It was a dramatic thing that had to be done.

"We had to go all the way down to the steel. It was just like revitalizing the community, going to the core and getting everybody involved. Each coat of paint that went back on symbolizes the same kind of issues the community went through. It sounds kind of geeky, but you have to get to the base of what your economic problems are in the community, you have to get focused on it. By doing the ketchup bottle, we met the people with something that they knew would be a detriment if it was lost. It was a wake-up call.

"And the response was incredible."

People reaching out to save the ketchup bottle went beyond Collinsville. The ketchup bottle preservation group connected with a lighthouse preservation group outside Detroit and sold $10,000 worth of ketchup bottle T-shirts just in the Detroit area.

In November, 1994, while selling commemorative T-shirts at the bottle site, DeMoisy received a ticket from Collinsville police for violating the local sign ordinance. Someone had posted two T-shirt advertising leaflets on nearby utility poles, not knowing that it was against the law. A St. Louis paper ran the story with the headline, "BOTTLE BACKERS IN PICKLE OVER CATSUP TICKET." The charges were later dropped.

Interest in the ketchup bottle has grown so much that last month, the International World's Largest Catsup Bottle Fan Club was formed. A $10 donation includes a membership card, a quarterly newsletter, special invitations to ketchup bottle-related events, and discounts on ketchup bottle merchandise. Fan club proceeds go towards future maintenance, promotion and heritage educational programs. And the bottle's juicy Web site is awesome. The all-volunteer Web site can be reached at *www.catsupbottle. com.*

Sparked by the ketchup bottle restoration, the Collinsville Library is coming back and the schools are improving. Just after I left, the downtown hosted its first Collinsville High School homecoming parade in a decade.

Many of the residents of Collinsville, pop. 22,500, work in St.

Louis. "We are a suburb of St. Louis, yet we are considered a rural southern Illinois town," she said. "We have a lot of different issues that impact the viability of the community. Being a bedroom community explains some of the timing issues with downtown store hours. How do you accommodate people who live here, but commute to St. Louis?"

Because of its bottom-of-a-hill proximity to old trees, the World's Largest Catsup Bottle makes for an excellent end-of-autumn visit. Bring a portable grill and have a weenie roast. Hold the mustard, of course. And if that doesn't twist your cap, try a taco at Bert's Chuck Wagon, 207 E. Clay in downtown Collinsville.

I visited the landmark on a day it was raining ketchup and dogs and still got charged up when I saw the roadside attraction. Why? "There's something fun about it," answered DeMoisy, who did graduate work in architecture at Miami of Ohio and did her post-graduate work in architecture and preservation at the University of Hawaii. "It requires nothing. It doesn't make you do anything but laugh."

While at the University of Hawaii, DeMoisy studied under Bill Murtaugh, one of the top preservation professors in America. He now does international preservation for Yugoslavia and other spots in eastern Europe. For 25 years, Murtaugh was keeper of the National Register in Washington, D.C.

A World's Largest Catsup Bottle 50th anniversary shebang on June 13, 1999, will also celebrate the bottle's inclusion as a structure on the National Register of Historic Places. "We'll have a 6-foot ketchup-bottle cake," DeMoisy said. "A ketchup-bottle parade. The annual Illinois Route 66 caravan will end here. [In the late 1950s, 66 re-routed through the north end of Collinsville.] Anyone who has a good sense of humor really appreciates the bottle."

Of course. Variety is the spice of life.

October 25, 1998

Hippie salute
Peace and love

ARCOLA, Ill.—Hippies are not high on the list of icons to be memorialized.

There are shrines for Elvis, Mr. Ed and elephants, but when it comes to old hippies, memory loss can be monumental.

The world's only Hippie Memorial recalls the free-form soul of the 1960s. The 62-foot-long metal structure sits adjacent to the historic 117-year-old Illinois Central RR depot in downtown Arcola (pop. 2,700), about 40 miles south of Urbana-Champaign.

Dedication of the memorial was set for Saturday during the first Hippie Memorial Festival in Arcola. On hand for it: "Tonight Show With Jay Leno" comedy writer Frank King and the Mighty Pranksters rock 'n' roll band. Even Oprah Winfrey sent two tickets to her show for an auction that benefits a local domestic abuse facility.

Courtesy of Arcola Chamber of Commerce.

The Hippie Memorial was constructed by Arcola artist Bob Moomaw. He died at age 63 of a heart attack in April 1998, and the memorial was bequeathed to Gus Kelsey, an Arcola native who lives in southwest Michigan. Kelsey spent $8,000 out of his own pocket to refurbish the memorial. The memorial was installed around Thanksgiving.

Kelsey thought it was appropriate to keep the memorial in Arcola as a tribute to Moomaw instead of moving it to a hippie bastion such as San Francisco, Woodstock, N.Y., or Wicker Park. Moomaw's 35-year-old son, John, was recruited to spin records from the 1960s at the dedication. And his widow, Sherron, was to attend.

At the center of the memorial's narrow stucco wall is a sandblasted peace sign that reads, "Dedicated to Hippies and Hippies at Heart. Peace & Love," and it bears Kelsey's and Moomaw's names.

The crossbars of the welded scrap-metal memorial denote the webs of Moomaw's life. The most vibrant piece of the sculpture is the center, where his work peaks at 6 feet with bright peace symbols and flowers. That represents the 1960s, which Moomaw felt was the best time for self-expression. Beginning with a rusted car muffler, the memorial downsizes into a dull industrial look that Moomaw related to the Ronald Reagan years.

"I'll build a patio where you can buy a memorial brick for your friendly hippie," Kelsey said, standing in front of the memorial.

If a Grateful Dead drum solo had form, it would look like the Hippie Memorial.

"I'll go ahead and put a John Lennon brick in there because he probably won't buy one," Kelsey said. "I'm going to install a flagpole with the American flag and a Hippie Memorial flag. And a buddy is going to make a twirling, three-sided neon peace sign."

Kelsey took a drag from his Antonio y Cleopatra cigar and added, "We'll have a couple of benches so people can just sit here and *groove*." Other expansion plans include a vintage Volkswagen bus and Beetle. Kelsey is even talking to the owner of the Letterman's Club tavern across the street from the memorial to turn it into the Hippie Memorial Bar.

What a long, strange strip it will be.

Kelsey, 47, is married, with a daughter, Stephanie, 23. He is operations manager at South End Beverages, an Anheuser-Busch distributorship in St. Joseph, Mich. Kelsey and his daughter also own a graphics company in Benton Harbor, Mich.

A couple of weeks ago, Kelsey become a grandfather for the first time when Stephanie gave birth to William Ellis.

"He came out with a full head of hair," said the balding Kelsey. "Which says something about the hippie movement."

In 1983, Kelsey ran for mayor of Arcola, losing by one vote, before leaving town in 1984. He knew Moomaw fairly well.

Kelsey said, "I used to walk by Bob's [sign] shop on Main Street. I'd look at his paintings. They were all anti-government, things like that. He was a unique guy. He'd make up words while he was talking to you. That was his hobby. I always just thought he was deep. I'd walk away thinking, 'What did he just say?' "

Moomaw said the Hippie Memorial should be "raw like life, and that life is just junk collecting rust."

Moomaw began assembling the memorial in 1992 behind a yellow wooden fence at his shop. Kelsey was living in Bridgman, Mich., about 35 miles from South Bend, Ind. He was working for former Arcola and Barrington high school basketball coach Dean Sanders, who now owns South End Beverages.

"In 1993, I came back to Arcola and the memorial was gone," Kelsey said. "I called Bob and said, 'What are you going to do with that Hippie Memorial?' He said he was going to offer it to the city. I said, 'Bob, the city would just take it out to the dump. They won't understand that it's a man's soul.' He asked me what I wanted it for. Well, I was one of the first hippies here. There were three longhairs in the whole town."

Later in 1993, Moomaw gave the Hippie Memorial to Kelsey. The town is divided on Kelsey's devotion to the project. The city gave Kelsey permission to install the memorial on land it leases from the Illinois Central RR, but it has no other involvement with the project.

"It's a mixed bag," said Mary Dilliner, executive director of the Arcola Chamber of Commerce. The 136-member chamber is sponsoring the Hippie Memorial Festival.

"Some are having fun with it; others hate it," said Dilliner, a 40-year-old native of nearby Tuscola. "There's a flier bandit in town who takes festival fliers down every time we put one up. The chamber on a while has been pretty supportive. They gave me no budget. They said I could do the festival if I could come up with the money. Maybe that was their way of thinking I'd never come up with the money, but that just makes me try harder."

So far, she has raised $1,850 of her $2,000 budget.

Some locals even questioned Dilliner's choice of Beth's Place domestic abuse center in Tuscola as the beneficiary of the charity auction.

Dilliner explained that Moomaw "felt that what was good about the hippie movement is that it gave Americans the freedom to stand up and speak out for what they believe in. That's what people who leave domestic situations are saying. They're not going to take it anymore. I think it fit."

Kelsey added, "Some people don't understand this because

Arcola doesn't have a memorial for Vietnam veterans. But they don't understand I paid for it. Hey, I'll build a memorial for Vietnam and I'll do it for the cost of the materials. And I think we should have one. The Korean War, too."

Archie Edwards, 72, is one of three Korean War vets in Arcola. He served in the Army, and for 33 months he was a prisoner of war near the Yalu River in Korea. He lives a couple of blocks from the Hippie Memorial.

"It looks like a bunch of scrap iron welded together," the Arcola native said with a laugh in a phone conversation. "It don't bother me. I'll go to the dedication if I'm around. I've been in and out of the VA hospital. But Korean War veterans should be remembered, too. Korea was the bloodiest war in the 20th century."

The Hippie Memorial is just another attraction in a predominantly Republican community that is also the birthplace of the creator of Raggedy Ann (Johnny Gruelle) and the center of the state's broom corn industry. Broom corn is a tall, unusual variety of sorghum used in the manufacturing of brooms. Even the memories of old hippies can't be swept away.

Kelsey said, "This town has been unique as long as I can remember. We have a big mix of Mexican people who came up to work in the broom industry. A lot of people also came up from Kentucky. They were called 'Broom Corn Johnnies.' They cut that broom corn with a knife. And they stayed, too. This is not only Bob Moomaw's memorial, but it keeps me in Arcola, too."

June 27, 1999

The warmth of the Kitch-Inn
Mendota diner marks its 90th anniversary

A sweet story of homespun success stands amid the cornfields of Mendota, Ill., a two-hour drive from Chicago. The Kitch-Inn diner and candy store is celebrating its 90th anniversary this year.

The Kitch-Inn has been in the same family since 1909, when Ted Troupis bought the Mendota Candy Kitchen from fellow Greek immigrant James Stasinos.

Today the Kitch-Inn, 710 Washington St. (815-539-9206) in downtown Mendota, offers a full menu with daily luncheon plates and kitschy delights like the nutty carrot muffin (chunks of walnuts, slivered carrots, pineapple and raisins for $1.29).

The Kitch-Inn is owned by Ted's son Andrew and his wife Genevieve.

They met when she was a high school waitress at the confectionery.

But you probably knew that.

"They'd hire high school kids and teach them how to make change," Genevieve said as she walked out of the kitchen at the end of a summer workday. "Old-timey things like that."

Sitting on a nearby diner stool, Andrew, 70, added, "You can punch the register and it will tell you the change, but I don't allow anybody who works for me to do that. They have to count the money back to the people."

That's hand-to-hand spirit.

There's no better time to visit Mendota than during the 52nd Annual Sweet Corn Festival, which kicks off Thursday and runs through Aug. 15 in downtown Mendota. The Del Monte corn processing plant is on the east side of town.

One of the weekend's highlights will be the Sweet Corn Festival Grand Parade, which will kick off at 1 p.m. Aug. 15 in downtown Mendota. The Jesse White Tumblers will appear in the parade, and House Speaker J. Dennis Hastert (R-14th) is the grand marshal. He joins a list of fine marshals who include ex-Baltimore Oriole Boog Powell (1984), bandleader Lawrence Welk (1950), Baseball Hall of Famer Bill Veeck (1959) and beloved WLS-AM rock jock Clark Weber (1965).

Photo courtesy of Andrew and Genevieve Troupis.

Andrew and Genevieve Troupis of Mendota's Kitch-Inn.

Free sweet corn will be available beginning at 2 p.m. Aug 15 in downtown Mendota. The Kitch-Inn is closed on Sunday and Monday, but it is open from 7 a.m. to 4 p.m. Tuesday through Thursday, until 6 p.m. Friday and until 3 p.m. Saturday. If you can't stand the heat, get into the Kitch-Inn.

The 1948 Sweet Corn Festival featured Genevieve (Weiss) as an attendant in the Sweet Corn Queen's court. "They ran our picture on the front page of the Chicago Sun-Times," she said. "I was a junior at Mendota High School. I wore my prom dress. It was innovative. There weren't as many festivals as there are now." In 1959 Veeck called the queen and her court "The prettiest infield I ever had," according to the book *Mendota, Illinois 1853-1978.*

Andrew and Genevieve knew each other in high school.

"Pretty well," he said.

She said, "We didn't like one another very much."

He said, "I married you, didn't I?"

She said, "I thought you were kind of a hunk, but you were dating other girls."

He said, "You were out [of high school] a year and I married you."

They smiled and laughed together.

Diner talk.

The Kitch-Inn seats about 50 people in seven Chinese-orange booths, two tables and 11 diner stools. Many times the staff will just stuff the money inside an old taped-up Dutch Masters cigar box.

The fountain behind the counter features a vintage pink 1940s malt dispenser and a 60-year-old Hamilton juicer. Genevieve nodded toward the orange juice machine and said, "It's the only one I ever knew." She then smiled at her husband of 49 years.

The candy kitchen moved two doors east into its current location at Washington and Illinois Avenue in 1941. The business evolved from a candy store into a restaurant in 1953 when national ice cream companies began squeezing out ma & pa shops.

"Ice cream makers like Sealtest were crowding us," Andrew said. "Dad used to make 20,000 gallons of ice cream a year. When I quit making it [in 1966] I was down to 1,200 a year. We changed the name to 'The Kitch' in 1957. A salesman said, 'Why don't you call this place "The Kitch-Inn?" You have a restaurant now.' It seemed to fit. I've got the old 'Kitch' neon sign behind my barn out in the country."

As a flickering homage to another time, Troupis still makes homemade candy, available from October through April. Working from a basement candy kitchen filled with copper kettles and marble tables, he makes peanut and coconut brittle, peanut and pecan clusters, cashews and caramel.

"I've had people want to buy the [secret] recipe for the pure cream caramel," he said with a sly smile. "I'll tell you this much—when I make a [40-pound] batch of caramel, I use one gallon of 36 percent butterfat cream. Last year I sold 800 to 1,000 pounds of caramel before I quit [in April]."

These days Troupis buys his ice cream from the Valley Maid ice cream company in Aurora. But he makes his own syrups, which include—in order of popularity—chocolate, strawberry and vanilla.

His father came to America in 1906. Ted's first job was making phonograph cylinders at Thomas Edison's laboratory in Menlo

Park, N.J., before moving to Illinois and working as a candymaker in Quincy and Taylorville. In 1906 Stasinos opened an ice cream and candy store in Mendota and hired Troupis. Ted Troupis bought the other half of the Mendota operation in 1909.

"When I was a boy, downtown Mendota was booming," Troupis said. "There was an A & P grocery store, a National Tea [grocery store], a Kroger's. My father had a '29 Buick, and on a Saturday night he'd park it in front of the candy kitchen and my brother and I would sleep in the car. All the farmers came into town. If you walked around the block, you had to step off the curb—there were that many people downtown. All the railroads were here, too."

The Illinois Central, Milwaukee and C.B. & Q. (Chicago, Burlington and Quincy) rolled through the farm town, just two blocks east of the Kitch-Inn. Today, Mendota (pop. 7,200) is still an Amtrak stop.

The since-razed Union Depot included a hotel and restaurant. The past is preserved in the three-year-old Union Depot Railroad Museum, 783 Main St., which features an operating small-scale layout of downtown Mendota, circa 1930.

"Before Interstate 80 was built, all the east-west traffic came through Route 34 [Ogden Avenue] and Mendota," Troupis said. "Back then we were open until 6 in the evening." Mendota was true to its Native American name of "Meeting of the Trails."

The elder Troupis died in 1960 at the age of 72. Andrew and Genevieve have four children. Andrew, 37, runs a medical company in Chicago; George, 44, is a high school teacher in Lake Geneva, Wis.; April (Bettilyon), 47, is a first-grade teacher in Bensenville, and Ted, 49, works for an industrial company in Ladd, a small town west of Mendota.

Andrew pointed to his oldest son in a family picture near the fountain and said in reassuring tones, "We were married 49 years. But he was *legal.*" All the children worked at the Kitch-Inn while growing up, but none are involved with the restaurant today.

Besides Andrew and Genevieve, the Kitch-Inn has a staff of seven people. Andrew has had two by-pass surgeries and he wears a pacemaker. He tries to help out whenever he can. But as much as Andrew loves to talk about the past, he can't help but think about the future.

"We'll sell the restaurant to somebody," he said as he shrugged his shoulders against the afternoon shadows. "But I don't want to sell it to just anybody." It makes sense. Everybody is somebody at the Kitch-Inn.

To get to Mendota, take Interstate 355 south to I-88 West, exit I-39 South to Mendota exit (73). Head west into Mendota. A more scenic journey is Route 34 out of the Aurora-Naperville area directly into Mendota. For a complete Sweet Corn Festival schedule, call the Mendota Area Chamber of Commerce, (815) 539-6507.

August 8, 1999

On Shakey ground
Last slice in Cal City

For a guy who owns a Shakey's, Brian Wilkes keeps a stiff upper lip.

I bought two slices of pizza for the drive home from Shakey's, 675 River Oaks Dr. in Calumet City, the chain's last restaurant in northern Illinois. Wilkes gave me the pizza in a 40th anniversary cardboard container. He softly read the boxtop aloud: *"Shakey's— The pizza that started it all."*

He's closing the restaurant at the end of the year.

The last several years have been a struggle for the Shakey's chain, founded in 1954 in a grocery store in downtown Sacramento, Calif. A fire hit the original Shakey's in January, 1996, and that building remains boarded up. In 1957, Shakey's created America's first pizza franchise by opening restaurants in California, Washington and Oregon.

At one time, Shakey's had more than 700 restaurants across the world. Today there are 108 in America and 200 abroad. Founder Sherwood "Shakey" Johnson sold his interests in 1967 and is retired and living near Yuba City, Calif. He does not give interviews. He got out while the getting was good.

I remember Shakey's from the early 1970s for its *21* varieties of pizza (*Wow!*) and the help who wore bow ties, red-striped shirts and round skimmer hats. How could you forget the image of being served by people who looked as if they had stepped out of "A Clockwork Orange"? And every Shakey's of the 1960s and '70s had a banjo player and a player piano

They never sang the blues.

"In the late 1980s, Calumet City was the No. 1 store in the country," Wilkes says during an interview at his restaurant. "At its peak it brought in close to $3 million in sales. After 1989, sales started downward. A million things happened. The area is changing. Our taxes went up. We used to be the only buffet around here; then many others opened up. It all faded out."

Because Shakey's catered to families, the restaurants always had an inherent sense of purpose. Wilkes, 34, and his partner bought into that. A native of Schererville, Wilkes has worked for Shakey's since 1983. He managed the Calumet City store for two years before buying it in May, 1994.

His partner and co-owner Mark DeJarlis, 37, started at the same restaurant as a 15-year-old busboy. "It's the only job he's ever had," Wilkes says, staring across an empty banquet room.

DeJarlis and Wilkes purchased the Calumet City operation in 1994 and a Shakey's in Highland, Ind., in November, 1995 (they will keep that restaurant open).

The Shakey's in Calumet City would have celebrated its 30th anniversary Jan. 19. DeJarlis and Wilkes have been keeping it open at a loss, often paying for expenses out of their own pockets.

The 350-seat restaurant is in need of some gentle remodeling, a fact that Wilkes acknowledges. Some of the woodwork has yellowed with time, yet there's a nostalgic charm to the stained-glass Shakey's light fixtures that hang in the hallway.

A game room with nearly 30 coin-operated machines such as Jungle Jive and Feed Big Bertha comes off as a last-chance stab to attract families. The game room is empty. Big Bertha is starving.

"You can't keep running a place that's not making money," Wilkes says. "It's hard to make ends meet with a buffet, which has been here since 1976. It's funny, the old-timers still call it 'bunch of lunch' (even though it's all day long). In 1989 this store had 130 employees and seven full-time mangers. Now there are 50 employees and one full-time manager, my partner and I."

Many of the Calumet City employees are firmly rooted. Food preparation cook Bernie Diana has worked at the restaurant since it opened. Her husband even played banjo in the parlor. She will be asked to go to Highland.

Assistant manager Sharon Zasda has been working at the Calumet City restaurant for 18 years, and she will move to Highland. So will assistant manager Beth Crosslin, a Hammond resident who has split her 13 years at Shakey's between the Calumet City and Highland stores.

"Shakey's had that worldwide presence," Crosslin says working the buffet while her 2½-year-old son Jeremy watches. "I remember someone coming in here wanting to open one in Egypt. Five years ago, a customer showed me pictures of a Shakey's in Jamaica. It was a grass hut with big chairs in an outside bar. But they had the actual Shakey's sign on the roof."

Actually, in 1989 Shakey's was acquired by an international firm, Inno-Pacific Holdings, based in Singapore. Last month,

Shakey's announced a new game plan: a Shakey's Cafe that features a new Santa Fe-inspired exterior design and an expanded menu that includes rotisserie and fried chicken, gourmet pastas and entree salads. The first Shakey's Cafe opened in October in Foothill Ranch in Southern California.

Mark Curran, 46, has been president of Shakey's Inc. since 1995. From his office in Irvine, Calif., Curran says, "We haven't changed the marketing position of what Shakey's stood for. Back in the '60s it was a good value for feeding the family and a lot of fun. Except we've evolved. In the past, you might have gone in and gotten a pizza, a beer and a player piano with the family. Today, you can have a nice glass of Merlot; the kids can still have their pizza and go back in the game room while you relax."

Wilkes and DeJarlis have seen the Shakey's Cafe specs, but it's too early to tell if the Highland store will make the change. It's too late for Calumet City. "You wouldn't believe how it used to be here," Wilkes reflects. "People waited in line for an hour. They used to wait outside, but the former owner enclosed the sidewalk so they didn't have to be outside.

"There used to be a Toys R Us next to us, and now it's a strip mall. When Toys R Us pulled out, that took a big chunk of business. It's tough. You hate to see this one go."

It is tough. Sometimes you go out to look for the past and you get a taste of the future.

December 14, 1997

Still shaking
'Curbies' recall the simple
beginnings of a roadside classic

NORMAL, Ill.—The good news is that the site of America's first Steak 'n Shake restaurant is going to be saved. The bad news for burger lovers is that you will only be able to order pizza.

Normal residents Gus and Edith Belt started Steak 'n Shake in the 1930s. There are now 354 Steak 'n Shakes in 16 states. Parent company Consolidated Products of Indianapolis plans to operate 600 Steak 'n Shakes nationwide by 2004.

But in the chain's hometown, the original Steak 'n Shake building is giving way to a Monical's Pizza parlor. The location is 1219 S. Main St., on old Route 66, slicing through downtown Normal. Monical's will remodel the building and erect a marker to recognize its historical significance.

The restaurant is in a flood plain bordered by old willow trees and Sugar Creek—an area that would be in the center of flood waters during a 100-year storm. The Monical's chain gained approval from the Illinois Department of Natural Resources because Monical's plan increased the amount of water that will stay on the property. Steak 'n Shake's plan decreased the amount of water that remained on the property.

So last August Steak 'n Shake took the high road and opened a new restaurant on 614 W. Raab Rd., just west of Main Street in Normal. In January they sold the original parcel to Monical's for $250,000.

A colorful group of four original Steak 'n Shake "curbies," soda jerks and regulars get together over breakfast four times a week to talk about old times at the new Steak 'n Shake.

"Gus opened it in 1933 as the Shell Inn," says Mel Tulle, a "curbie" from 1941 and '42. "It was all the beer you could drink and all the chicken you could eat for 35 cents. There was also a Shell [gas] station on the property. Prohibition came, so he started selling steak [hamburgers] and shakes."

Belt used to bring in steaks during the restaurant's busiest times and grind them into burgers while customers sat at the counter watching. That's how the restaurant's slogan, "In sight it must be right," came about.

The original Belt building was mostly destroyed by a fire in the 1960s. One wall remains from the site, but that won't stop the pizza chain from celebrating all that is Steak 'n Shake.

Monical's is installing cream-colored stucco that replicates the original Steak 'n Shake. Monical's also resurrected a 30-year-old black and white laminate counter and red-top vinyl diner stools with chrome bases.

"The counter doesn't go back to Steak 'n Shake One, but its goes back a long time," says Chip Rorem, architect for Monical's. "We saved what we could. And we're still going to have a drive-through."

Belt renamed the roadside diner Steak 'n Shake in 1934. A butter-grilled steak hamburger was a quarter. It came with home baked beans and potatoes. "Mrs. Belt's Personal Specialties" included homemade chili (seasoned with ground Spanish cumin seed, paprika, and chili powder) for 15 cents a bowl, accompanied by crackers and sliced dills.

A few things set Steak 'n Shake apart from other roadside diners:

- They slice pickles the long way. "They had a long wooden board with a blade in it," Tulle explains. "The pickles came in a barrel. They'd lay the pickles over the board to slice them, which was the easiest way to do it. They also fit the bun easier that way."

- There are "Four Ways to Enjoy: Car, Table, Counter, and Takhomasak."

- Sun-Times film critic Roger Ebert is a Steak 'n Shake fan, having been weaned on the burgers in his hometown of Urbana-Champaign, not far from Bloomington-Normal.

Tulle says, "Steak 'n Shake was real busy. People were driving circles around the restaurant because there was no place to park. The menu was limited so they could move the traffic. They even had a Normal policeman out there directing traffic in the evening."

Bob Rogers worked the Steak 'n Shake grill in 1939. "A drive-in with curb service was a novelty," he says. "High school kids would drive around the lot. They called that 'buggin' the Shake.' "

Rogers left Normal for the Pacific between 1942 and 1945 to

serve in the 24th Cavalry Reconnaissance during World War I. Tulle enlisted in the Air Force in 1942 and flew the hump in the China-Burma operation. Flying the hump is a lot tougher than buggin' the shake. Tulle was discharged in 1946.

Like all fellow "curbies," Rogers and Tulle returned to their hometown. Between 1964 and 1967 Rogers even came back to Route 66 when he owned and operated the Redwood Motel on the old road. "That was a bad mistake," he says. "Route 66 was changing at Lincoln and bypassing Normal. I told my wife I had to get out of there. The new line took all the old business."

Now, here's what I like about old-fashioned road reporting: Folks talk to you as if you know everyone in the community. Dave Graves was an original Steak 'n Shake "curbie" from 1938 to '41. "When they got busy, Gus would come out jerkin' trays and stuff," Graves says. "I was working up front with Les Baylor. I had six milk shakes. So I'm comin' around the corner with the milk shakes and Gus is comin' the other way with two empty trays— and BOOM! I got six milk shakes right over Gus Belt. I thought he'd fire me."

Another night around 1940 a fancy stretch limousine backed into the north end of the Steak 'n Shake lot. Graves was working the area. "The procedure was to walk up to the driver's side where he'd give you the order," Graves says. "I walked up to the driver's side and nothing happened. Pretty soon two guys get out of the back on each side. Big guys. Panama hats. They ordered."

Graves returned to the limousine while juggling three trays. He asked the gentlemen to roll down a window. "They said, 'We ain't rolling down no windows,' " Graves says. "These two guys ate theirs on top of the car. They tipped us a buck—Wow, man! They pulled around to the gas station. They were probably going to St. Louis. This time the driver rolled down the window to pay for the gas. The attendant looked in the window.

"And he saw Al Capone."

But the "curbies" agreed the most lavish tips came from out-of-state license plates.

Around 1938 the Belts hired an "efficiency expert," in the words of Graves. The consultant observed the staff and took notes. Graves recalls, "All the curb boys had nicknames. Mine was 'Ding'—like a bell. There was 'Buck,' 'Pete.' He decided to do away with these hokey names. He gave us numbers."

"Ding" became "Number Five."

That plan lasted about two weeks. Edith "Edie" Belt insisted the curb boys' nicknames be reinstated. Customers told her they hated the numbers. But as years passed, Steak 'n Shake became No. 1 in the minds of folks motoring through America's heartland.

July 16, 2000

A postcard paradise

You can see all four corners of the world from the Lakewood Forest Preserve in northwest suburban Wauconda. That's the home of the Curt Teich Postcard Archives at the Lake County Museum.

More than 2 million postcards are stored in acid-free boxes in a quaint 1920s white farmhouse surrounded by apple orchards. The world's largest public postcard collection covers 360,000 different views, according to archive curator Katherine Hamilton-Smith.

That's a gob o' greetings.

The American postcard was born in 1893 in Chicago. "The first picture postcards that didn't have to be put in an envelope were printed [in 1893] for the Chicago World's Columbian Exposition," Hamilton-Smith said.

The Curt Teich (pronounced "tyke") Co. put its stamp of approval on the archives. The postcard company operated between 1898 and 1978, before Curt's son Ralph donated its archives to the museum. The company was at 1755 W. Irving Park, which is now Post Card Place lofts.

Curt Teich (1877-1974) was a German printer who immigrated to Chicago in 1895. In 1905, he barnstormed alone by train to the West Coast, getting off at every point to photograph local points of interest.

It was Detours, circa 1905.

Local merchants paid him $1 per minimum order of 1,000 cards, and in 90 days, Teich sold $30,000 in orders. The company became the largest volume printer of advertising, scenic postcards, maps and brochures in the world, wisely saving 15 copies of every printed piece. That's invaluable stuff for a curator like Hamilton-Smith.

"Ralph first approached the Chicago Historical Society with the collection, which is the logical place to go," Hamilton-Smith said. "They said they'd take the 11,000 views of Chicago but nothing else."

Ralph Teich, 74, lives in Lake Forest. "I told them [the historical society] 'No way,' " he said in an interview. "I tried several other museums and it was the same situation. They only wanted local cards. But the [then] director [Gary Keller] of the Lake

County Museum was interested in the entire collection. It was important to keep it together."

Hamilton-Smith has been with the archive since 1982, when the Teich collection landed in Lake County. She said, "It came with a lot of money. The [now-defunct family] Teich Foundation gave an initial grant of just under half a million dollars for a five-year setup, and they recently gave another half a million dollars to serve as the core of an endowment from which the archives will draw money for its budget. The first eight years of the project were entirely privately funded."

The Teich collection is the core of the archives, but they also accept postcard donations from other parts of the world. They do not buy collections.

The archives are open to researchers, collectors, illustrators, writers and architectural groups. They accept queries from any-where in the world. The first hour of research is free for non-profit reference. After that, the archive charges a fee of $12 an hour.

In order of popularity, the most common requests from the public are views of Route 66 (at least once a week, according to Hamilton-Smith), World War II, hometowns and Chicago views. "We work remotely most of the time," Hamilton-Smith said. "It's unusual that people come here and knock on the door."

The archive staff spent most of the summer posting postcards online as part of a state-library funded project called "Wish You Were Here, Illinois!" Postcard images important to Illinois her-itage have been digitized and put on the Internet *(www.north starnet.org/Digitize)*.

Under the direction of 22-year-old editor Steve Ferrigan, the archives cataloged and digitized 5,000 images of 526 towns and locations in Illinois. For example, the Starved Rock State Park is its own location. Directions and any information from the backs of the postcards are also included.

National magazines like Rolling Stone use the archives for illustrations. Rolling Stone recently contacted the archives for an article on affordable higher education—not on the Marvelette's 1961 hit "Please Mr. Postman."

"They sent us a list of 25 colleges and universities the writer was featuring," Hamilton- Smith said. "This is the only collection in the country where you give them all those views as opposed to having to go to all the schools. We negotiate for-profit prices."

"So we function in a quasi-weird environment because we

have people whose mother has a 75th birthday coming up, then we get a call from Vanity Fair or Rolling Stone."

The archive staff also does style research for Lettuce Entertain You Enterprises. Staff researcher Debra Gust said, "We help them get a feel for their restaurants. They look at images of certain things. When they were doing Wildfire, we looked at rustic places with open-pit barbecues."

Postcard views may not be as ornate as they used to be, but actual postcards are still popular. "The rack cards you get in urban clubs and restaurants are hot for postcard collectors now," Hamilton-Smith said, "because they're just as evocative of culture today as advertising cards at the turn of the century. Postcards have always been used for advertising."

The exhibit "Bringing the World Home" will open in spring 2000 at the Lake County Museum. The 3,000-square-foot exhibit will address the history and significance of postcards worldwide. Visitors will enter the exhibit by walking under a reproduction of the Eiffel Tower and through on-site Internet, people will be able to send actual or e-mail postcards.

The first card the Curt Teich Printing Co. produced was of the Masonic Temple in Chicago. The last card they printed was of the Memorial Arts Building in Milan, Ohio. The cards are organized chronologically from card No. 1.

"They also saved the original art material that went into producing the postcards," Hamilton-Smith said. She then pulled out one of the files on the (Joe Louis') Rhumboogie Club, 343 E. Garfield, circa 1943.

"There's about 110,000 of these files," she said as she delivered a like-new Rhumboogie postcard from a steel case. "We also have the original photographs for everything used in the postcard and the layout that the type company art department would have done." Some files even have pieces of carpet, which were saved to match colors.

Hamilton-Smith, 43, came to the archives just out of graduate school at the University of Chicago. She was born in Kearney, Neb., and raised in Omaha. "Yes, we have several hundred views of Kearney," she said, answering a wise-guy question.

Hamilton-Smith studied art history in college.

"I was a medievalist," she quipped. "That's why I'm working on 20th century postcards."

The Lake County Museum is at Fairfield Road and Route 176. Call 847-526-8638.

August 22, 1999

Kane County splendor
Grande dame of a hotel stands proud in St. Charles

The Hotel Baker was once known as the "Best Little Hotel in the World." And she is coming back in a big way. The elegant hotel along the west bank of the Fox River in downtown St. Charles commemorates its 70th birthday this year.

The grand old lady had been retired since 1969—in fact had been used as a senior retirement center. In 1996 St. Charles businessmen Craig Frank and Neil Johnson bought the hotel and began a two-year, $9 million renovation of the property, which is on the National Historic Register.

The hotel reopened to the public last November.

She features an Art Deco-tinged Charlemagne Lounge, a restaurant and a 200-seat oval ballroom with a dance floor encircled by a columned balcony. Ellen Johnsen, 85, one of the hotel's former employees, led the $50,000 restoration drive for the dance floor with more than 2,600 red, green, blue and amber lights beneath glass blocks. And just north of the hotel restaurant along the river is an award-winning 70-year-old rose garden. The hotel is a remarkable place to stay when visiting Kane County.

The Hotel Baker's warmth and history remind me of the Peabody hotel in downtown Memphis—although the St. Charles hotel has bigger rooms. Every room at the Hotel Baker is individually decorated with restored antique pieces that are original to the hotel. The marble bathrooms have been redone. And three of the rooms have all-season hot tubs on an enclosed veranda.

The hot tubs came in after the senior citizens left.

Hotel founder Edward "The Colonel" Baker would approve of the sporty activities. The honorary title of "Colonel" was given to Baker in the early 1930s because of his affinity for horse racing. Pictures of the Colonel abound throughout the hotel, and indeed, with his signature straw skimmer and cigar, he looks like a bleary-eyed guy who spent a lot of time watching horses.

The riverfront Mediterranean-style restaurant is named "The Trophy Room" in tribute to the hardware Baker won through his horse races. Breakfast, lunch and dinner are served in The Trophy Room, with dinner entrees such as lamb chops ($28.95) and grilled

Photo by Lisa Day.

Mediterranean spiced chicken breast with chickpea vinaigrette ($16.95).

In 1918, at the age of 50, Baker inherited nearly $20 million from his sister, Dellora Baker Gates. She was an heir of DeKalb area barbed wire baron John Warne "Bet-A-Million" Gates, who also founded the Texaco Oil Co. Baker did not go straight to the track with his newfound fuel.

Instead, using only the interest income from his inheritance, Baker commissioned local architects to design his 54-room hotel. He insisted that the guest rooms be like race horses: No two were alike in either layout or decor.

Baker even ordered custom-designed light fixtures, a kitchenette and a spiral staircase for his private digs on the fifth floor (now the Colonel Baker Suite), the cozy apartment in which he died. Final construction costs exceeded more than $1 million when the hotel opened on June 2, 1928.

Baker was not a shy guy, as illustrated by the opulent stained glass peacock over the main entrance on Main Street. The peacock seems to greet visitors and has become something of a Hotel Baker trademark.

Naturally, with all the big bucks and being on the fringe of burgeoning DuPage County, Baker was a staunch Republican. Notable GOP members like Sens. Everett Dirksen and Gerald Ford have stayed at the hotel, but that didn't preclude visits from Democrats like John F. Kennedy (who stayed at the hotel in the 1950s, before he became president) and Mayor Richard J. Daley. Baker died at the age of 90 in 1959.

Co-owner Frank, 44, was born and reared in St. Charles. He runs the family-founded Frank's Employment Agency across the Fox River from the hotel. The hotel employs 75 people.

The employment agency is in the historic 71-year-old Arcada Theatre building, which the family also owns and restored. Every Tuesday is "Balcony Night" at the old vaudeville house, which still has but one movie screen.

"When the hotel opened, George Burns and Gracie Allen would do vaudeville at the Arcada and then stay here," Frank said during a hotel tour. "I have good memories here. I had my high school prom here. I had a great aunt who lived here when it was a senior center. So when Lutheran Social Services decided they couldn't handle the hotel [as a senior center] anymore, this came up for auction. I teamed up with Neil [a local land developer], and we decided to go for it."

Since the hotel reopened, she has attracted corporate clients visiting the Chicago area and international guests who attend the Arthur Andersen training center in St. Charles. Flea market fans stay at the hotel every month, and when former Beach Boy Brian Wilson gave his spring recital at the Norris Cultural Arts Center in St. Charles, musicians and executives from his Giant Record label took over the hotel.

"It was a fun weekend," Frank said. "We knew we had a number of celebrities coming. They registered under bogus names. So we had guests like Johnnie Walker and Jim Beam."

Hotel General Manager Keith J. Sennstrom has been in the hotel business for 23 years. He's been general manager at the Knickerbocker Hotel in Chicago, oversaw the renovation as general manager of the Whitehall Hotel in Chicago and was the general manager of the Radisson Hotel in Lisle. Sennstrom understands the charms of a small hotel.

"Nothing compares to this," he said. "It's the warmth you get when you're in an old building like this. When I first came to this hotel I stayed here. I've been in this business a long time. I've traveled all over the world. And I've never slept in a more comfortable bed."

Sennstrom said that since the hotel reopened, nearly half of the guests inquire how to buy the mattresses they slept on. The mattresses are covered by soft all-Egyptian cotton sheets, with no less than 300 count, a very tight fiber weave that gives a silky finish to the sheets.

"We are now selling the hotel mattresses," Sennstrom said. "Not the ones they slept on—but we can have them shipped to their house. Colonel Baker built the property to be the best little hotel in the world. It had that title at one time.

"Of course, there are a lot of wonderful hotels in the world. But we still think we're one of the best."

Rates range from $149-$200 per room, and suites are $299-$600 per room. The Hotel Baker is at 100 W. Main St., St. Charles, (630) 584-2100.

July 19, 1998

MISSOURI

FLEA MARKET

HARVEY HOUSE

KANSAS CITY

INDEPENDENCE
HAIR MUSEUM

ST. LOUIS
JASPER'S RADIOS

Map by Lisa Day.

Radio collector Jasper Giardina displays a dial for every smile

ST. LOUIS, Mo.—When Jasper Giardina speaks, everyone listens.

You can't tune out a guy who owns 8,000 radios. That's the largest radio collection in the world. The booty includes boom boxes. Crystal sets. Weird promotional transistor radios depicting hot dogs, french fries and Elvis Presley. Expensive Catlins, the Cadillacs of the radio community. A very loud tractor radio from the 1940s. Floor models.

And they're all on display at Jasper's Antique Radio Museum in the historic Cherokee Street antique district, a few hops down the road from the Anheuser-Busch factories.

Life is a rock and Jasper will roll you.

"Radios tell a story," Jasper says while wandering through his two-story red brick building that dates from the mid-1800s. "Early battery sets are from the '20s; you hit the '30s when you get the round cathedrals. In the '40s you see the small table models; in the '50s you go with the plastics. Radios reflect the eras we live in."

Jasper stops in a narrow hallway. Radios are stacked ceiling-high on shelves on each side of the 68-year-old St. Louis native. With his left hand, he makes a short wave at the long rows of radios.

Jasper used to live in the apartment upstairs from his museum. But the radio collection overflowed into the apartment and he moved out. The upstairs highlight is a 1932 coin-operated radio that used to be in a Lawrence, Kan., whorehouse. A customer would drop anywhere from one to 20 nickels to play the music. The racy radio was owned and operated by L & P Radio Sales, 1302 N. 14th Ave., in Melrose Park.

Deep in the museum's dank basement, Jasper has constructed a simulated radio station complete with turntables, vintage country and gospel records, weather clocks and an old United Press International ticker. Surely Thomas Edison didn't have all this in mind.

Some of Jasper's radios are for sale, others are not. He also

Photos courtesy of Jasper Giardina and the Antique Radio Museum.

Celebrities with St. Louis native Jasper Giardina, his radios, and his fruit baskets: Geraldo Rivera *(above)*, Bill Murray *(right)*, and Richard Simmons *(below)*.

helps collectors by finding parts and tubes, and he assists with restorations. Notable visitors include singer Tony Bennett, actor Dom DeLuise and St. Louis-based sportscaster Bob Costas.

"Jay Leno was here," Jasper says. "All he was interested in was car radios. Merv Griffin came in a couple of years ago. He bought a radio for one of his gambling boats in Metropolis, Ill. President Jimmy Carter came in."

I own some old radios, about 7,992 less than Jasper. I've found that certain types of music sound better on different radios. My pink plastic kitchen radio is perfect for '60s rock kitsch. But the sprightly bass of big band music sounds delightful over my 1940s Zenith robot dial, replete with one AM band and two short wave bands.

"The 1940s Zeniths are perfect for big bands," he says. "All radios reflect different times. I was the oldest of five kids. My father died when I was 15. We had a big radio with tall legs—like the one over here," and he walks over to a four-legged 1929 Apex Highboy console model.

"We used to crawl *under* the radio and listen. I don't think I went to my first movie until I was 20 years old. We'd fight for the best spot to listen to the radio. We listened to [the Wheaties-sponsored All-American boy] Jack Armstrong every day. After all those fights, I told my brothers and sisters someday I'd get them a radio for every room."

Jasper used to run four antique shops in downtown St. Louis. His interest in radios piqued from antiquing. "Now I've started collecting microphones," he says. "I've got too many radios. But I don't know the first thing about microphones." Last summer Howard Stern did stop into Jasper's to pick up a phallic microphone.

But radios and microphones only speak for a part of Jasper's business. When Jasper is not conducting tours ($1.50 per person) of his museum, he can be found in the back of his store carefully arranging baskets for Jasper's Tropical Gift Fruit Basket Co. His father, Sam, was in the wholesale fruit business. Jasper even designs and writes his fruit basket brochures: *The Welcome Gift for All Occasions: for Love, for Happiness, for Real Estate Closings, for Bon Voyage, for Doctor Referrals . . .*

"People don't know how the radio and fruit goes together," Jasper says with a laugh. "But the fruit pays for this crazy hobby. I'm getting ready now for the Christmas rush. I don't make a lot of money. But I have a lot of fun." Of course, Jasper listens to the radio while he works; specifically, talk radio on KMOX-AM. He's a frequent guest on the station.

Jasper isn't married.

More than 8,000 radios can cause a lot of static.

"I've just had a gal leave me on account of this," he says. "Two weeks ago. We went together 45 years ago. We reunited through KMOX. Her mother heard me on the air and wrote her daughter in Florida. She said, 'That guy's on the loose.' So I sent her a great big fruit basket in Florida. We started going together. It was good for the first couple years . . ." and Jasper's voice drifts off to a faraway place. ". . . but she didn't like the radios."

Jasper has 30-year-old daughter, Alisa. She's in line to inherit the museum when Jasper rolls through that big transmitter into eternity. Alisa's working to get the museum online, actually a very un-radio thing to do. "I don't want it," Jasper says. "I told her I still use pencils with erasers on them."

There's a lifetime of memories in 8,000 radios. I asked Jasper to choose a favorite radio from his collection. After a thoughtful pause, he points to a 1938 gold-trimmed walnut Austin table radio with a clock.

"I have a fetish for clock radios," he says. "I bought this in Olney, Ill. The wood is perfect. The knobs are all matching. It's the perfect radio. It hasn't been Frankensteined and all butchered up. You listen to it and it reminds you that radio remains great because you use your imagination.

"The sound of people talking behind a microphone! The sound effects of people walking, that *clomp-clomp* on a table, and the sound of music. All you have to do is close your eyes."

And time stands still.

November 23, 1997

Fast food won the West
Fred Harvey was tourist oasis

KANSAS CITY, Mo.—The Fred Harvey Co. created America's first interstate restaurant chain. During the early 20th century, the Kansas City-based firm built its Harvey House along railway lines in the Southwest.

They were appetizers for American culture.

Fred Harvey came to America from England in 1850 at the age of 15. A gangly and spirited former dishwasher, Harvey struck a handshake deal in 1876 with representatives from the Atchison, Topeka & Santa Fe Railway to provide quality food service for passengers who were accustomed to miles of bad roadside cuisine. Trains were not equipped with dining cars.

Rail passengers disembarked from the train to eat at a Harvey House, usually within an allotted half-hour time frame. Fast food. By 1901 the Harvey Co. operated 16 hotels/restaurants and 26 restaurants along the Santa Fe line from Kansas to California. And Native American artists who lived along the route sold their work to tourists rolling through the region. An average tourist would pay $2 for souvenir-type items.

On one level, this unique arrangement launched the tourism industry in the Southwest. On a deeper level, the Harvey Co. taught Americans about humility, always the lasting treasure of travel.

"Experiencing on the senses of a world different from their own, travelers realize their provincialism and recognize their ignorance," wrote essayist Paul Fussell.

The Nelson-Atkins Museum of Art exhibition "Inventing the Southwest: The Fred Harvey Co. and Native American Art" is a fascinating story told through more than 300 objects, including Native American blankets, pottery and baskets as well as heartland marketing tools that the Harvey Co. used to promote the Southwest.

"Before the turn of the century there was no such thing as the Southwest as a [tourist] destination," said David Binkley, the Nelson-Atkins Museum curator of the arts of Africa, Oceania and the Americas. The exhibition was organized by the Heard Museum in Phoenix. Binkley served as a consultant. "It was through the contract between the Harvey Co. and the Santa Fe that they created a [tourist] structure. That's why it's called 'Inventing the Southwest.' And what do you need to be a tourist?

"You need an environment that has to appear welcoming. So pueblo women are foregrounded in a way. They're shown as art producers. They're smiling, with children, and they meet you at the train. You then have to determine how the Harvey Co. acquired the materials [some of which the Nelson-Atkins Museum purchased from the company before the museum opened in 1933]. And you have to have reliable food that's uniform in quality."

The Harvey Co. made the Southwest more visitor-friendly through several techniques. Most visible were the company's Harvey Girls. They were courteous, squeaky-clean women ages 18 to 30, who were hired from the East and Midwest to work as waitresses. Judy Garland starred in the 1946 film "The Harvey Girls," which featured the hit song "On the Atchison, Topeka and the Santa Fe" in its Oscar-winning score.

Harvey Girls were always single. Some archivists suggest that by marrying their road-weary customers, they helped civilize the Southwest. Thousands of Harvey Girls were tested with questions like: "What service requests should a guest never have to make?" (The answer: "Salt, pepper and sugar.")

Also, between 1925 and 1931, the Harvey Co. introduced Indian Detours, which featured touring vehicles called Harvey-cars that took passengers down the rough backroads to view the pueblos, Spanish villages and landscapes of Arizona and New Mexico. Indian Detours couriers (or guides) were young, college-educated women wearing Western outfits featuring velvet blouses and Navajo jewelry.

These excursions were another way for Native Americans who were far removed from the railroad to sell crafts directly to the tourist. Yet the visitor and the artist never came face-to-face. As train travel became more popular, the size, design, color and cost of the art became more market-driven.

Some contend that this sanitized the Southwest.

Native American silversmiths Gail Bird and Yazzie Johnson create stunning narrative jewelry pieces based on their experiences in the Southwest. Their "Route 66 Tourism Belt" is a highlight of "Inventing the Southwest." Heard Museum curator Diana Pardue brought Bird and Johnson into the exhibition after seeing their work at the annual Indian Market in Santa Fe, N.M. Pardue wanted to include current pieces that were also representative of the Harvey Co. collection.

Strung on leather with a sliver background and dotted with 18-karat gold, the Bird-Johnson piece is an elaboration on the Navajo concha belt, which typically has a dozen similar-looking, shell-shaped metals, or conchas. Bird and Johnson's conchas are all different and are cut in irregular shapes. Since 1979 they've produced 33 different belts. They only make one belt per theme, so the piece in "Inventing the Southwest" is unique.

Bird and Johnson's tourism belt depicts lightning bolts, hitchhikers' thumbs, pickup trucks and Route 66 icons such as the neon-drenched Blue Swallow Motel in Tucumcari, N.M.

"I don't feel devalued at all," Bird said from her home in northern New Mexico. Bird, 48, was born in Oakland, Calif. She is of Santo Domingo and Laguna extraction. Johnson is Navajo. Bird's father was reared on the Santo Domingo pueblo, halfway between Albuquerque and Santa Fe, off of Route 66. "I see how certain people can feel devalued. Anybody can allow themselves to become a victim. But there are certain ways people survive.

"And they survive by using the most exterior part of themselves in order to make a living and make some statement to the world. Art can help you do that. You don't reveal everything. There are all sorts of stories how Indian people will do a weaving or a textile, yet they'll retain a part of it so that it doesn't reveal all. Plus, it provides a way of maintaining some sort of sense of what happened."

Pueblo potter Maria Martinez (1880-1980) is the most recognized Native American artist of this century. She is depicted in the exhibition's re-creation of a lifesize diorama that was on view at the Nelson-Atkins Museum from 1933 to the early 1970s. "The diorama was a way to interpret Native American art to an audience in the Midwest," Binkley said.

The artist originally commissioned to work on the diorama was John G. Prasuhn, who had retired from the Field Museum in Chicago. Prasuhn traveled to the San Ildefonso Pueblo in San Diego, asked Martinez if she'd be willing to be photographed, took measurements and made a sculpture of her that was brought back to Kansas City.

Martinez came to Kansas City in 1954 and approved of the diorama. She requested one modification. She wanted the background changed from its classic tiered Taos Pueblo background to reflect the black mesa influence of San Ildefonso Pueblo, where she lived in 1915 when the Harvey Co. hired Martinez and husband Julian to demonstrate pottery-making at the Panama-California Exposition. The museum complied. And the Martinez diorama was brought back for the "Inventing the Southwest" exhibition.

Women played a major role in the Harvey Co., especially unusual for the early 20th century. Most of the Native American art was made by women while men worked in the fields. The Harvey Co. employed women to interpret Southwestern culture. And the Harvey Co. hired architect Mary Jane Colter (1869-1958). Among her Native American/Art Deco-inspired works were the Spanish rancho La Posada (the Resting Place), which opened in 1930 in Winslow, Ariz., and in 1922 she designed the El Navajo Hotel in Gallup, N.M. In 1925 Colter decorated the Fred Harvey shops in Chicago's Union Station.

The last remnants of Colter's work are the Phantom Ranch cabins, as well as the Lookout and Hermit's Rest curio shops in the Grand Canyon. The Grand Canyon is also the site of the Hopi House gift shop, located in the lone surviving Harvey House building.

"Roughly 85 percent of this exhibition was made by women," Binkley said. "Silver was produced by Navajo men. But basketry, blankets, household containers—it was all done by women. Some of the baskets are so incredible, so tight, they could even hold water.

"In the 19th century, the image of Native Americans was always masculine and of warriors. That changed dramatically with the arrival of the train. Harvey Co. was creating a whole marketing program. I don't think there was another moment in the early 20th century that was comparable to that—at all."

December 7, 1997

A flea market like no other

KANSAS CITY, Mo.—The Westport Flea Market is the only place in America where you can barter for treasures after eating a Cajun chicken salad and downing one of 26 different draught beers.

The indoor flea market and bar and grill is a must stop for anyone who visits the trendy Westport neighborhood, three miles south of downtown Kansas City. The popular catchphrase with locals is *"Get drunk and buy junk."*

"Many times men come here with their wives," said flea market general manager Barbara Cornelius. "They hang out in the bar area, drink and watch sports. The women go shop."

The bar and grill portion of the Westport Flea Market, 817 Westport Rd. (816-931-1986), is open from 11 a.m. to 11 p.m. Sunday through Thursday, and the bar stays open until 1 a.m. on Friday and Saturday. The roadhouse-inspired grill can seat between 150 and 200 people. The menu includes mighty fine cheeseburgers, chile con carne, salads and Friday night catfish.

Eight bar stools are lined up along a modest bar, not far from a CD jukebox, a foosball machine and a cardboard sign that reads, "No Spittin' On The Floor, Please."

The flea market, which features 30 full booths that snake throughout the complex, is open 10 a.m. to 5 p.m. Saturdays and Sundays. Dealers rent the space for an average of $40 for a weekend. The flea market is housed in a former potato chip factory. It is one of the oldest buildings in Westport. The glazed white brick building was erected in 1914.

As settlers headed west in the early 1900s on the Santa Fe and Oregon trails, they stopped in Westport to outfit their wagons before continuing their journey. Among the 1836 population of 50 people in Westport were scouts Kit Carson and John Sutter, who vamoosed to escape his creditors—and to become a key figure in the California Gold Rush.

Westport became part of Kansas City in 1899. The area underwent a major renaissance in the early 1970s when developer and former Dixieland jazz club owner Don Anderson came up with the idea for a Midwestern version of San Francisco's Ghirardelli Square. Anderson converted a run-down block of brick buildings along Westport Road into quaint retail shops and offices.

The Westport Flea Market even has a private Sante Fe Trail party room, which is used for business meetings, overflow lunch crowds and bachelorette parties. "Not too long ago we had a wedding reception in there," Cornelius said. "The groom's father was a regular customer here."

Flea market owner Mel Kleb, II bought the "flea," as he calls it, in 1979 when it had 30 percent occupancy, a $10,000 debt and was a week away from bankruptcy. "Within six months, I had 100 percent occupancy," said Kleb, a Kansas City native and former steakhouse owner. "But we had no food service."

In 1981 Kleb installed the bar and kitchen to increase the cash flow which would provide extra parking. "On the first day I had more staff than customers," he laughed. "I took four of my most well-endowed bar maids and we went on the streets and distributed over 35,000 two-for-one coupons in one week. I couldn't afford to advertise. All of a sudden people found us.

"And after all this time, I'm pretty sure this is the only flea market in the country like this. I've been contacted by four other cities who wanted to mirror this image and put a restaurant in a flea market, but it's hard to do. This one is so unique."

Kleb, 55, also owns the Holiday Inn adjacent to the flea market, which accounts for notable flea market visitors like actor Ed Asner, country singer Charley Pride and the country band Little Texas.

The flea market is known around here for a couple things:

- The Flea Market Burger ($5.45), is regarded as one of the best hamburgers in Kansas City, a lean 10-ounces of ground chuck from McGonigle's Meat, area prime beef butcher. "We go through 300 to 400 pounds of hamburger every other day," said Cornelius, also a Kansas City native.

- During the mid-1980s antique dealer Robert Andrew Berdella operated a booth he called "Bob's Bizarre Bazaar" near the front of the flea market. Berdella sold New Guinea ancestral figures, African ceremonial bones as well as paintings, old record albums, furniture, axes and jewelry he designed.

When Bob wasn't manning his booth between 1984 and 1988, he was busy killing at least six young area men. After Berdella's 1988 arrest, police found artifacts that included 2,000-year old Roman vials filled with tears and Tibetan exorcism knives, all stacked throughout his Kansas City home.

According to the 1995 book *Mass Murder and Serial Killing Exposed,* Berdella "sedated his victims with animal anesthetics and tranquilizers, then restrained them with ropes, gags and a dog collar around the neck." And it gets worse.

In October, 1992, Berdella suffered a fatal heart attack while serving a life sentence without parole in a prison in Jefferson City, Mo. He was 43.

"The bottom line with that story is how well you know your neighbor," said Cornelius, who has worked at the flea market since 1985. "And what are they doing in their basement? He had a lot of imported jewelry from Africa. Earrings. He even had voodoo dolls up there. But no one had a clue.

"After he was arrested we had a lot of people come through here for curiosity, but the newspaper made it sound like he owned the place."

Kleb added, "All we knew about him was that he was a tenant who paid his rent on time. He was rather shy, but he was visible and involved in fund-raising in the community. People were shocked. It was part of our history and we never ducked it. But everyone moved past it all pretty quickly."

It wasn't difficult for Cornelius to move on. The 45-year-old former waitress constantly keeps an eye open for that special flea market find. Cornelius looked back toward a cluttered booth and said, "As a matter of fact I'm just taking home stuff like Ginsu knives and antique sterling silver serving forks for pickles that I bought over the weekend. If you take the time to look around, you can find a lot in here."

It's food for thought.

November 1, 1998

Hair museum saves strands of history

INDEPENDENCE, Mo.—This is not just another other piece about hair. It's a hair piece, all right, but with cultural waves. First-time visitors will flip their wigs when they walk into Leila's Hair Museum in the Independence College of Cosmetology, 815 W. 23rd St., just outside Kansas City.

The walls of the small museum are covered with more than 150 framed wreaths made of human hair and 2,000 pieces of jewelry (earrings, hat pins, necklaces) containing, or made of, human hair. There are hairy postcards and even a 5-inch bookmark made entirely of hair. That's for when you're reading about Harry Truman, Independence's most famous son.

Hardee, hair-hair.

Another highlight of the museum is a matching set of late 1800s hair wreaths from two sisters who sheared their hair before joining a convent in Sedalia, Mo. A couple of other pieces even include black horse hair.

Collectively, it all seems a little creepy—until you meet museum curator-founder Leila Cohoon. She is a sweet woman who is truly devoted to collecting hair arts and crafts that date back to before 1600. Cohoon, 67, is a native of Marceline, Mo., the hometown of Walt Disney. A hairdresesr by trade, Cohoon founded the college of cosmetology with her husband, Don, in 1960. She used to dress the hair of Disney's redheaded schoolteacher.

Cohoon snagged her first hair wreath in 1958. She was en route to buy a pair of Easter shoes in downtown Kansas City, Mo. "I went by an antique shop and saw a hair wreath," says Cohoon. "On the back, in German, it says, 'Mama and Papa, 1852.' I didn't know they made anything out of hair, much less decorations. I was hooked. It didn't make a difference how long it would take or how much it would cost, I was after everything I could get my hands on. I couldn't believe the art form. I still can't."

Cohoon gets to the roots of hair art.

After collecting just two Victorian-influenced hair wreaths, she began to study the intricate designs that went into the pieces, such as assorted flowers and even a tiny rooster. Using her hairdressing knowledge, Cohoon learned how to duplicate the detailed, original styles. She now can authentically restore some of her pieces.

"Then, other times, the background is dilapidated," she says. "Sometimes I have to find a new frame. About half of the wreaths are in their original frames. There's only one product I clean them with. You can't have any moisture because wires that hold the hair together would rust."

I know that problem.

Today, hair crafts are virtually a lost art. Cohoon may be the world's foremost expert on the art form, which she has traced back to the 15th century. Just last month Cohoon helped form the Victorian Hair Weavers Society, which had its first meeting in Kansas City, Mo. "There were six hair weavers at this convention," Cohoon says. "That was a thrill. I've spent all these years trying to find people who know how to do this."

Comic Phyllis Diller sold a hair wreath to the museum. She found the four-generational piece in an antique store. When Diller's daughter sent it to the museum, Phyllis attached the note, "This hair wreath comes to you from a woman who has outlived her hair." Cohoon's rules of induction insist the piece must be at least 100 years old. That's why the museum has no other celebrity pieces and why we'll all have to wait for the Fabio

Photo courtesy of Leila's Hair Museum.

One of over 2,000 examples of Victorian hairwork on
display at Leila's Hair Museum in Independence, Mo.

hair wreath.

David Letterman's producers thought about booking Cohoon on the show but then backed off, saying the hair museum "wasn't funny enough." Cohoon, however, does plan to write Oprah Winfrey for assistance in tracing the genealogy of one of her rare acquisitions. Cohoon works on her pieces with fortitude and a tender blend of wonder and nostalgia.

"We certainly don't have the patience today the old-timers had," she says. "I remember my grandmother making a remark, 'That person doesn't have the patience to count hairs.' And I wonder if it isn't because of this art form that my grandmother said that. You never hear anybody saying that today.

"And to do this [art], you do have to know how to count hairs. The hair has to be going the right direction because it has a cuticle on it, which tangles if you work with it upside down. The hair in each one of these [wreaths] usually comes from an entire family. So I can't take a piece of one and put it in another one."

One of the museum's prize items is an 1852 floral tapestry featuring the locks of 156 members of a single family. Frankly, I didn't know the Osmonds went back that far. Cohoon strolls over to a matched set of hair wreaths, each piece containing brown hair beautifully woven around 4-inch-long evergreen branches. "Who would think to do that?" she asks. "The hair looks like it's coming out of the branches. It's the only matched set I have in here."

For many people, wreaths of hair can seem sad and without flair.

Au contraire!

"Hair wreaths are not memorial pieces as in *mourning,*" she says, nodding toward a wedding hair wreath. "This was a happy occasion. That's the bride and groom's hair [shaped as two hearts]. The rest of it is [hair] from the wedding party. The amazing thing is the lady had to get the wedding dress [a portion of which served as a white background] and collect the hair from all those people in order to give it as a gift the day of the wedding. I'd say 50 to 60 people were involved in that.

"There's a lot of different colors in there."

Cohoon has been married for 46 years. She's used to the jokes, inspired by her husband. "He always started it," says Cohoon, who has children 44 and 45 years old and seven grandchildren. "He would tell people, 'She's got hair under the bed,' 'She's got

hair in the closet,' and they'd all laugh. I imagined people thinking I cut hair and it just rolled in those places. But he'd let me
explain this is where I hid my hair pieces when I'd buy them. I
didn't want him to know how much money I was spending.
Finally, I couldn't hide them anymore. I had to start the museum.
All this is my paycheck down the years. But it's been a labor of
love."

Every day is a good hair day in the museum on 23rd Street.
Cohoon greets visitors with a broad smile and a hair brooch on her
gold jacket. "The Victorians were very sentimental," Cohoon
says. "At one time the price of hair cost more than gold. I have
another brooch at home with the hair from two children who
passed away within a short time of each other. So the mother had
a brooch made, which I'm sure she wore.

"The older child was 11, and her hair is in the background, and
the baby's hair is laying on top of the older child's hair. And when
I wear a brooch, I know that mother would be very proud." Leila
Cohoon wears the tradition well.

Leila's is open from 8:30 a.m. to 4:30 p.m. Monday-Saturday.
Admission is $3 for adults or $1.50 for seniors and kids under 12.
Call (816) 252-HAIR.

July 12, 1998

VE HICLE

MICHIGAN

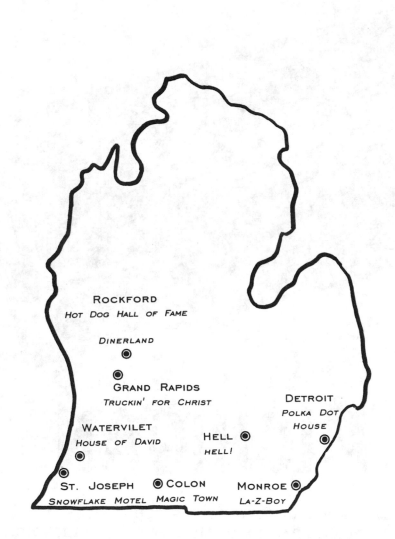

ROCKFORD
HOT DOG HALL OF FAME

DINERLAND
◉

◉
GRAND RAPIDS
TRUCKIN' FOR CHRIST

DETROIT
POLKA DOT
HOUSE

WATERVILET
HOUSE OF DAVID

HELL ◉
HELL!

◉

◉

◉
WATERVILET
HOUSE OF DAVID

◉ COLON
MAGIC TOWN

MONROE ◉
LA-Z-BOY

◉
ST. JOSEPH
SNOWFLAKE MOTEL

Map by Lisa Day.

Road to Hell leads directly to . . . Michigan?

HELL, Mich.—This road trip is paved with sizzling jokes.

I've been to Hell and back.

Let's go to Hell.

Too easy.

Hell is an easy-going borough of 247 people about 50 miles west of Detroit and 20 miles north of Ann Arbor. Hell is known for horseback riding, fishing and hiking on more than 11,666 acres of hilly countryside. Hell is located in the state-operated Pinckney Recreation Area.

The focal point of social activity is the Hell Country Store and Spirits, 4025 Patterson Lake Rd.—formerly the Devil's Den. Across the parking lot from the store is the Dam Site Inn restaurant and tavern. Hell's Halloween activities will take place in the parking lot, adjacent to Hell Creek.

A big bonfire is planned for Devil's Night (Saturday), and on Halloween people will be bobbing for apples and entering costume and pumpkin-carving contests. All events are free.

There's not much else to do in Hell. But "Mayor" Odum Plenty aims to make it a vacation hot spot. In real life Plenty is John Colone, the former owner of a Chrysler Plymouth Dodge Jeep Eagle dealership four miles down the road in Pinckney (pop. 1,400).

Two big things happened in Hell the day before I got there.

Colone celebrated his 54th birthday. And he sold his dealership to spend more time in Hell. "My goal is for Hell to be the Halloween capital of the country," Colone says during a scenic tour of the community. Colone owns the country store and the adjacent five acres of land.

Next month work begins on remodeling a former party store on the Colone property into the Hell's Bells ice cream and souvenir shop. And a new "haunted" bed and breakfast is in the works on a nearby 12-acre plot of land that Colone has an option to buy.

Hell Creek Ranch, established in 1963, is one of the oldest

ranches in the state. The 3,600-acre ranch at 10866 Cedar Lake Rd. offers camping, canoe trips, ice fishing and horseback riding. There are nine wooden bridges which frame the 140 miles of hiking trails in the Pinckney Recreation Area that is part of Hell.

"Hell is one of the best destinations for motorcycles in the state of Michigan," Colone says. "There's great roads here, and we're close to Detroit. We get 60,000 bikers a year that come through here."

In mid-May the town hosts a HellFest, where local ministers bless motorcycles and street rods. (The festival used to be called BuzzardFest because buzzards roosted in the area every May.)

All year long, visitors from around the world sign a guestbook in the country store with commentary like "Dad drove us to Hell." One tourist recently came to Michigan from Hell, Sweden.

Actor Jeff Daniels lives near Chelsea, 15 miles south of Hell. Rocker Ted Nugent resides on a remote compound in Jackson, 30 miles east of Hell, but he comes to Hell often to visit his hunting buddy, "Tattoo Donny."

Colone was born and reared in Pinckney. He couldn't escape Hell.

The town got its name in 1841. Founder George Reeves would grind barley, corn and wheat in the family mill. "But he also had a still," Colone says. "The first six or seven bushels were made into moonshine. A lot of time the horses would come home by themselves; wagons would show up with no driver. Things had gone to hell. When it came time to name the town they said, 'Why don't you call it Hell? Everybody else does.' "

Colone is trying to build a still to commemorate Reeves, and he's applying the finishing touches on a wind chime made out of bowling balls. He points out, "When it clangs, run like hell." And in front of the country store is a National Weather Service Observation Station where the daily temperature and barometric pressure are posted, just in case it gets hot as. . .

Well, it can get cold in Hell. Colone points out, "Last January was the first time I saw Hell freeze over in about eight years. It takes three or four days of minus degrees to get that dam to freeze."

Colone has had some hell in his life, which explains his dreams of a little heaven on earth. He was squad leader of the 3rd/506 Infantry, Company A, 4th Platoon of the 101st Airborne Division in Vietnam. He was seriously wounded and spent nearly two years in hospitals in Da Nang and Saigon of what was then South Vietnam. "I was actually found naked and toe-tagged in a body bag," he says in soft tones. "During the Tet Offensive of '68. My platoon walked into an ambush. There was 21 of us. And 17 of them were . . .

". . . I was shot five times. In my leg, arm, head, hands," he says. Colone pats his right knee and continues, "I saw my lieutenant two years ago. That was the first time we got together. Nobody wanted . . . I just wanted no part of anything . . ."

Colone stops talking. He looks at the water which gently runs down the dam. The clear water cannot wash away the rush of memories.

"I remember going in the service and instead of using Pinckney as my home-town, I'd just say Hell," he continues. "I always thought there was great possibili-ties to use the world 'Hell' in fun. So last year I formed a company called Abaddon Enterprises."

In the Old Testament, Abaddon is the angel from hell.

In the early 1960s Colone even named his '59 Plymouth Fury "Abad-don."

"I've been in the car business 33 years," Colone says. "I bought the deal-ership 21 years ago. And yesterday I agreed to sell it. We're one of the top 5 percent dealers in the country [in cus-tomer satisfaction, according to his par-ent Chrysler Five-Star Program]. But the car business isn't fun anymore, and I want to do something else. This gives me the money and the time to. . ."

Bumper sticker courtesy of Hell, Michigan.

Colone can't help himself. He says, ". . . go to Hell.

"So I got together with six of my friends that didn't know each other, but have all had some hell in their lives. We formed a [six-person] board for Abaddon. One member was a chopper pilot from Vietnam. Another is a minister. Another is a wonderful lady who got married at 40 and adopted seven physically challenged children. They all live within a 10-mile radius of Hell."

Abaddon Enterprises will invest $1 million over the next three years to get Hell off the ground. Colone pledges that his group will keep Hell family-oriented. He explains, "On our Web site [*www.hell2u.com*] we've had people want to do X-rated things, and we want no part of that. We don't allow any religious things. That's why I bought up all the property."

Colone and his wife, Annie, live in Pinckney. They've been married 33 years and have two daughters, Laura, 31, and Michele, 30. Colone and his wife own a four-bedroom lakefront cottage directly behind the country store.

There's no real mayor of Hell, and Livingston County police patrol it. Colone likes to joke that Hell once had a church. It burned down. "We still performed seven weddings here last year," he later says, smiling through a red plastic pitchfork in the country store. "Out in the back here. We want to build a little chapel."

About 10 years ago the Hell Country Store and Spirits got permission from the U.S. Postal Service to run a post office in the store. People love to send correspondence postmarked from Hell—especially on April 15.

The store sells Bloody Mary mix—Bloody Mary From Hell—and Salsa From Hell as well as a real square inch of Hell with a certificate of authenticity signed by county soil conservationist "Jim Sparks." The dirt comes in a heart-shaped plastic box. The order number is 7734, which when read upside down is hell.

Colone explains, "The beauty of it is that because there is no government here, we fall under the [1992] Rural America Act where there's all kinds of grants and 2 percent and 3 percent loans so we don't lose these little towns. That's what we're about. Communities are built on business, not by residence."

Not everyone buys into Colone's dreams for Hell.

One resident wrote Colone a letter with "Gang Leader" scrawled on the envelope criticizing the "mayor" for his greed. "Hell, I put on a car show every year at my dealership and we raise $14,000 to 16,000," Colone says. "Every dime goes to charity. We don't allow commercial vendors to sell food or anything in

Hell."

Abaddon did conjure up the mythical "Damnation University," or "Dam U," as graduates call it, which offers degrees in everything. "To people with great hindsight we even offer analvision," Colone quips.

Just last month, before a show in Auburn Hills, Mich., Mayor Odum Plenty presented Bruce Springsteen with a dual Dam U degree for philanthropy and for leading the best rock 'n' roll band on the planet.

Colone explains, "I had a home remodeled and I became friends with this guy from the flooring company in New York. He called me one day and said he was coming to work on a $2 million home in Ann Arbor. He came out here, had too much to drink, so we took him to a hotel.

"He had a great time in Hell"

During the course of the evening's activities, Colone mentioned that he was searching for Springsteen tickets. "The guy said, 'Oh, I can get you those.' " Colone says. "After a few beers you can do anything. Well it turned out he had put floors in Bruce's house in New Jersey. We got tickets and backstage passes.

"We gave Bruce the degree and at first it was like 'What is this stuff?' but then he came back with a big hug and said, 'I can't believe how nice this is.' " All degrees are personalized with items that Abaddon creative director Todd McKinney digs up on the Internet.

It's hard to leave Hell after a visit on a splendid autumn day. Armed with my own Dam U journalism degree, some Greetings From Hell postcards and Hell boxer shorts I bought for my angelic girlfriend, I bid goodbye to Colone, McKinney and the gang at the Hell Country Store and Spirits.

I thank them for their warm hospitality. Everyone laughs.

In these parts, there's nothing like fanning the fire.

Hell is a four-hour drive from Chicago. Take Interstate 94 to Chelsea, Mich. (Route 52), about 30 miles east of Jackson. Exit 52 north to Werkner Road. Go right on Werkner to Territorial Road. Turn right on North Territorial and go through the small town of Inverness. As you exit town, look for Hankerd and turn left on Hankerd. That will take you through the Half Moon Lake beach area before Hankerd dead-ends on Patterson Lake Road. Turn right and head into Hell. Motels are in Chelsea and Howell,

Mich., each about 12 miles from Hell.

For more information, call Hell Country Store and Spirits at (734) 878-3129.

October 24, 1999

A bit of Frank Lloyd Wright in an unlikely place

ST. JOSEPH, Mich.—Last call was on the horizon last Friday at the Snow Flake Lounge, in the Frank Lloyd Wright-inspired Snow Flake Motel south of St. Joseph. A local Elvis Presley and Patsy Cline husband-and-wife impersonation team was hosting karaoke night.

It was a blizzard of the bizarre.

Joe Atkins had just gotten off the late shift as press operator at Wolverine Metal Stamping across the street from the motel. He's a sharp soul singer in the three-octave style of Luther Ingram. "Stretch," a 6-foot-7 Benton Harbor rock 'n' roll booking agent, strolled in for a nightcap. And "Rubber Duckie" was singing all night. He used to be in the Navy. Pretty soon Joe, Stretch and Rubber Duckie were harmonizing on Boyz II Men's "The End of the Road." Never has a song seemed so symbolic.

"It's unnatural. . .," crooned the men, with "Elvis" and "Patsy" looking on with bliss. *"You belong to me/I belong to you . . ."*

The morning after, motel owner Pradyuman Patel was standing in the motel office. He looked frazzled. His long black hair dangled in front of his tired eyes. "This is all very tough," he grumbled—and he hadn't even been in the lounge the previous night.

Patel grabbed a clipboard showing the roll call of his Friday night clients. There were six names on a white sheet of paper. That meant 51 other units at the Snow Flake had sat vacant. There were more visitors at the lounge than people staying at the motel. Patel shook the clipboard and said, "This is a negative cash flow."

Things turned positive this week.

Patel's property will become the Travelodge/Snow Flake Motel (Inspired by Frank Lloyd Wright) as early as late winter. Glenn Anderson is Travelodge/Knight's Inn director of franchise sales at the parent company Cendant Corp. (Also the parent company of Welcome Wagon!) Last Monday, wheels were set in motion for a $500,00 bank loan that will help Patel restore his motel as a

Travelodge historic property.

In an interview from his Des Plaines office, Anderson said, "He will repaint it, renovate the interior rooms and put in electronic locks. There will be new landscaping. He gets to restore the original sign. We do motorcoach tours, and this is part of the Lake Michigan tour we want to put on the chart."

The Snow Flake Motel was built between 1961 and 1962. Wright died in 1959. No one is sure on how involved Wright was with the motel, but the plans were completed by William Wesley Peters, Wright's chief apprentice and son-in-law, in 1960.

Wright's is best-known as a residential architect who strived to get away from the boxed-in feeling of houses. His vision of the motel came from above. From the sky, the six wings surrounding the now-desolate courtyard-garden appear as a six-pointed snowflake star. A hexagon-shaped pool filled with debris is covered by the skeleton of what's supposed to be a Plexiglas dome.

The motel was originally painted blue and white to denote a crisp Michigan winter. Today, it is a faded brown and white and is in a state of disrepair. A few people have written newspaper articles about the Snow Flake.

It seems like even fewer have actually stayed there.

The Snow Flake was even overlooked by completist filmmakers Ken Burns and Lynn Novick, whose two-part biography on Wright aired last week on PBS. Earlier this year the sleek, organic motel was listed in the National Register of Historic Places.

Patel felt burned by articles that described the motel as a dump, but the truth is, he has given up on some of the rooms. From my patio window I saw a row of empty rooms with ramshackle drapes and overturned mattresses. The place had the feel of an abandoned space shuttle.

My room was OK. I've had worse for $37.80. The renovated rooms have a loft-like feel with exposed white brick, dark brown wood and modern ceiling lights. The best word to describe the bathroom is industrial.

I cranked up the heat and pulled in some Chicago stations on my non-cable television set. Original built-in Jetson-style wall fixtures remained for wakeup calls and telephone calls, but they did not work. Check out the motel room's aqua blue and wood chairs while you can. New furniture will be part of the renovation.

Patel, 45, bought the motel two years ago for $850,000. He put $450,000 back into the motel and changed the name to the St. Joseph Inn—although everyone else still calls it the Snow Flake Motel. Patel was in the hotel business in Detroit for 11 years. Frank Lloyd Wright was the only reason he purchased the motel. "But now, no one cares," he said.

Anderson elaborated, "Someone wrote an article that just ripped the place. [Patel] put $450,000 into something that was a complete wreck, he was trying to get a loan for another half million, and someone burned him to death. This poor guy is on his last leg. He doesn't want to talk to another reporter. He tries hard. If you would have seen what that place looked like before he had it. . . . It's 100 percent better, and it's got another 100 percent to go."

Patel has written to the Frank Lloyd Wright Foundation in Chicago, the William Wesley Peters Memorial Library at Taliesin West in Scottsdale, Ariz., and Taliesin in Spring Green, Wis., for assistance, but they have not responded. They can't help, since the Snow Flake is not a Wright building.

"There is a conservancy for Frank Lloyd Wright buildings," said architect Charles Montooth from Taliesin in Spring Green. "But this motel was designed by William Wesley Peters. I was by the Snow Flake two summers ago, and I feel for the fellow [Patel]. There's not a lot we can do. We're trying to get financial help to keep Taliesin going, too. Taliesin is Wright's landmark home, studio and gardens in southern Wisconsin."

Montooth, 78, worked with Wright from 1945 until Wright's death in 1959. He said, "I doubt if Mr. Wright even saw the [Snow Flake] drawings. It certainly was inspired by him. It's a beautiful design with an interesting roof. The whole pattern followed the principles of Mr. Wright. The pattern develops around the court-yard in the geometric figure of a hexagon.

"But also, what you see is what you get. In summer, the leaves are out and they add enrichment. In the winter, the icicles are dramatic as they hang from the snowflake-patterned awnings. All these things work together. Mr. Wright had a favorite expression, 'There's a reward for honesty.' So if you had an honest design and the design expressed the structure and vice versa, good things would come of it. Like light coming in. I know someone who stayed there, and I was pleased to know some of the original rooms still have life in them."

The Snow Flake Lounge has different management from the

motel. Jay Patel leases the lounge from Pradyuman Patel. They are not related; in fact, they don't get along that well. Jay Patel also owns the rustic Silver Dollar Cafe and Mickey's Lounge near downtown St. Joseph.

Elvis and Patsy perform at Mickey's on Thursday night, and they bring their 1,400 CDs and $8,000 worth of video and sound equipment to the Snow Flake Lounge every Friday. (Elvis and Patsy are a lock for New Year's Eve at the Snow Flake—book your room now.)

Elvis and Patsy, a.k.a. Mike and Katie Martin, have been married 11 months. Katie, 47, is a waitress at the Snow Flake Lounge. Her grandfather, Jesse A. Kraft, played for the House of David baseball team out of Benton Harbor. Her father, Edward Krajecki, started 16-inch softball in Michigan before bringing it to Chicago. Mike, 52, is a millwright at Bosch Braking System, another factory across the street from the Snow Flake.

Remember, this is a small town.

Mike explained, "She was in love with me 30 years ago, and I was married. I divorced that woman, married someone else and started doing karaoke at the bar and met her," and he nods toward Katie. "Things felt right at home, and this is where I'll be the rest of my life.

"And we're going to do music the rest of our life."

The Martins are not as theatrical as the Milwaukee-based Thunder and Lightning/Elvis & Patsy impersonation team. Besides covering Patsy Cline, Katie also does Shania Twain and Reba McEntire. Mike does a killer of Faron Young's "Hello Walls." He said, "I also do Conway Twitty and Willie Nelson, but no matter who I sing, everybody says I still come out like Elvis."

And so goes another American Trilogy on Midwestern backroads: Elvis. Frank Lloyd Wright. Immigrant motel owners trying to make their way. Frank Lloyd Wright said it best when he said, "Looking *in* is not so easy as looking *at*."

The Snow Flake Motel, 3822 Red Arrow Highway, is open year-round. It is about a 100-mile drive from Chicago: Take I-94 East, get off at Exit 23 and turn right. Call (616) 429-3261.

November 15, 1998

Michigan town casts a spell on visitors

COLON, Mich.—It's no illusion. Colon is the most magical city in America. A three-hour drive from Chicago, the Michigan resort town has a Magic City Hardware, Magi Cafe and the Magic Carpet Restaurant.

The Colon Magi High School's mascot is a fighting white rabbit.

Gee. Every little thing they do around here is magic.

That's because Colon—population 1,200—is the home of Abbott's Magic Co., 124 St. Joseph St., a block west of the only blinking light in Colon. The traffic light signals entry into a downtown decorated with street planters that resemble magicians' top hats.

Chicago-born Harry Blackstone Sr. was the first magician to settle in Colon. In 1927 Blackstone and Australian vaudeville act (ventriloquist, juggler, magician) Perry Abbott created the Blackstone Magic Co. Their partnership lasted 18 months before they went separate ways. In 1934 Abbott formed his own company, which is still going strong today.

TOP 10 ROAD TUNES
For your drive to Colon, Mich.

1. "Strange Magic," Electric Light Orchestra
2. "Do You Believe in Magic?," Lovin' Spoonful
3. "Into the Mystic," Van Morrison
4. "Magical Mystery Tour," Beatles
5. "Magic," Cars
6. "Magic Carpet Ride," Steppenwolf
7. "That Old Black Magic," Frank Sinatra
8. "Spooky," Classics IV
9. "This Magic Moment," Drifters
10. "Trick Bag," Earl King

Every summer Colon celebrates its heritage with an annual "Abbott's Magic Get-Together," which this year runs Aug. 4-9.

Magicians from around the world will levitate to Colon. Confirmed acts include Japan's Mahka Tendo, Germany's Topaz, Circus Boy, Ice McDonald and Hungary's Mr. Jupiter. That lineup sounds more like next year's Bulls to me.

Abbott's is owned and operated by Greg Bordner, whose father, Recil, started the 1934 business with Abbott. When Bordner, 48, graduated with a degree in political science from Michigan State University in 1974, he began working at the magic company. His father died in 1981.

Bordner still lives in the area.

"I live in the suburbs," he says. "Semi-Colon."

I laugh really hard.

With a straight face, Bordner says, "Some people don't think that's funny. You've been on the road too long."

Blackstone settled in Colon because he was a regular performer at the still-standing State Theatre in Kalamazoo, Mich. "And Colon is halfway between Chicago and Detroit," Bordner says. "In the 1930s the big magicians had their own railway cars which enabled them to do the vanishing camel or the vanishing elephant onstage. The railroad went through town. Colon was also a great place for recreation. Vaudeville theaters weren't air conditioned, so they took the summers off when lesser acts played the houses. They came here to start the new show up and create new tricks."

Colon remains a magnetic force for magicians worldwide. About a dozen magicians live in Colon; even more are buried in Colon Lakeside Cemetery, State Street and Farrand Road, a mile west of town. They're listed on a printed handout titled "Their Final Act."

Harry Blackstone Sr. is buried beneath a mysterious white marble headstone that can be interpreted as either a rose or a flame. Although he died in November 1965, he is still trying to fool people. Three generations of Blackstones are buried in Lakeside Cemetery.

Entertainer Karrell Fox's (a.k.a. "Milky the Clown" in the Detroit area) headstone (1928- 1998) simply says, "It Was Fun." And humorist-magician "Little Johnny Jones" (1898- 1995) has a headstone adorned with the picture of a magician. The epitaph

BLACKSTONE

HARRY BOUTON

SEPTEMBER 27, 1885
NOVEMBER 16, 1965

Photo by Lisa Day.

reads, "Now I have to go and fool St. Peter."

Standing in the cemetery on a bright blue day, Bordner explains, "It's sort of the elephant's burial ground for magicians. During magic week we have an annual celebration of life for somebody new who is being planted. This year it is Ricki Dunn, who was a pick-pocket. He worked in Las Vegas." In the showrooms, I presume.

A party in Dunn's memory will be held at 5 p.m. Aug. 6 at the Abbott Magic Co. The party is open to the public.

But for the living, Abbott's is a treasure trove of tricks. The mostly mail-order store carries several thousand magic items, including advanced levitations (starting at $500 and rising, of course) a bouquet of trick flowers ($8.50) and books about Blackstone, Harry Houdini and others. Abbott's manufactures some items; others are imported. "We've got orders going out to Saudi Arabia and South Africa," Bordner says as he wanders around the 2,400-square-foot showroom, which is open to the public.

Abbott's leather and canvas straitjackets (starting at $200) are most compelling. The leather straps are installed by Miller's Harness Shop in an Amish colony nearby. "About 10 percent of the area is Amish," Bordner says. "And they all have their own little business, whether they sell eggs, chickens or whatever. They're real hard-working people."

Even in a bind.

Bordner can't understand the attention bestowed on younger magicians like David Blaine. This spring Blaine received national publicity for a New York stunt when he was buried alive for seven days in a three-ton water-filled tank that covered a Plexiglas coffin.

"Lots of the tricks he does are available in magic shops," Bordner says. "Maybe not being buried alive, but I have books on the subject. I couldn't believe he got his own television special. He's doing stuff I sell, which is great for me because people will say, 'Give me that [folding] coin where it looks like you're breaking the end off.' That's a $10 trick we sell."

Another good trick is to figure out how Colon got its name.

Local lore has it that in the 1830s a man known as Indian Trader Hatch and settler Louravasis Shellhous surveyed the plot of land which is nestled between Palmer Lake and Sturgeon Lake. They supposedly chose "colon" because they position of the lake and the St. Joseph River two miles north of the lakes correspond exactly to the position of the colon.

"That's one story," Bordner says. "The other is a guy [Shellhous] just opened the dictionary and stuck his finger at the word 'colon.' I can't believe they didn't change the name. Because there's so many easy jokes, like 'We're just passing through.' "

Photo by Lisa Day.

Abbott's magic store in Colon, Michigan.

Michigan's Colon is so small, it has no hotels. Magic week visitors stay in nearby Sturgis and Three Rivers.

"Some visitors stay in people's homes here," Bordner says. "I'll ask someone if they can keep a magician or a magic fan, and they tell me they've had magicians stay with them for 30 years. Friendships have developed over the years from that."

To get to Colon, take Interstate 80/90 east to the Howe/La Grange (Ind.) exit. That's highway M-66. Follow it 13 miles through Sturgis, Mich., directly into Colon.

St. Joseph is the first street in Colon where you can make a left turn. Take it, and poof! You're there.

July 11, 1999

Snapshots in recliner history courtesy of La-Z-Boy.

A pilgrimage for the armchair traveler

MONROE, Mich.—Gen. George Armstrong Custer took a stand, but the townspeople of his boyhood home in Monroe would prefer to take a seat.

This is the home of the La-Z-Boy Museum & Archives.

There may be bigger and fancier museums, but Monroe can lay claim to the world's most comfortable museum. La-Z-Boy is the nation's largest manufacturer of upholstered furniture and the world's leading producer of reclining chairs. Monroe, pop. 22,902, is on Interstate 75, just 35 miles south of Detroit and 20 miles north of Toledo, Ohio. The La- Z-Boy Museum makes for a perfect Labor Day getaway.

With seat reclined, cruise control and the Beatles' "Golden Slumbers" on the radio, of course.

And since the intrepid general was born down the road in New Rumley, Ohio, Monroe does offer a "Traces of Gen. George A. Custer" tour that covers nearly two dozen sites that relate to his life.

Custer only lived to be 37. La-Z-Boy celebrates its 70th anniversary this year. The company was founded in 1928 by cousins Edwin J. Shoemaker and Edward M. Knabusch in Monroe. Around town they were affectionately known as "The Two Eds."

Now, with annual sales of more than $1 billion, the company employees 13,000 people in 29 manufacturing facilities and subsidiaries throughout the world. La-Z-Boy is no longer the butt of old guy jokes.

Featuring more than 45 pieces of vintage La-Z-Boy furniture, original machinery, homespun memorabilia and advertising relics, the museum is housed in the Two Eds' original building, erected in 1927 at 1284 N. Telegraph Rd.

The La-Z-Boy Museum is a half-mile north of the 25-year-old Danny's Frozen Custard stand, 1020 W. Elm (734-242-5477). Before visiting the museum, I had some custard for Custer. I like to live life large.

Knabusch died in 1988 at the age of 88. Shoemaker, who designed the original La-Z-Boy reclining porch chair, died earlier this year in his winter home in Sun City, Ariz. He was 90.

Shoemaker had gone to dinner with some friends. When he

returned home, he fell asleep in his favorite La-Z-Boy recliner and died. That's the ultimate La-Z-Boy endorsement.

In his final years Shoemaker worked with museum director Judith Carr, interpreting the museum and archives. "I have a letter he wrote me just before he passed away, talking about the projects he planned on working on when he came back," Carr said during a museum tour. "He wanted to make some more miniature model chairs. They were salesman samples that show how the mechanism works. You can't see the mechanism on a full-fledged chair." Many of Shoemaker's handcrafted maple model chairs are on display.

The museum and archives project were the idea of La-Z-Boy President Charles Knabusch, Edward's son. Knabusch died last year of a heart attack. He was 57. "By working with the family on this, we all learned to appreciate what they went through," Carr said. "They started the company in 1928, and Wall Street crashed in October, 1929. They went through that first decade with very little capital and experience. It's amazing they survived."

A museum visit begins with one of the first upholstered La-Z-Boy chairs, kicking back in a cozy alcove area adjacent to a private showroom. The alcove backdrop replicates the Shoemaker family farm in Monroe circa 1928.

"The company was not started to make La-Z-Boy chairs ," Carr said. "The company began by building novelty furniture. It was called the Floral City Furniture Co. [because of all the Monroe nurseries]. Mr. Shoemaker was the master engineer, and Mr. Knabusch was the guy who went out and made contacts, the true entrepreneur."

The museum offers a tender look at the Two Eds' childhood creations, such as a miniature cabinet Shoemaker made for his sister when he was 11 years old. The cabinet was built from cigar boxes and orange crates. And when the elder Knabusch was 12, he made his mother a bedroom outfit. Carr looked at the immaculately crafted wares and said, "The fact that young boys would even think of such a thing is incredible."

In 1928, Shoemaker conjured up the idea for a reclining wood-slat lawn chair by hinging the seat and back together so they moved at the same time. The Two Eds took the chair to a department store in Toledo.

"People tell stories of seeing them in the parking lot with little cardboard mechanisms and saying to each other, 'Gee, Ed, if it pivots, it oughta work that way,' " Carr said with a smile. "But the department store manager said, 'Fellas, it's a nice idea to recline like that, but it's seasonal.' "

The Two Eds recovered their idea in upholstery.

The original reclining La-Z-Boy chair is in the museum. Made out of hard maple, it reflects the rustic Adirondack lawn chair in its design. In 1929 Shoemaker and Knabusch had an employee contest to name the Floral City company's new product. La-Z-Boy also-rans include Sit-N-Snooze and Slack Back. In 1941, the Floral City Furniture Co. officially changed its name to La-Z-Boy.

The Two Eds applied for their first patent in 1929, a move depicted in the museum's original squeaky spring recliners. An advertisement from the March 6, 1930, edition of the Monroe Evening News reveals the prices of the La-Z-Boys at $49.50 and $59.50. Today, a La-Z-Boy retails for around $400.

"To survive in the 1930s, Mr. Knabusch came up with the idea to sell refrigerators, rugs and lamps besides the chairs," Carr said. "They would set up a tent in the parking lot and give away shrubs. Mr. Shoemaker brought in a mouse circus to entertain the kids."

Pictures and paintings from the 1930s can be found in a stairwell leading to the basement, which includes an original drill press, lathe and the original upholstering work station. The basement museum also includes upholstered army tank seats that La-Z-Boy made during World War II.

"We're in the process of recreating the basement in the way it looked in 1944," Carr said. "We know what it looked liked because we have two vintage photographs showing this area. The whole basement area will become a miniature factory of the way chairs used to be made."

In recent years La-Z-Boys have become big-ticket items at antique shows and flea markets. The museum's 1970s "Sofette" is a two-seater sofa; each seat has its own individual footrest and reclining mechanism. Sofettes and La-Z-Boy love seats were actually designed with the romantic spirit of car seats. "The advertisements show them with a man and woman sitting in the Sofette together," Carr said. "One is reading a paper, the other is watching television."

And take the 1950s "Posture Chair." Please. The company billed the sleek vinyl lime green chair as "The only form fitting chair with [attached] floating seat and back." Carr looked down at the pseudo-casting couch with deep sympathy and said, "It was our Edsel. Because like the Edsel, it had an unusual design and it didn't sell very well. It wasn't in the line very long. And it quickly became a collectible."

Another short-lived contraption was the original "Tranquil-ator," an interior vibrator that during the mid-1950s was installed in several different La-Z-Boy recliners.

But a 1954 platform rocker represents a critical moment in La-Z-Boy history. It featured the company's first built-in footrest—but the rocker didn't recline.

"Finally, in 1961 La-Z-Boy put it all together and introduced a chair that rocked, reclined and had a built-in footrest," Carr said. Shoemaker put a footrest inside the chair that could be activated by a handle.

"They called it the Reclina-Rocker," she said. "That's when La-Z-Boy went from being a little furniture company in Michigan to the largest upholstered furniture manufacturer in the United States."

The only downside about the museum is the temptation to test out all the La-Z-Boys. "We don't allow people to sit in them," Carr said. "They're old, and we're trying to preserve them."

The museum also includes archival advertisements featuring late actor Jim Backus endorsing La-Z-Boy both as Backus and as his comic character, Mr. Magoo, and casual testimony from Bing Crosby, Ed McMahon and former Detroit Lions start Alex Karras.

Carr, 58, is a native of Monroe County, Mich. She joined La-Z-Boy in 1974 as a clerk-typist and went to work as a buyer in the purchasing department. Carr has been married since 1957 and has several kids and grandchildren. Carr became part of the La-Z-Boy family through sweet midwestern serendipity.

She was working as a waitress at the Holiday Inn in Monroe when Shoemaker came in for dinner with a licensee from Australia. "The gentleman from Australia said, 'Judy, what is Monroe famous for?' " Carr recalled. "And I said Monroe was famous for Gen. George Custer and La-Z-Boy. And he said, 'How would you like to meet the man who invented the La-Z-Boy?'

"I did not know the Shoemakers. I said, 'Mr. Shoemaker, can I work for you when I grow up?' I was in my early 30s. [She laughed] And Mr. Shoemaker's wife, Ruth [now deceased], poked him in the ribs and said, 'Eddie, that's the kind of girl you need at La-Z-Boy. Somebody enthusiastic!' "

Carr looked around the museum that reflects so much of her life, which has been a good life. The big, warm nature of 45 empty La-Z-Boys in one room invites immediate friendship. "More and more people are becoming interested in La-Z-Boy," she said. "You get a warm and fuzzy feeling. It's a feeling of security in the way that life goes on and everything is all right, no matter what we've been through."

Carr gave it a rest.

Then she said, "I guess you can tell I like telling these stories."

The La-Z-Boy Museum is open to the public by appointment only. The company accommodates tour groups, school groups and La-Z-Boy cultists. To make a reservation, contact Judith Carr at (734) 242-1444, ext. 6058.

September 6, 1998

House of David lives on
Museum preserves colorful history of southwestern Michigan sect

WATERVILET, Mich.—The House of David sect has a slight problem. During the mid-1900s the Christian organization operated a baseball team, vegetarian restaurants and even ran the world's largest miniature railroad out of Eden Springs Amusement Park near downtown Benton Harbor, Mich.

But there were no raves with these Daves.

There were celibate.

No one could pass down their lore. And that's where Chris Siriano came in. He operates the new House of David Museum, which takes up most of the Old World Antique Gallery, 349 Main St. in downtown Watervilet, about 10 minutes east of Benton Harbor (616-463-8888, exit 41 north on I-94).

"The House of David history needed to be saved," Siriano said during a tour of his definitive museum. "It's been an important part of this area for almost 100 years. I wanted to set up a museum where the House of David could be researched—schoolchildren, college students or anyone else could come in to appreciate what they were about."

Siriano's museum has more than 2,500 House of David items, including 1,000 rare photographs, 700 pieces of artwork, more than 100 wooden souvenirs and several original House of David baseball and basketball uniforms. Some of the smaller pieces are for sale.

Chris Siriano passes down
the lore of the celibate House of David sect in this Waterlivet museum devoted to them.

Photo by Lisa Day.

The House of David was organized as a commonwealth, according to the apostolic plan (Acts 2-3), in spring, 1903. The group claimed to be one of the Biblical lost tribes of Israel. Founder Benjamin Purnell believed the upcoming millennium would usher in the new dawning of the Garden of Eden on the site of the since-demolished Eden Springs Amusement Park.

"Get Ready," as Michigan's Rare Earth sang in 1970.

By 1916 there were nearly 1,000 men and women living in the Israelite colony. They concluded the old world would be destroyed once Christ's elect 12,000 members from each of the 12 tribes of Israel gathered in Benton Harbor. And a thousand years of harmony and tranquility would begin.

House of David members turned in all their worldly possessions to a commonwealth fund, from which they received support in sickness and in health, and contributed labor according to their capabilities. Their motto was to look forward and not backward, which is why the members' backs are to the cameras in some pictures.

Most of the men never had haircuts or shaved. They wore long hair and a beard because Jesus did. *The What? Where? When? Why? and How?* booklet, published by the House of David in 1931 pointed out that "Jesus, being a Nazarite, never transgressed his Father's commands."

The House of David was built with single guys and gals. To engage in sex would cross the word of Jesus. The members believed they could only have children after the millennium. Just like what I'm thinking.

Siriano said there are six House of David members alive today. They are in their late 80s and early 90s and still live in the old mansions that housed the membership. Siriano talks to them three times a week.

One House of David member, 88-year-old George Anderson, once faced Hall of Fame baseball pitcher Satchel Paige during the summer and guarded Meadowlark Lemon of the Harlem Globetrotters in winter basketball games. Made up only of House of David members, the baseball and basketball teams barnstormed across the Midwest, playing pick-up teams and all-star aggregations like the Globetrotters and Negro League All-Star squads.

The House of David baseball stadium was located on Empire Avenue in Benton Harbor. The outfield fence remains today, while the dirt diamond has been transformed into a House of

An early-1900s view of the House of David Administration Building.

Postcard reprinted with the permission of the House of David Museum.

David Trailer Park. The trailer park is operated by Paul Johnson, the last person who joined the House of David (in 1953).

Siriano, 37, is a Benton Harbor native.

He remembers how his parents took him to Eden Springs to ride miniature trains and race cars. "That's about all that was left when I was a child," Siriano said on a dark winter Saturday afternoon. "The vaudeville shows were gone. The bands and orchestras were gone. The baseball teams quit playing in the 1950s because the guys got too old. The zoo was closed.

"They still participated in the food market in Benton Harbor, and the House of David still had their own hotel and vegetarian restaurants through the beginning of the 1970s. I loved their ice cream. They made their own ice cream, and they patented their waffle cones. Everyone went there to try their world-famous waffle cones. It was such a unique taste."

The House of David compound is located on nearly 100 acres of land on Britain Avenue, off Michigan 139. What remains is closed to the public. Siriano said, "The hotel and restaurant are still standing, but they're in disrepair and ready to be razed. The train tracks are still in place. [Walt Disney once bought one of the miniature trains for his studio.] It took three years for them to build a miniature stone house for kids. They used thousands of hand-carved stones cut like diamonds, and that's still there. But it's all private, and the remaining members don't like people poking around."

So, Siriano's museum affords one of the best ways to get in touch with the House of David. Museum visitors can buy an original House of David amusement park pennant for $25, an original packet of postcards for $20 and reproduction House of David baseball jerseys from 1931 and 1935 for $125 each.

One of the collection's most precious items is a 1932 red "midget auto," one of 14 original cars from the amusement park. The amusement park was particularly popular during the Depression, when visitors—including many Chicagoans—could go there to have fun without spending lots of money.

Siriano tapped the midget auto as he celebrated the fact it was built from old bed frames and used parts from Model A's and Model T's. "Those cars became famous," Siriano said. "People enjoy that when they come here. And the baseball stuff is popular. House of David baseball memorabilia is super-hard to find because they barnstormed with the Negro Leagues and they are considered part of that history."

Siriano even has a 6-foot-tall 1920s groundup fishscale finish and handcarved teakwood column that came from a float the sect entered in Southwest Michigan's annual Blossom Parade. The House of David entered the parade every spring. And every spring their float won.

"In fact, in the 1950s they were asked to take a couple of years off to try and encourage the parade's corporate sponsors to continue to spend money, and maybe they'd be awarded first place," Siriano chuckled. "This is one of the last pieces of big statuary that's left anywhere.

"The House of David made a lot of sculptures, but they kept them in the upstairs of their art department. In 1965 their art department burned to the ground, so it's unusual that something that big from the art department got out into the public." Siriano found the statue at an estate sale northeast of Watervelt. He makes no money from the House of David Museum, although he accepts donations. Siriano draws his income from his antique business.

Some people who live around Watervliet and Benton Harbor don't exactly view the House of David in the spirit of Disneyland magic. House of David founder Benjamin Purnell was a traveling preacher, and for a while he was a broom-maker in Richmond, Ind. He loved music, particularly Hawaiian steel guitars, Marimbas and African-American spirituals. Benjamin was known to ride around the House of David property on a white horse, wearing a flowering white robe and jewel-encrusted sombrero. He met his wife Mary in Ohio.

According to a 1953 Sun-Times article, Benjamin—as he was known around the House of David—said a dove perched on his shoulder and directed him to Benton Harbor. That suggested divine intervention.

In 1927, allegations of fraud and sexual misconduct were made against Benjamin, which led to the most celebrated civil trial in Berrien County history. The case ended with a guilty verdict on charges of teaching and practicing perjury, but the decision was later reversed on appeal.

Benjamin died of diabetes and tuberculosis 11 days after the civil suit's conclusion. He was 66. After his death, his wife started the competing City of David, virtually across the street from the House of David.

The House of David sect, of course, believed the chosen dead will rise again, so Benjamin's body lies mummified in a glass-covered coffin in a chapel in the still-standing Diamond House (so named because in the sun it sparkled from the stones and minerals from which it was built). Only members can view his coffin.

"When the others died, their bodies were placed in Crystal Springs Cemetery in Benton Harbor," Siriano said. "There's no headstones; a few had a number on a stone, but most of them are unmarked graves."

So for now, the most passionate tribute to the colorful sect can be found in the aisles of a dusty antique store on a sleepy main street in southwest Michigan. It could make for a memorable pre-millennium pilgrimage.

January 10, 1999

POSTSCRIPT:

The House of David Historium has moved to a bigger location at 4040 Fikes Road in tiny Riverside, Mich. (616-849-0432). The museum is separate from the adjacent Golden Ember antique shop. Riverside is a 10-minute drive north of St. Joseph, Mich.

In summer 2000, the House of David offered to sell an original amusement park train to the historium. "I'll put the train in a building by itself and run it on weekends," said museum operator Chris Siriano. "We're going to acquire a mile of track and lay it out on the property. We have three acres to play with. It will give people a taste of what the House of David used to offer. Really, there's only five House of David members left."

Doing Detroit in polka dots

DETROIT, Mich.—A house is a house, of course, of course.

That is, of course, unless the house is talking to Tyree Guyton.

In 1986 the 43-year-old folk artist was cleaning paintbrushes on an abandoned house in the 3600 block of Heidelberg Street on the blighted near east side of Detroit.

According to Guyton, the house began to speak to him.

He answered the call with the help of his grandfather, Sam "Grandpa" Mackey, a retired house painter (now deceased), and Guyton's former wife Karen. They covered the two-story frame home with old signage, household items, toys, dolls and other urban junque.

Over the next few years Guyton's muse spread down the block to include polka-dot painted houses, trees and sidewalks, abstract portraits painted on discarded car hoods and a 1955 passenger bus wildly decorated in commemoration of Detroiter Rosa Parks and her stance for equal rights. It's all documented in "Come Unto Me: The Faces of Tyree Guyton," which airs at 11 a.m. Wednes-

Photo by Lisa Day.

Detroit folk artist Tyree Guyton

day on the Cinemax "Reel Life" series.

Many neighbors, however, regarded Guyton's colorful work as an eyesore. What became known as The Heidelberg Project has locked horns with two successive Detroit administrations. "Art is not good when it's outside," one resident complains during the 29-minute documentary. Filmmaker Nicole Cattell spent several years following developments surrounding the project.

About half of the project—including the original talking house—has since been dismantled by the city, but it is still worth a look, especially if you tag team the visit with a trip to Tiger Stadium, just a few blocks away. The home of the Detroit Tigers will be dismantled after this baseball season.

"My great-grandparents moved in this neighborhood in 1947," Guyton said during a conversation on a sultry Saturday afternoon in front of his "O.J. (Obstruction of Justice) House" and studio at 3680 Heidelberg. "It was a German neighborhood. I remember being a kid, playing up and down the street. It was beautiful. It had a strong block club, and my uncle was president of the block club."

Heidelberg Street was a great place to be young.

And Guyton's playful, primitive work makes everyone young again.

"Somehow things happened in this neighborhood," Guyton said as his voice trailed away. "I believe it was the [civil rights] riots of 1967. It brought about this great change and separation amongst the people."

The Guyton family remained true to the turf. Guyton and his mother currently live at 3658 Heidelberg, a.k.a. "The Polka Dot House." Guyton painted the home in assorted polka dots, which represent people of many colors. The home has been in the Guyton family since 1947.

But the house that Guyton first heard was demolished by the city in 1991.

"What I heard was so beautiful," he said with little bitterness. "I saw what this neighborhood could become. Before I started, it was a war zone. There was homelessness, prostitution and drugs. But from the house, I heard this voice and a melody that told me to do something. It reminded me of classical music. Sometimes I feel like I'm the conductor and my art is the orchestra."

The "O.J. House" is in a "limbo state," according to Jenenne

Whitfield, executive director of The Heidelberg Project. In 1995 the non-profit Heidelberg Project purchased back due taxes on the house in the name of the project. She said the project is in the process of acquiring the title of the home and studio from the state of Michigan. No one lives in the house.

Meanwhile, the city continues to try to clean up the project.

"We look at art as an industry in Detroit," said Greg Bowens, press secretary for Detroit Mayor Dennis Archer. "And we try to promote and facilitate the growth of that industry. The Heidelberg Project is no exception. It is one thing to create art and promote a particular

Photo by Lisa Day.

Heidelberg Street's "Polka Dot House," has been in Guyton's family since 1947.

brand of art, but it is another thing to impose your will on the people who live around you. Tyree sold art and gave festivals, but no one in the community was able to benefit from it. But they had to suffer all the inconveniences of having to put up with what is essentially a commercial venture on a residential street."

On Sept. 12, 1998, Archer called Whitfield and said the city was going to remove anything related to the project from Heidelberg Street. He suggested that Guyton store anything he wanted to save.

"We don't know what the city's motives are," said Deborah A. Bonner, attorney for The Heidelberg Project. On Sept. 21, 1998, Bonner filed a complaint and request that artwork remain on the street. The next day Wayne County Circuit Court Judge Claudia

House Morcum ruled that the city could not remove anything from Heidelberg Street in that Guyton had ownership interest in land and in the items that were to be destroyed.

After Morcum failed to be re-elected in February, the case was reassigned to Judge Amy Hathaway. She lifted the injunction on Feb. 4. On that afternoon the city removed Guyton's artwork from three trees along Heidelberg Street and bulldozed Guyton's abandoned home studio on Canfield Road, about a mile west of The Heidelberg Project. The home had been donated to the project. "Tyree's name was on the deed," Bonner said. "There was no question he owned it."

Guyton currently has a pending lawsuit against the city of Detroit. He is asking for $3 million in damages (including $1 million in artwork stored in his razed studio) and that what is left on The Heidelberg Project remain.

Bowens added, "Even in Tyree's exuberance to create art, he ended up causing harm to the environment by destroying 12 trees on that street because he nailed art to the trees. That caused the trees to die. The taxpayers did not pay to have The Heidelberg Project created and they should not have to pay to have things removed. The total cost of the trees was $25,000."

The city will bill Guyton for the trees, according to Bowens.

Whitfield said, "This is a very old and economically poor community. There has been no development in this area for 80 years. Well, something's up now. We could be the blockage for some kind of development."

In late 1997, the Eastside Industrial Council of Detroit obtained a $52,000 grant from the Hudson Webber Foundation to learn how to develop areas that are too far gone to be brought back residentially but can be developed for industry. The Heidelberg Project was in a priority neighborhood.

Bonner said, "After they got that grant, everything turned."

Bowens countered, "There's no industrial plan for that neighborhood. It's a stable neighborhood. Some of our friends in the media have tried to characterize those residents as being poverty stricken, but just because you're retired and on a fixed income doesn't mean you're poor. And just because you're black doesn't mean you're in dire straits. Tyree Guyton would like to paint himself as a savior of the people, or some kind of economic hero, but if you've seen any kind of economic spinoff for those folks, I'll give you my paycheck.

"It just didn't happen."

The "Come Unto Me" documentary points out the battles Guyton had with previous Detroit Mayor Coleman Young. Bonner said, "People liked Coleman, and he said, 'This is the way I can shut up the neighbors and keep you here—I'll bulldoze these houses and you keep going.' There's never been an attempt to eradicate the entire project, which is what has happened now."

The city isn't even a fan of the Cinemax documentary.

"As far as we're concerned, that documentary is an infomercial for Tyree's products," Bowens said. "They didn't bother to call anyone in city government to try and find out what our position was. It's not a balanced view."

Guyton often spends 15, 16 hours a day at the project site. He is constantly working on the "O.J. House," shifting things around, adding some elements while removing other items. "It's a work in progress," he said. "I hear that house talking to me. And I still listen. A couple days ago I added a big [roadside] mouse on the roof. The city fabricated this lie that there are rodents over here. So we put a big rat up there for them."

Guyton supports himself with proceeds from sales of his paintings and construction pieces. Some of his car hoods top off at $8,000. An index card-size painting sells for $500 to $750. Whitfield serves as his agent in America, and Guyton also has a European agent.

A photo exhibit of The Heidelberg Project has toured to Budapest, Tokyo, Moscow and Dusseldorf, Germany. Guyton has received critical acclaim with exhibitions at the Detroit Institute of Arts and galleries in New York and Detroit.

"I was in Hungary for an installation about five months ago," Guyton said. "I made some polka dots in Hungary. So I see the message spreading all over the world. I love opposition. It makes me great masterpieces. They tear it down, I put it back. I'll polka dot all of Detroit. And I've started."

Guyton walked southeast down Heidelberg Street. He pointed to a vacant burned-out frame house. "The city council called our project an 'eyesore,' " Guyton said as he looked at the charred house, punctuated by a half dozen red blue polka dots. "If our project is an eyesore, what do you call this? I told the city I would polka dot anything I saw that was blighted. And we have blight all over the city."

Guyton spun around and looked at an abandoned film factory.

He spruced up the broken-down building with polka dots. "Over the last month I've been working on these buildings," he said. "The polka dots are about all people. I collect jelly beans, and polka dots are like that, a brotherhood of all races that will bring about change for humanity. I don't see black and white.

"I just see everyday groovy people."

June 13, 1999

A burger and sculpture to go
Diner mogul serves fun on the run

ROCKFORD, Mich.—The deer and maybe even some antelope play in the frozen tundra of central Michigan.

There's miles and miles of nothing on 14 Mile Road in rural Rockford, 15 minutes north of Grand Rapids.

As a tired and hungry driver rolls down the two-laner, four chrome and steel objects pop up on the eastern horizon. They look like old kitchen appliances.

This is the home on the range.

Jerry Berta's Dinerland consists of a diner art gallery, a diner, a fancy diner and a private diner meeting room, all on 4.5 acres. Dinerland is the only place in the world where there are four classic diners in one location.

Berta is to diners what Ted Nugent is to firearms.

"There's five acres of land behind us that we have the option to buy," Berta says. Berta, 46, talks kinda fast, like he's placing an order to go. "So I've proposed building a 1950s Main Street back there—with a functional barber shop, beauty shop and a small movie theater that would be a video store. The [Algoma] township is behind it 100 percent."

Main Street would complement the 18-hole miniature golf course that Berta built in 1993. Nearly every hole is denoted with a huge cement sculpture of food or diner art.

Berta's culinary compound is a faraway place and time that he calls "Dinerland," a registered trademark. A sculptor by trade, Berta makes ceramic diners, movie theaters and chili peppers. His artwork retails for $150 to $2,500. Berta also custom-makes diners. Clients include Michigan rocker Bob Seger and Christie Hefner, who picked up one of Berta's toaster-sized Star Theater movie palaces (which advertises "It's a Wonderful Life" on the marquee") at an art show in Coconut Grove, Fla., and gave it to her father.

"Diners take us back to simpler times," Berta says. "They look like an old appliance with their rounded corners. And when you walk in, everyone is friendly. The buildings are friendly. People look at my work and ask if they're made out of 1950s toasters or bumpers. I take it as a compliment."

Photo by Lisa Day.

Rosie's Diner of Rockford's Dinerland.

Berta just linked a licensing deal with the Cavanagh Group in Atlanta to re-create a limited-edition line of diners, a movie theater and a teapot. Cavanagh will steer Berta's replicas into the collector's market, as it has done with Coca-Cola and Harley-Davidson memorabilia.

But in 1987 Berta got a taste of the real deal.

He purchased the abandoned Uncle Bob's Diner in Flint, Mich. It had been on the market for two years. Uncle Bob's was built in 1947 by the Jerry O'Mahony Dining Car Co. It was Michigan's last remaining diner. Berta bought the diner for $2,000 and moved it to Rockford. After a beautiful restoration, Berta opened the Diner Store, a gallery and studio, to display artwork by himself and his wife, Madeline Kaczmarzyk.

Berta stuck a neon sign in the window: *No Food, Just Art.*

Customers ignored the sign.

Some people would just take down the sign. Not Berta. He opened another diner. On the way to an art show in New York City, Berta and artist assistant Fred Tiensivu stumbled across Rosie's, a 1946 Paramount Dining Car Co. diner that was for sale in Ferry, N.J. The owner couldn't give the joint away, although it soaked up infamy as the location for the *quicker-picker-upper* Bounty paper towel commercials starring Rosie the waitress (actress Nancy Walker). Not even the Smithsonian was interested in saving Rosie's.

But Berta purchased the wide-bodied Rosie's for $20,000 and transported it 700 miles in two sections back to Rockford. In 1991 Berta opened Rosie's Diner, a full-service diner next to the Diner Store. Rosie's drew up to 1,300 people a day to a barren land, a half mile east of U.S. 131 (at Exit 101, call 616-866-2787).

"I didn't know how to run a restaurant," Berta said. "But I knew how to be a customer. The food had to taste good and the waitresses had to smile. It's common sense stuff. My dream diner meal? It would be meat loaf, a side of green beans, mashed potatoes and gravy and great coffee.

"And don't forget a good piece of pie. We've won awards for our pies. We have about 10 different pies [including carrot cake, chocolate peanut butter, cherry, Dutch apple, blueberry . . .]. I realized we should have a grandma making our pies. Most restaurants don't make their own pies; it's not business-wise. But we peel the apples, cut 'em up add some brown sugar. The diner itself brings them in the first time. It's the food that makes them come

Photo by Lisa Day.

Sculptures in Jerry Berta's gallery of diner art.

back."

Rosie's was a hit. Berta had only one solution to handle the overflow crowds: Buy a third diner. In 1994 he purchased and moved in the Garden of Eatin' from Fulton, N.Y. Berta renamed it the Delux Diner and set up the operation for a casual diner dining experience, complete with beer, wine and business lunches. Finally, in 1995 Berta, Tiensivu and an area contractor expanded the Delux by adding an Art Deco diner meeting room to the rear. Even the Dinerland bathrooms are decorated with ornate tile art depicting diners. In peak season, Berta's Dinerland employs 45 people.

"I didn't know all this would happen," Berta says. "In 1976 I just started with them as a sculptural medium. I thought they were all old train cars."

Tiensivu smiled. A hard-core blues fan, when Tiensivu deals a large grin, a blue bicuspid can be seen in his top row of teeth. Locals affectionately call the 46-year-old Tiensivu "Blues Tooth."

Tiensivu explained, "There's a misnomer that people think diners were all train cars at one time. They did borrow those streamlined, stylized fronts from the trains of the 1930s, but true diners are made much as pre-fab homes or mobile homes. They're meant to be shipped to a site and set up in one day's time. None of our diners were ever train cars."

Berta and Tiensivu restore the diners to represent the period in which they were originally built, right down to funky Formica tops and stained mahogany booths. In 1969 Tiensivu was voted best artist in the Rockford school system.

Berta grew up in Utica, Mich., north of Detroit. He received a bachelor of fine arts degree from Wayne State University in Detroit. The most frequent question Berta hears is, "Why Rockford?"

Well, one good thing about having nothing within miles is the available parking for Rosie's Deer Hunters Breakfast (served only during rifle season) or Motorcycle Night, held on Thursdays during the summer.

"A guy came out from Consumer's Energy [an area utility company]," Berta says. "He asked how we did site demographics. He said, 'Look at all the people here. This is incredible!' I said, 'Do you see that road over there? I live down it.' When I opened my gallery I didn't want to drive to work. The guy thought I wasn't telling him the real reason. We just lucked out. Because we're on this highway and everybody saw a diner, they stopped in looking for food.

"Some days I'll walk out of here like I'm really making art. My mind is just on art and I'll look out the window. When the light is just right, I'll go, 'Where did that come from?' Then I realize there's this whole little village of diners out there. It's one big piece of art. Then I remember, 'That's right! I own it.'

"Or it owns me."

SOUND TRACKS: There have been some great diner songs, like Tom Waits' "Eggs and Sausage" from his "Nighthawks at the Diner" record and George Clinton's "Do Fries Go With That Shake?" But last year Martin Sexton recorded "Diner," the highlight of his "Black Sheep" CD (Eastern Front Records). The sprightly song is full of diner lyrics such as:

". . . The cashier she always squints/By the gum and the bowl of mints/She's tapping her toe/To the Dean Martin on the consolette/Booth service and a cigarette, we're loving it so . . ."

"Me and diners go back to my early years," the 31-year-old Sexton said recently from his home in Northhampton, Mass. "Dining with truckers in Syracuse, N.Y., and just grooving on the chrome, Formica and pink waitress skirts." Sexton sings, and plays electric guitar and salt and pepper shakers on "Diner." He wrote the song with backing vocalist Ned Claflin.

"Actually we were trying to write about something completely different," Sexton said. "It wasn't getting anywhere. We had a cup of coffee and he asked me, 'What do you really love? Maybe we could write about that.' I told him I loved diners. So we made a list of what I loved about them, what you find in them, where do you find them, who goes to them. Then the song came out in 10 minutes. The Dean Martin line comes from the Blue Bonnet, one of my favorite diners in Northampton. They have Dean Martin on the consolette."

January 25, 1998

Woman bites 42 dogs—and survives

The Hot Dog Hall of Fame—
now that's a mouthful

ROCKFORD, Mich.—Most halls of fame honor noble accomplishments that forever stand tall. There's hallowed spots for astronauts. Cowboys. Even rock 'n' rollers, where you can hear Paul Revere and the Raiders sing "Hungry (For Those Good Things)."

But there is one place where weenies go down in infamy.

That is the Hot Dog Hall of Fame, located in the Corner Bar and Restaurant, 31 N. Main (616-866-9866) in this scenic community of 4,500, located about 10 miles north of Grand Rapids.

Anyone can gain immortality into the Hot Dog Hall of Fame.

Just eat a dozen chili dogs in four hours.

"I'll tell you, if you get full at 11 or 12, it doesn't matter if you have a dozen hours," said 69-year-old tavern owner Don Berg (no relation to Chicago frankfurter king David Berg). "You just can't eat any more."

An entire wall of the cozy 125-year-old bar is devoted to the 4,700 Hot Dog Hall of Famers who downed a dozen or more tube steaks in the allotted time period. Berg has sold more than 1,200 miles of hot dogs since 1965, when he purchased the tavern on the ground floor of the oldest brick building in town.

The Corner Bar serves nine different hot dogs in a bun, including the pizza dog ($1.50), the burrito dog ($1.50) and the New York-inspired slaw 'n' chili dog ($1.25). The chili dogs are $1.08, plus 30 cents off every sixth dog. I was full after eating one burrito dog and one chili dog.

The Babe Ruth of the Hot Dog Hall of Fame is Sharon VanDuinen, a 41-year-old dental hygienist from nearby Jenison. She set the house record in March, 1982. She ate 42¾ chili dogs in four hours, chased by 15 mugs of Diet Pepsi. Sharon is 5-foot-3, 110 pounds.

The Hall of Fame record still stands. So does Sharon.

"The first hour, I ate 25 chili dogs," Sharon recalled during an interview from her home. "The only thing you were allowed to leave out were mustard, onions and catsup. You had to have the chili sauce.

"I had 18 to go to break the record [42 set by Dizzy Densmore of Greenwood, Mich.] and three hours to do it. The first hour wasn't bad. After that, they all started tasting pretty pasty.

"Every hour on the hour, they'd bring me six chili dogs. It took the entire three hours. On my last dog, everyone in the bar was pounding on their tables, 'Come on!' 'Come on!' I had to walk outside to get air. Do you know how you feel when you're getting car sick? I was feeling pretty *bog*."

After setting the record, Sharon wandered down the street to dance at the Las Vegas night at the Lions club. "The whole town was in an uproar because I was beating [as in eating] this record," she said. "Everyone at Las Vegas night knew about it. We went there afterward, but it's kind of a blur. They said I was dancing. Someone also said I was eating peanuts."

In June, 1981, Sharon set the Hot Dog Hall of Fame record/ woman's division by eating 20 chili dogs. "Just because I could," she said. "My ex-brother-in-law is the salesman of all salesmen. After I ate the 20, we went back to the Corner Bar and he was pumping me the whole time, saying, 'Shari, I know you can beat the record,' So we get in the bar and he announces that I'm going to do this. I figured I'd do the best I can."

Sharon rolled the dice and paid a price.

She gained 10 pounds after her frankfurter feat. She also couldn't sleep the night after she set the record. "I was too full," she admitted. "But the next day I wanted to eat a whole roast by myself. My stomach was that stretched out. It took me a month to lose that weight."

In May, 1982, Corner Bar manager Jim "Harpo" Richard orga- nized the rematch that rocked Rockford: Sharon vs. former champ Densmore. Sharon reminisced, "Dizzy practiced eating hot dogs from March until May. We had a weigh-in. Dizzy weighed 220 pounds. I weighed in at 110 pounds."

It would appear that Sharon was the underdog.

"He ate 12 hot dogs and barfed," she said. "I ate 13 hot dogs in 16 minutes and whupped his butt again."

Happily married with two children, Sharon returns to the Hot Dog Hall of Fame a couple times a year to bask in her glory of gluttony. She does have some appetizing tips. "When you start eating, it takes 20 minutes to feel full," she said. "So you have to eat as fast as you can, as much as you can. There's no technique. It's just getting them down."

Although Sharon set her amazing record in a tavern, alcohol was not involved. She drank Diet Pepsi and she recommends water for power pup consumption.

The Hot Dog Hall of Fame was officially established in 1968 after Detroit Lions football players Milt Plum, John Gordy and Ron Kramer dropped into the bar after playing Rockford high school teachers in a benefit basketball game. Berg said, "They had eight or 10 hot dogs [each]."

Other notables who have sampled a Corner Bar dog include former Detroit Tiger Mickey Lolich, Chicago Bears Football Hall of Famer Dick Butkus and the late actor Dick ("Bewitched") York, who lived outside Rockford.

The bar's autographed pictures of Linda Ronstadt and other musicians come courtesy of Berg's daughter Suzanne, a former vice president at Elektra Records. She now works at Impulse Records in New York.

The elder Berg conceded that Sharon's record is tough to break.

"The only one who came close was a guy who came in a few years ago around 1 a.m.," said Berg, whose Chicago roots go back to uncle Ray MacMeal, who ran the Maywood Hotel. "This guy at 35 hot dogs, but we had to kick him out at 2:30. It was bar time. He was on his way to breaking the record."

Berg used to sample a dog a day just to make sure the home-made chili was kicking in. The secret chili sauce was concocted in the 1930s by previous tavern owner George Myers, a former Army cook.

"The chili varies," Berg said. "Sometimes it's real spicy, sometimes the meat absorbs it, sometimes the meat doesn't." That's the legacy at the Hot Dog Hall of Fame, where the bite is always better than the bark.

January 11, 1998

Retiree keeps on truckin' for Christ
Ex-driver covering nation with Bibles

GRAND RAPIDS, Mich.—A majestic map of the United States hangs like a gospel note in the offices of Highway Melodies Inc., located in an upstairs storefront on the southeast side of Grand Rapids.

More than 650 brightly colored pins are stuck in the map.

Each pin denotes a truck stop where someone has placed a paperback copy of the New Testament. There is a pin in every state in the contiguous 48. The pins stand for beacons in the night, especially during the holiday season.

Teaching truckers how to convoy with Christ is the mission of this nonprofit corporation, founded in 1974 by the late Raleigh Huls, who drove trucks for a local bakery. He began by spreading the word over CB radio.

Yes, there can be a very good buddy out there.

"We're in Mount Vernon, Wash., this way" says retired truck driver Sid Cnossen, pointing to the top left corner of the map. His hand gently sweeps to the right. Cnossen continues, "In Holton, Maine, here, then Vero Beach [Fla.] this way." And his rugged hand drops with the grace of the snow that is falling outside.

"Once my wife [Tess] and I took our ['87 Cruisemaster] motor home down U.S. 10 from Jacksonville, Fla., to Ontario, Calif." Cnossen says. "We dropped off Bibles at every truck stop along the way, about 30 to 35 stops."

This is not the most popular trucker stereotype.

Think "American trucker," and most people picture hell on wheels. They see black T-shirts and thick smoke rings. They hear Dave Dudley's gnarly "Six Days on the Road" and "Rolaids, Doan's Pills and Preparation H."

But since 1987, truckers and friends of truckers have gently placed 500,000 New Testaments in truck stops across the great 48. "We're still trying to figure out how to get in Hawaii," Cnossen quips. Highway Melodies also offers free Bible studies for adults and children, evangelistic audio cassettes and a quarterly newsletter called Homeward Bound.

The latest issue of Homeward Bound features an interview

with Martien Stam, an ex-driver who operates a similar trucker's ministry, Chauffeurs Evangelisatieteam Holland in the Netherlands. Stam tells the newsletter he is fascinated with roadside restaurant lingo in America: "The waitress asks you what you want with your main meal and you say, 'I'll go with the potato.' When I heard that my reaction was you are not going with the potato—the potato is going with you . . ."

But it is the Lord who travels with roughly 100 Highway Melodies volunteers who place the New Testament in truck stops. Besides truck drivers, church people and retirees help spread the good word along the road.

Grand Rapids, population 181,000, is a logical home for Highway Melodies, which operates on a staff of three volunteers and one paid office worker from its humble office. The Christian Reform Church of North America is headquartered here. About a quarter of the town's population have brought their Dutch Reformist roots to the scenic borough along the Grand River, about 25 miles east of Lake Michigan. Soul singer and evangelist the Rev. Al Green hails from Grand Rapids. So does Kevin Smith of the gospel-rap group DC Talk.

"I was raised in the Christian Reform Church," says the 70-year-old Cnossen, who was born near rural Cadillac, 100 miles north of Grand Rapids. He's been married to Tess for 47 years. A former teacher, she also grew up near Cadillac. The Cnossens have five children between the ages of 36 and 46. They all attended Grand Rapids-area private Christian schools, with tuition paid for by their father's trucker's salary.

From 1946 until he retired in 1986, Cnossen hauled appliances across the heartland in an 18-wheeler. "When I started, my boss didn't even want an AM radio in the truck," he says, looking slightly guilty. "He thought it would distract us. So sometimes we'd carry one that some radio repairman fixed up for us. After we left town, we'd plug it into the cigarette lighter. I'd listen to bluegrass music all night long; Bill Monroe and Ralph Stanley out of New Orleans. But we'd sure pull out the radio before we'd reach the terminal."

Cnossen estimates he's plugged in 7,500 volunteer hours at Highway Melodies since he walked away from his big rig. He's the distribution coordinator for Highway Melodies. Tess is Bible study coordinator.

"I always was a Christian driver," he says. "I was in a bad accident in 1951. I hit a double-bottom gasoline tanker east of

Lansing, Mich. It never caught fire. I only got a compound fracture of the leg.

"Sometimes I feel I've been kept here for this purpose."

Cnossen met Raleigh Huls in 1948 at a truck stop near Detroit. They talked about trucking and shared their Christian beliefs over a couple of cups of coffee. Huls died in August after a long battle with cancer. He was 77.

"I felt close to Raleigh because of his Christian beliefs," Cnossen says. "But by 1987 things weren't going anywhere. I told him I'd like a case of Bibles. I wanted to distribute them. I didn't know how it was going to work."

Cnossen took his first display case into the Tiki Truck Stop, just off Interstate 80 outside of Chicago in Peru, Ill. "I prayed before I walked in there," he says. "Since that time, I've personally put [23,600] Bibles in 475 truck stops in the United States."

Typically a Highway Melodies trucker walks into a truck stop with Bibles and a cardboard display case. They'll ask a manager where they can leave their materials. People have to search out the Bibles—the trucker does not impose on customers. "We'll set up wherever the manager says we can," Cnossen says. "By the fuel desk. In the driver's lounge. Every truck stop is different."

Some truck stops can be intimidating.

Photo courtesy of Tess & Sid Cnossen of HMI Ministries.

Cnossen will never forget the vibes he felt about placing Bibles at a trucker's home in Las Vegas. "I walked in," Cnossen says, laughing. "There's slot machines all over. The guy behind the fuel desk is about 300 pounds and his hair is back in a ponytail. He looked like a bouncer. I had a copy of the New Testament and I said, 'This may be a foolish question . . .' He was fine with it and told me to put the display case right at the edge of the fuel desk . . . 20 feet from all those gambling machines."

But Cnossen is most proud about placing Bibles in the mammoth Iowa-80 Truck Stop in Walcott, Iowa. Set on 55 acres with parking for 750 semis and 150 cars, that is the biggest truck stop in America. "People pick up 14 a day there," he says proudly. "They give us a nice display spot. Everyone walks right by them."

Highway Melodies board member Stan Barnes, 55, was a sports producer at WFLD-TV (then Chicago's Channel 32) between 1965 and 1967. He says, "Our mission statement is short: to spread the word of God to our nation's truck drivers. That's it. It's like the picture of Christ on the outside of the door and the handle is inside. Somebody has to make the first move. We're not preaching at them.

"But this didn't explode until Sid and Tess got involved and opened up the truck stops. Raleigh was one guy, a very small ministry. Sid and Tess are God's field troops. There's a number of trucking ministries. We don't have the largest budget [less than $100,000 annually, supported by local churches and business people], but we're the largest as far as the lives we reach. We don't want to make money. We just want to get Bibles out there."

Each New Testament has the number (800) 452-0951 printed on the inside cover, where truckers can reach Highway Melodies Inc. The four-person volunteer staff does not directly contact the truck driver.

"They're a rugged bunch," Cnossen says. "There's Christians amongst them, but there's still a lot who aren't. Depending on who you talk to, there's 6 to 8 million drivers out there, and if you consider how many lives the trucking industry touches, who knows?

"Since deregulation, everything is going by trucks today that used to go by rail. The drivers are a younger set. They love speed. It's just a wild bunch. You hear them on the CB and, 'Oh, my.' It's a rough road out there."

Tess adds, "By the time we get the phone call, they've gone

full circle into a relationship with Christ. They're calling to say 'Thanks.' We just had a call from a trucker who was ready to commit suicide. Another driver handed him a New Testament and he sat in his cab and read it. It turned his life around."

Of course, it costs money to print the Bibles, which are published at the Bible League in suburban South Holland. Truckers can fill out a business reply card, and in return they'll get background information, including a log with listings of 450 truck stops across America. Should the truckers want to distribute Bibles, 44 New Testaments per case are $36.52 plus shipping (or 83 cents each).

Barnes says, "You pay for them yourself or get your church to underwrite you. We do have a Bible fund to get you started, but eventually we cut the cord. Some never follow up. Most do. It's drivers, truck stop operators, pastors, retirees. When you go on your trip, take a case of Bibles and stop at truck stops. You'll love it!"

There's a country song in there somewhere. And it has a steadfast melody.

December 28, 1997

INDIANA

VEHICLE

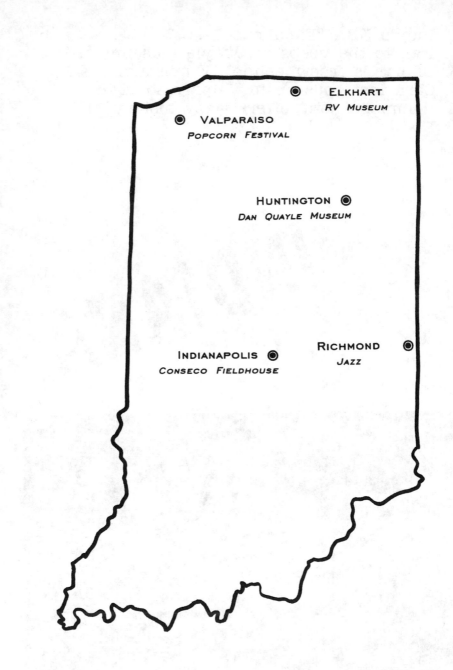

ELKHART
RV MUSEUM

VALPARAISO
POPCORN FESTIVAL

HUNTINGTON
DAN QUAYLE MUSEUM

RICHMOND
JAZZ

INDIANAPOLIS
CONSECO FIELDHOUSE

Map by Lisa Day.

Indianapolis waxes nostalgic in NBA 'Fieldhouse'

INDIANAPOLIS, Ind.—Just prior to tipoff of an Indiana Pacers game at the new throwback Conseco Fieldhouse, grainy 1950s black and white footage of local prep basketball players appear on the scoreboard. Suddenly, in self-assured Midwestern tones, a voice booms, *"In 49 states, it's just basketball—but this is Indiana!"* The first-place NBA Central Division Pacers are introduced and the game begins.

This is the way it's always been.

And it's the way it always shall be.

Indiana is a basketball mecca. Besides Conseco Fieldhouse, Hoosiersteria incorporates the 72-year-old Hinkle Fieldhouse in Indianapolis, where the final scenes of the hit film "Hoosiers" were shot; the Steve Alford All-American Inn in New Castle, Ind., and Larry Bird's native French Lick, Ind.

But the $186 million Conseco Fieldhouse, which opened in November, is the centerpiece of any roundball road trip. The quaint 18,500-seat facility is already known as "the Fieldhouse" instead of "arena" or "stadium."

It was built to honor Indiana's basketball past. Hinkle Fieldhouse was even used as a model. The Fieldhouse replicates Hinkle's arched barrel-style roof with open beams and huge upper windows on each side of the court.

Indiana has produced more basketball royalty than any state in America. Basketball Hall of Famer Oscar Robertson attended Crispus Attucks High School in Indianapolis. UCLA coaching legend John Wooden is from Martinsville, Ind., north of Bloomington. NBA twins Tom and Dick Van Arsdale are from the south side of Indianapolis, where they played at Manuel High School.

Appropriately, the Fieldhouse is the Camden Yards or Wrigley Field of pro basketball. I've never seen anything like it. And the closest throwback collegiate gym I've visited is the 48-year-old Memorial Gymnasium at Vanderbilt in Nashville, Tenn., where team benches are under the basket at each end of the court.

The Pacers dispatched Kansas City, Mo., architects Ellerbe Becket to at least 15 old gymnasiums across America to capture

Photo courtesy of the Indiana Pacers.

The $186-million "retro" Conesco Fieldhouse in
downtown Indianapolis, home to the Indiana Pacers.

the retro feel. "It's the finest facility of its type in the world," said
Pacers announcer Bobby "Slick" Leonard, who coached the Pacers
to three championships in the old American Basketball Association.

A native of Terre Haute, Ind., Leonard has been with the
pacers since 1968, when they played at the Fairgrounds Coliseum,
now 60 years old, north of downtown. In 1974 the Pacers moved
downtown to Market Square Arena (which will be razed this
spring), where they played until this season. Conseco, a Fortune
500 financial services organization based in the Indianapolis
suburb of Carmel, agreed to fork over $40 million over 20 years for
the naming rights.

The Fieldhouse scoreboards are hand-operated, à la Wrigley
Field. A 1940s train station arrival and departure-like clacker
board in the main lobby updates NBA standings. Leonard laughed,
"That lobby reminds me of Pennsylvania Station [in New York
City], all marble, the clacker board. This *is* tradition!"

Advertising is presented in 1930s-'40s style. Signs are not
backlit. They are all lit from the front, creating a billboard effect,
or use neon. Most impressive is RCA's small-town 1950s store-

front, replete with nine old-time television screens that actually run vintage black and white basketball footage. There's even a nearby park bench for old-timers like the Pacers' 38-year-old reserve forward Sam Perkins.

"We wanted to create a basketball gathering place," said Pacers media relations director David Benner as he stood in a sea of kelly green seats before the old-school Pacers took on the new-school Philadelphia 76ers. "The state boy's high school finals are coming here. They've been at the [bigger, 30,000 seat for basketball] RCA Dome for the past 13 years. We wanted to make this the most distinctive place going."

The Pacers' practice facility is within the Fieldhouse. The gym is bricked and accented with trophy cases to recreate the feel of a high school gym. It is the only NBA practice court that is

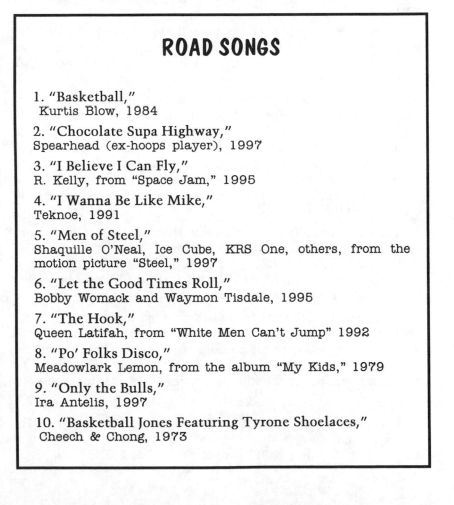

ROAD SONGS

1. "Basketball,"
Kurtis Blow, 1984

2. "Chocolate Supa Highway,"
Spearhead (ex-hoops player), 1997

3. "I Believe I Can Fly,"
R. Kelly, from "Space Jam," 1995

4. "I Wanna Be Like Mike,"
Teknoe, 1991

5. "Men of Steel,"
Shaquille O'Neal, Ice Cube, KRS One, others, from the motion picture "Steel," 1997

6. "Let the Good Times Roll,"
Bobby Womack and Waymon Tisdale, 1995

7. "The Hook,"
Queen Latifah, from "White Men Can't Jump" 1992

8. "Po' Folks Disco,"
Meadowlark Lemon, from the album "My Kids," 1979

9. "Only the Bulls,"
Ira Antelis, 1997

10. "Basketball Jones Featuring Tyrone Shoelaces,"
Cheech & Chong, 1973

viewable from the street.

A couple of hours before game time, Pacers head coach Larry Bird was in the gym tutoring gangly 6-foot-11-inch Pacers forward Jonathan Bender, who at 19 is the youngest player in the NBA. The teacher and student were alone in the gym, with street curtains drawn.

"We'll raise the curtains when Bird is done," Benner said. "Reggie [Miller, the Pacers' 34-year-old all-star guard] will come in and shoot before the game. The fans will see him warming up. He doesn't mind.

"Older guys seem to appreciate this more than younger players because they've played in older buildings. Chris Mullin [36-year-old reserve forward who still sports an old-time crew cut] has said several times the Fieldhouse is like the old high school gym. We love it."

Indeed. On the night of my visit the old school ruled as the Pacers spanked the '76ers. It was the Pacers' 17th consecutive home victory, a franchise record. The Pacers are currently an NBA best 24-2 at home.

Fans enter the Fieldhouse through a retro pavilion that incorporates a hardwood motif. Quotes from Hoosier hoops legends like Butler University coach Tony Hinkle drape the entryways. Hinkle said, *"Some people call basketball a craze in Indiana. It is not a craze because a craze is something that lasts briefly."* Ushers wear nostalgic bow ties, vests and kelly green striped shirts. They look like they are on their way to a barbershop quartet convention.

The pavilion hallways are lined with cases containing memorabilia from Indiana basketball history. Ex-Pacers center Mel Daniels was the Most Valuable Player of the now-defunct American Basketball Association's 1971 All-Star game. Fans can see his MVP check for a whopping $875.

The court is visible as fans walk through the doors. The Best Locker Room restaurant uses actual never-worn black Chuck Taylor Converse high tops to hold condiments. The Fieldhouse even has a Starbucks/gift shop. It is also done in hardwood. The best part about the coffee shop is a defining Detours moment:

The World's Largest Basketball.

It's 18 feet in diameter and is suspended from the ceiling. "It's a replica right down to the number of dimples on an NBA ball," Benner said. "It's like 8,000 dimples."

Indianapolis-based fans Mike Morrison, 37, and Gary Springer, 39, liked the Fieldhouse but were jaded about the Starbucks thing. "This looks a lot like Hinkle Fieldhouse," said Springer, a local engineer who had attended 20 games at the Fieldhouse. "But Hinkle's louder than hell. This is a little slick for Indianapolis. No offense, but it oughta be in Chicago."

Morrison added, "Anyplace that has a cappuccino bar seems like a bit much for us. A biscotti and a beer and a coffee? I mean, we're at a basketball game."

Although the Fieldhouse has been open only a few months, other sports fans are making pilgrimages to downtown Indianapolis to travel in the past. "Even among my colleagues," said Benner, who attended Center Grove High School, south of Indianapolis. "A writer from New York came in and he said he was bringing his son back. He wanted his son to see this."

Trash talking and talk back have given the NBA a serious image problem. The TV ratings for this year's NBA All-Star game were the lowest ever. A warm and fuzzy Fieldhouse may be just what the league needs.

"Dallas is building a new facility," Benner said. "They've been

Photo courtesy of the Indiana Pacers.

The new warm and fuzzy Conesco Fieldhouse
even has a cappuccino bar.

here twice to look at us. Charlotte has had people here. Sacramento's owner was here the other day, and he took a tour. We're able to pull this off a little better than most, because of the history

When Elvis' building has left . . .

Elvis Presley's final concert took place on June 26, 1977, at Market Square Arena, 300 E. Market St., in downtown Indianapolis. It was the 68th birthday of his manager, Col. Tom Parker. Presley's 80-minute set included a stirring version of the Simon and Garfunkel hit "Bridge Over Troubled Water."

The arena will be razed this spring, so a plaque commemorating the King's last gig has been moved to Conseco Fieldhouse, Delaware and Pennsylvania Avenues, five blocks south and two blocks west of Market Square. Details? Elvis never cared about details anyway.

The plaque can be found in a Market Square Arena memorabilia case in the Clarian Health Pavilion on the south side of the Fieldhouse. It reads:

Dedicated to Market Square Arena

Elvis's last concert, June 26, 1977. Adored by millions, the American dream and more, a legend in the beginning with no end, like there never has been before. May the melody of his songs stay in the hearts of all people and keep the American dream young and pure forever. The love and goodwill he spread throughout this world through us will still be carried out.

TAKING CARE OF ELVIS FAN CLUB

With Market Square Arena joining the King at that big rock festival in the sky, Elvis roadologists can check out the antiquated Allen County War Memorial Coliseum, 4000 Parnell Ave. in Fort Wayne, Ind., where Presley appeared three times: March 30, 1957; June 12, 1972, and October 25, 1976.

When it was built in the early 1950s, the coliseum was the largest free span structure in America. Between 1952 and 1957 it was the home of the NBA's Fort Wayne Zollner Pistons. In 1957 they left Fort Wayne to become the Detroit Pistons.

of basketball in Indiana."

The 1986 film "Hoosiers" solidified Indiana's reputation as a basketball mecca. Actor Gene Hackman grew up in Danville, Ill., a long bounce pass away from Indianapolis. Hackman played the role of Norman Dale, the former big-time college coach who takes a small-town Indiana high school basketball team to glory and discovers self-redemption in the process. The film was loosely based on the 1954 Indiana state champions from Milan. The rural school won the title on a last-second 18-foot jump shot by its star Bobby Plump.

"There was a certain kind of subdued quality to people of that era," Hackman told the Arkansas Democrat-Gazette in 1987. "They certainly didn't swear as much as we all do now. There were certain kinds of values that were different. Many of those things are negatives in terms of drama. They're not overt, flashy things to do. If you can make a film work within that context, you've accomplished something."

That's how the Fieldhouse works.

It also hosts concerts. Bruce Springsteen was the first concert there, and Hoosier native John Mellencamp performed on New Year's Eve.

Leonard, 67, saw all kinds of arenas as a head coach in the American Basketball Association and the NBA. In 1961-62, he was a starting guard for the Chicago Packers of the NBA. In 1962-63, he was a reserve with the NBA's Chicago Zephyrs.

Leonard coached the Pacers between 1968 and 1980, winning 529 games. In the American Basketball Association years of 1967-76 the Pacers played in the Mid-South Coliseum in Memphis (which hosted the Beatles on Aug. 19, 1966), the dark and dingy Denver Auditorium and the Salt Palace in Salt Lake City.

"We played in an open-air stadium in Coconut Grove [Fla., during the early 1970s]," Leonard recalled with a laugh. "The ref called a bad foul. You know how refs are. He set the ball down at the end of the floor. I'm screaming at the refs, but they wouldn't look at me. The timeout was over and the fans were laughing. The ref reached down to get the ball to give it to the team that had it out. Well, the damn floor wasn't level and the ball rolled to the other end of the court. He didn't even know what people were laughing at."

Did Leonard ever anticipate an arena like the Fieldhouse?

"I didn't have that kind of vision," said the Jimmy Stewart

look-alike. "To see the progress of this franchise? And for that matter, Indianapolis itself. I feel it started 30 years ago with that Pacer ballclub. [In 1969-70, Leonard's second year as coach, he won an American Basketball Association championship with a 59-25 record.] I've seen it all, and I really believe if it wasn't for the Indiana Pacers, we wouldn't have the [NFL's] Indianapolis Colts or the RCA Dome.

"It was just progress, but somebody had to get it started."

March 5, 2000

Hail to the veeps

Quayle museum pays tribute to America's second bananas

HUNTINGTON, Ind.—The Highway of Vice Presidents is not a dead end.

In fact, the Dan Quayle Center and Museum is one of the liveliest steps on a 100-mile section of Indiana 9, south of Fort Wayne, which features the hometowns of three American vice presidents.

"It's a very unusual stretch of state highway," understates Michael R. Sellon, executive director of the Dan Quayle Commemorative Foundation, during a tour of "America's only vice presidential museum."

"Three of the 45 vice presidents [Quayle, Thomas Marshall and Thomas Hendricks, who died eight months into his 1885 term] were born or raised along one area of highway in Indiana. That's why it was declared the Highway of Vice Presidents by the state assembly."

Pass at your own risk.

Since the Quayle museum opened in the fall of 1993, it has attracted visitors from every state and 45 foreign countries. The museum averages 575 visitors a month. Admission is free; a donation is suggested. The good folks at the museum take their Danness in stride. They do not refer to him as "Vice President Quayle"; instead, he is "Dan." Like "Elvis" or "Lassie."

And while Sellon, his three-person staff and 32 volunteers are proud to point out that Indiana has produced five vice presidents, they love to quote Vice President Marshall, who served from 1913 to 1921 under Woodrow Wilson.

Sellon drops Marshall's lines like Kenneth Starr subpoenas when he speaks to area civic groups: "I was the Wilson administration's spare tire—to be used only in case of emergency." *Chi-ching.* Marshall coined the phrase, "What this country needs is a good 5-cent cigar." Then there's Marshall's parable about two brothers. Sellon recalls, "One ran away to the sea, the other became vice president, and neither was heard from again." Dan fit the bill perfectly.

"In order to gain the public's attention, you can't be serious all

Photos courtesy of the Dan Quayle Center and Museum.

Dan Quayle *(left)* and Thomas Hendricks *(depicted below)* are two of three U.S. VPs born along one stretch of Indiana Highway. The third was Thomas Marshall.

Close-up caricature of Thomas Hendricks portrayed as a locust in the September 2, 1885 *Puck Magazine*. The full cartoon shows President Grover Cleveland protecting the "Government Farm" against the swarm of "political locusts" with the "fire" of his civil service reforms. Ironically, Hendricks of Indiana was Cleveland's vice president.

From the collections of The Dan Quayle Center and Museum, Huntington, Ind.

the time," Sellon says with a straight face. "The vice presidency has been the butt of many jokes, and you can't ignore that if you want to give and honest overview of the vice presidency. It's certainly an important position, because 14 of our vice presidents have later become president.

"But the people who framed the Constitution in 1787 didn't think the vice presidency was very important. That's reflected in the Constitutional mandates of the vice president's duties: 1) You sit around and wait in case the president dies, resigns or is impeached, and 2) You get to be president of the Senate, which is largely a ceremonial position because you can only vote if there's a [rare] tie."

Sellon concedes the vice presidency was filled with riffraff until the early 1900's. Vice President Schuyler Colfax served under Ulysses S. Grant. A native of New Carlisle, Ind., Colfax planned to run for president after Grant.

But in 1872 Colfax was implicated for allegedly accepting stock in a railroad holding company, while a congressman, in return for tacitly allowing corruption to continue. And Sellon recalls how Abraham Lincoln's first vice president, Hannibal Hamlin, spent the entire Civil War living in Maine. Lincoln dumped Hamlin for his second term in favor of Andrew Johnson.

Sellon says, "You cannot overlook the fact that before the turn of the century the vice presidency was plagued with incompetence, scandal and absenteeism."

With that kind of colorful background, the history of the vice presidency is more interesting than Dan himself. I did see Dan's second grade report cards—his worst marks were a B in art and a B+ in English—his first lock of hair, and Sellon took my picture with a life-size cardboard cutout of Dan. Yes, I guess I was living large.

"The one exhibit most people come to see is the [permanent] one on Dan," Sellon says. "We really trace the story of his life, from his baby book through law school to when he became the youngest senator ever from Indiana [at age 33] to the vice presidency."

Like the Roy Rogers Museum in Victorville, Calif., the Quayle museum draws on a legacy that's rich in detail. Dan's framed law degree from Indiana University has a big chunk missing from its bottom right corner. Dan's dog Barnaby took a bite out of the degree after snarfing it off a kitchen table.

Every vice president has his picture hanging in Dan's museum. Even the five vice presidential candidates from Indiana who ran and lost are winners in Dan's museum.

And here's something I didn't know: "Look at the Constitution," Sellon says, standing in front of the 12th Amendment, ratified July 22, 1804. "When the Constitution was formed, whoever got the most votes became president, whoever got the second-most became vice president.

"So you ended up with a Democrat as president, a Republican vice president, and that did not work at all. So the 12th Amendment took care of that." Without that amendment, we'd be talking Clinton-Dole right now.

The 4,000-square-foot Quayle museum is a block north of downtown Huntington (population 16,500). Be sure to have a cup of coffee at Nick's Kitchen, 506 N. Jefferson, which is Dan's favorite restaurant. The house specialty is the Quayle Burger, a half pound of ground beef, with grilled onion, lettuce, and tomato with fries for $4.95.

All this for Dan. And he wasn't even born in Huntington.

"He grew up here and spent part of his adult life here," Sellon says. "He was actually born in Indianapolis. He moved here when he was about 5, and stayed until 1955, when he moved to Scottsdale, Ariz. He [returned in 1963 and] graduated Huntington High School [now Crestview Middle School] in 1965 and lived here when he went through college and law school."

Dan then opened his law practice with his wife, Marilyn. They remained in Huntington until 1976, when Dan became a congressman. He served two terms and ran for the Senate in 1980, defeating Birch Bayh. Dan now lives in suburban Phoenix. He is a public speaker and runs Campaign America, a combination of the Quayle-Bob Dole ex-backers.

Dan's still a young man. He turned 51 earlier this month. I wondered if Dan ever comes to his museum and says, "Clear that space, I've been talking to Jack Kemp about the 2000 ticket."

Sellon says, "We're about the last to know. And we're supposed to be separate. We're nonprofit and nonpartisan. You don't have to be a Republican to work here or visit here. He's not on our board of directors, although we do have his brother and his father on our board."

Although Sellon can take an irreverent approach to the vice presidency, the museum won't carry stuff like Dan's greatest hits

("If we don't succeed, we run the risk of failure."—Dan, 1990) or back issues of the defunct Quayle newsletter.

"My profession is a museum director," says Sellon, 46. "I'm not a political analyst, so anything I tell you about Dan's legacy is personal opinion. But probably distancing himself timewise [from Dan's sometimes-befuddled vice presidency] has allowed more perspective. Very early he brought up items like family values, and at the time he was ridiculed. Over the past five years, family values have come to the forefront."

Sellon, a native of Peoria, has a graduate degree in anthropology with a museum studies emphasis from Northern Illinois University. He's married and has three children. With some prodding, he seems sensitive toward Dan.

"As a rule, the media tends to be a little more on the liberal side," Sellon says. "And I've been on the Web, I see the Dan Quayle quotes, and 98 percent of them he never made. So perhaps he wasn't treated as fairly as he could have been."

But time heals all syntax wounds. Dan will always speak eloquently to the humble hearts along the Highway of Vice Presidents.

The Dan Quayle Center & Museum is at 815 Warren, Huntington, Ind. 46750 (219-356-6356).

February 22, 1998

POSTSCRIPT:

Michael Sellon left the Dan Quayle Center in 1999. Appropriately, he has been replaced by Dan Johns, former Director of Developing and Marketing at the Muncie Children's Museum.

Freewheeling Artifacts
Museum displays RVs, motor homes

ELKHART, Ind.—Now, here's a museum that's going places.

After all, what other museum has a big button that reads, "You can't take sex, booze or weekends away from the American people!" preserved in a glass case near the front door?

None that I'm allowed to write about.

That freewheeling quote is attributed to the late John K. Hanson, founder of the Winnebago recreational vehicle. His words are the welcome mat to the Recreational Vehicle/Motor Home Hall of Fame, Museum and Library in Elkhart, about 100 miles from Chicago.

The 15,000-square-foot museum features 22 historic recreational vehicles (which includes trailers and motor homes) including the original 1967 model Winnebago—which sold for $4,995. It's like seeing Babe Ruth's locker at the Baseball Hall of Fame.

Apart from the recreational vehicles are four manufactured homes and housing units.

In 1976 the Department of Housing and Urban Development defined manufactured homes as residences and no longer as vehicles. That's when "house trailers" and "mobile homes" ceased to exist. Mobility was no longer their function; being a residence was the main gig.

The museum permits visitors to step right into a vintage yellow and white 1954 Shasta trailer, replete with hot plates for cooking, an icebox (instead of a refrigerator) and light-finished birch interior. "It was done in birch because there was limited illumination," said Recreational Vehicle/Motor Home Heritage Foundation Vice President Al Hesselbart. The foundation is the umbrella organization for the hall of fame, museum and library.

Down the road from the Shasta is the oldest known travel trailer in the world. Both the jet-black Earl travel trailer and the Model T Ford pulling it are authentic 1913 vehicles—not replicas. "The trailer was built in Los Angeles by a carriage maker of the time," Hesselbart said. "We don't know the identity of the manufacturer. It was built for a Mr. Earl. They had to have someplace to start, and the footprint followed a hearse."

In trailer life, what goes around comes around.

Winnebago founder Hanson graduated from the University of Minnesota in 1934 with a bachelor's degree in mortuary science and ran his father's funeral home before entering the recreational vehicle industry.

My favorite museum piece is a 1940 battleship gray New Moon trailer. New Moon was based in Alma, Mich. Lucille Ball and Desi Arnaz drove a New Moon in their 1954 film "The Long, Long Trailer."

"This is a remarkable home," Hesselbart said while standing in front of the 23-foot trailer with a masonite exterior. "It was the only home for the [Robert R.] Boatman family from their purchase in 1940 until mom died in 1988. The couple lived in this unit, and they raised one son."

Robert Boatman was a welder who worked for the American Bridge and Crane Co. of Chicago. He traveled around the country to work on municipal water towers. The trailer weathered a hurricane in Sarasota, Fla., (date unknown) and a tornado in Pryor, Okla., in 1942. The damage from the tornado, caused by a flying 2-by-4, can still be seen on one side of the trailer.

After retirement, the Boatman family took their trailer to a private lot in Garrison, Texas. Hesselbart said, "In 48 years they never replaced any original material. In 1988 they were still living with the original icebox, a gasoline cook stove and a kerosene furnace."

The museum also includes remarkable contraptions like the tiny 1956 Serro Scotty travel trailer that could fit into a garage. The aluminum trailer is only 12 feet long and less than 6 feet high. Hesselbart peeked into the trailer and said, "Characteristic of these early Scotty trailers was the hole in the floor that allowed you to stand up by the sink because the low roof prohibited you to stand anyplace else in the unit.

Equally remarkable is the fact Hesselbart has never owned a recreational vehicle or motor home in his life. "I've never owned, built or sold a motor home," said Hesselbart, 57. "I do houseboating, which just limits my highway."

The congenial Hesselbart and his family moved to Elkhart 20 years ago from west suburban Wheaton, where he was the Du Page County program director of the Boy Scouts of America. He also has a background in retail automotive sales. Hesselbart has been the Recreational Vehicle/Motor Home Heritage Foundation

Photos courtesy of Al Hesselbart and the RV/HM Heritage Foundation.

RVs of long ago *(above)* and not so long ago *(opposite)* at Elkhart's Recreational Vehicle/Motor Home Hall of Fame Museum.

facility manager and industry historian since 1994.

The library of the organization has more than 8,000 volumes of books and magazines dating back to the 1920s. It's the largest recreational vehicle/motor home library in the world.

The hall of fame recognizes 198 individuals who have had influence in the industry. There are four women in the hall of fame, including Chicago's Betty Orr (Class of '72) who in the 1930s and '40s ran Orr and Orr, her own trailer sales store in downtown Chicago.

The foundation operates on a tidy $300,000 annual budget with a staff of three. Hesselbart said the museum and hall of fame attracts about 10,000 visitors a year. Admission is free; donations are accepted.

As you drive south on Route 19 into downtown Elkhart, you begin to understand why the hall of fame and museum is here. The highway is lined with dozens of sales lots for recreational vehicles and motor homes. It gives you a good idea of what the rest of America will look like when all the baby boomers retire.

There are 107 manufacturers within a 25-mile radius of the hall of fame.

And if you really want to make a day of it, at least a dozen recreational vehicle or motor home manufacturers offer plant tours, including Coachmen Industries (219-262-0123) and Gulf-stream Coach (219-773-7761).

The hall of fame existed for 20 years as a paper entity. The current headquarters was built in 1990 when the volunteer board of directors decided to make the archives and artifacts accessible to the public.

"By this time Elkhart was recognized as the trailer capital of the world," Hesselbart said. "Transportation had a major role in that. In the 1920s through the 1940s, Elkhart was at the crossing of the New York Central and the Pennsylvania Railroad main line. At the same time U.S. Highway 33 [Washington D.C. to Minneapolis] and U.S. Highway 20 [New York through Chicago] crossed in Elkhart.

"And Elkhart had a reputation for entrepreneurial spirit."

But the spirit didn't reach as high as the ill-fated "High Rise

Mobile Home Parks," whose stacked prototype models are another museum highlight. "Several of them actually existed," Hesselbart said in amazement.

The June 18, 1971, issue of *Life* magazine screamed, "The World's First Multi-Story Mobile Manufactured Housing Development: The Upwardly Mobile Home." One late 1960s triple-deck high-rise mobile home park is still open for business on a hillside two miles from Morgantown, W. Va.

"There was a multitude of problems," Hesselbart said. "The biggest problem was that they required exposed plumbing. So in a northern climate they had problems with hard water in the wintertime. And since they were concrete structures, the bigger they got, the more they became akin to municipal parking garages. And we all know the conditions of parking garages in the city.

"That's not the environment you really want to live in."

The high-rise mobile home park concept was conjured up by Elmer Frey of Marshfield, Wis. That didn't prevent him from being part of the 1972 freshman induction class into the hall of fame. Frey also worked hard within the industry to change the identity of "house trailers" to "mobile homes."

"There's a very outdated stereotype of the product and the kind of people who live in manufactured homes," Hesselbart said. "The terminology 'mobile home' had been outdated since 1976, but we're so ingrained with the thought of trashy motor homes and similar people living in them—and unfortunately some of that was earned—it's a very hard stereotype for the industry to break.

"We had a couple here this morning in their early 50s who had both resigned their employment. They had a six-wheel trailer behind a pick-up truck. They worked as they needed to. They were leaving here for a three-month stint as staff members at Disney World in Orlando. After that they had employment at a KOA campground in the Florida Keys. They spent this summer staffing a campground on the outer banks of North Carolina. And you know what?

"They were having the greatest time of their life."

The Recreational Vehicle/Motor Home Hall of Fame and Museum is at 801 Benham Ave. Take 80-90 out of Chicago to exit 92. Follow Route 19 south into Elkhart. Turn left on Main Street and follow that south into downtown. After the bridge over the St.

Joseph River, look for Jackson Boulevard. Turn right on Jackson and proceed two blocks to 3rd Street. Turn left on 3rd, go through an underpass and catch the museum on your right. There were no recreational vehicles or motor homes in the parking lot during my visit. For information, call the museum at (219) 293-2344.

November 21, 1999

Valpo pops on
Plant closing; fest to stay

VALPARAISO, Ind.—The theme of the 21st Annual Valparaiso Popcorn Festival is "Popcorn Makes History." But the local Orville Redenbacher popcorn plant made ultimate history in May when parent company ConAgra announced it was closing the plant—in the very city where Redenbacher and partner Charles Bowman created gourmet popcorn.

ConAgra will consolidate the Valparaiso popcorn bottling and microwave packaging operations with those at other plants, including one in Marion, Ohio. Nearly 230 people will lose their jobs. A 15-person Redenbacher research department will remain in Valparaiso.

And that's enough to keep the popcorn festival cooking.

The 100-unit Orville Redenbacher Parade commences at 10 a.m. Saturday in downtown Valparaiso, a 45-minute drive from Chicago. The first parade got into the Guinness Book of World Records by way of a 12-foot-diameter popcorn ball produced by the Valparaiso Jaycees.

"Just like the Rose [Bowl] festival had floats built from flowers, we encourage everyone to build floats out of popcorn," said Glennas Kueck, popcorn festival executive director, during a conversation at Dottie D'Oeuvres coffeeshop in downtown Valparaiso. "Last year we gave them 50 pounds of uncooked Redenbacher popcorn to build from. This year it's 44 pound bags. ConAgra filtered off six pounds."

Everyone crackled.

Sitting next to Kueck at a round table were Bowman and Bill Oeding, president of the Greater Valparaiso Chamber of Commerce.

There's also a Popcorn Talent Show at noon Saturday on the Poppin' Fest Stage in downtown Valpo, and nearly 500 arts and crafts booths will be open from 7 a.m. until 6:30 p.m. Saturday throughout town. Kueck said that 800 pounds of popcorn will be popped to provide pep for the 70,000 people expected to participate on Saturday. (Valparaiso's population is 26,000.)

But my choice pick is the 5:15 p.m. appearance by the classic rock band Guns & Hoses on the west side of the 116-year-old courthouse on the town square.

Guns & Hoses is a five-piece band consisting of members of the Valparaiso police and fire department. The band's lead guitarist and vocalist is Mike Veal, a 26-year-veteran of the Porter County Sheriff's Police and currently commander of the detective bureau.

Oeding looked out on Lincolnway Street, renamed Redenbacher Way for the early September festival season. He said, "The Redenbacher plant has a substantial presence in this town. It started in the 1950s with a couple of guys and grew to 230 people. You hate to see a company of that size leave, but they're leaving in good standing." The popcorn festival and ConAgra will soon announce a continued partnership in the festival.

"We've been part of the popcorn festival since its inception," said Kay Carpenter, spokeswoman for ConAgra Grocery Products in Fullerton, Calif. "And Valparaiso was the home of Orville Redenbacher. We're leaving the community in essence, but the product is alive and well, and we want to support it."

A native of rural Brazil, Ind., Redenbacher died at age 88 in September 1995. He has a daughter who still lives in Valparaiso. His grandson Gary frequently appeared in television commercials with his grandfather. Gary, 44, lives in Northern California and has not attended the last few popcorn festivals.

Bowman, 80, met Redenbacher at Purdue University in West Lafayette, Ind., where Redenbacher graduated with a degree in agronomy. "I was in charge of all seed certification at the university, not just popcorn," said Bowman, who majored in agricultural education at Purdue. "I was actually the inspector going down to see if he was doing it right. One evening we were having a cup of coffee in a little restaurant in Princeton, Ind., and we started talking about making our own popcorn."

Arthur Brunson, a USDA popcorn breeder from Purdue, told the young man that people would pay for a higher-quality popcorn. "He planted the idea," Bowman said—no pun intended. "So the first thing we came up with was the word 'gourmet.' That brought up the question, 'How do you get gourmet popcorn?' "

And well . . .

Bowman smiled. He explained, "We went into a long lecture about the quality of the corn and how it was a different hybrid. The corn was from Indiana, but when I started in the late 1930s, most everyone grew popcorn in their garden. There was very little of it in the grocery, and what was there had not been bred for the consumer. Our hybrid did that."

In contrast to garden-variety popcorn, whose kernels expand about 20 times their original size when popped, Redenbacher and Bowman created a "snowflake" variety that expanded as much as 40 times, producing a lighter, fluffier *gourmet* popcorn.

In 1953 Bowman and Redenbacher began producing their popcorn at a seed corn plant they converted from an old three-story frame garage about 10 miles outside of Valparaiso. They first sold their fancy Redbo ("Red" as in Redenbacher, "Bo" as in Bowman) popcorn in 5-pound cloth bags along the Lincoln Highway (U.S. 30).

"People would stop, buy the popcorn and they'd always come back," Bowman said. "Popcorn was about 20 cents a pound. We were charging a dollar. They said ours was 'good old-fashioned popcorn.' We never knew what that meant."

Bowman recalled driving with Redenbacher to a Chicago advertising agency in the 1960s when the brand name was changed from Redbo to Orville Redenbacher Gourmet Popping Corn.

"This advertising writer wouldn't even buy the name 'Redenbacher,' " Bowman laughed. "She really played up *Orville, Orville . . .* So coming home from up there Orville said, 'What did you think?' I said, 'Man, we just spent a lot of money to change the name.' "

Orville Redenbacher Gourmet Popping Corn hit the gourmet section of food stores in 1972, but Bowman and Redenbacher didn't have the financing to get their goods in the general marketplace. In 1976 they sold out the brand to Hunt-Wesson Foods, now a division of ConAgra, a $24 billion diversified foods company.

Bowman isn't bent out of shape about Redenbacher getting most of the credit for the gourmet popcorn. "I had all the attention I needed," said Bowman, who is president of Chester Inc., an agricultural-technological plant next door to the Redenbacher plant on U.S. 30. He is currently perfecting a small line of organic popcorn.

Redenbacher's celebrity grew with his late 1970s and 1980s guest appearances on television commercials and talk shows. With his bow tie and thick glasses, the popcorn entrepreneur even became part of folklore when former WGN radio morning man Wally Phillips told a listener Redenbacher "invented" popcorn. "It's true," Bowman said. "He forgot about the Indians." Kueck—

a Native American from Oklahoma—added, "So much for those Aztecs and Mayans."

Bowman reflected, "We don't like it that ConAgra is leaving town, but they helped us get a lot of things done. And No. 1 was the festival. I was the chairman of the first festival, and in the early days, we had no experience. We had no idea what to do with 75,000 people coming to town." This year, throw a little salt in the wound, lick some chops and get ready to pop.

September 5, 1999

Indiana hotel offers jazzy history

RICHMOND, Ind.—The stars used to shine along the Old National Road that still hums along like a song through downtown Richmond. When the majestic Hotel Leland opened for business here during the fall of 1928, the borough near the Ohio border was the home of the Gennett Record Co.

The record company is long gone, but the hotel celebrates its 70th anniversary this year. The Clarion Hotel Leland (800-535-2630) stands tall at 900 South A St. in a revitalized central business district.

Jazz masters such as Louis Armstrong, Tommy Dorsey, Duke Ellington and Jelly Roll Morton came to Richmond to record their music at Gennett studios. Most of them stayed at the Leland, unless they were in a hurry to get to Chicago, now a four-hour drive from Richmond (pop. 41,350).

Located in a clapboard building in a railroad gorge near the Whitewater River, the studio was an offshoot of Richmond's now-defunct Starr Piano manufacturing company during the late

Photo by Lisa Day.

This tribute to Richmond's Gennett Record Music Co., the birthplace of recorded jazz, is located across from the old Leland Hotel.

1920s and early 1930s. The studio also recorded sides for the Decca and Remington labels. Even Gene Autry came to Richmond to record country-western music.

Hoagy Carmichael, who was born in Bloomington, Ind., wrote and recorded "Stardust" in Richmond. He was inspired by the hotel's second floor "Star Dust Ballroom," which is immaculately preserved with the original maple floor intact. Beautiful French doors open onto the Tea Garden built on the rooftop. A small stage is still used for area proms and dances. A mezzanine adjoins the peach and gray ballroom (capacity 445) and it is flanked by elegant stairwells.

"Stardust" was one of Carmichael's earliest compositions. The Carmichael songbook also includes "Skylark," "Georgia on my Mind" and "Up the Lazy River." As early as 1927 Carmichael was commuting between Indiana and Chicago, where he recorded "Washboard Blues" with the Paul Whiteman Orchestra (and the Dorsey Brothers in the lineup). A mural across the street from the Leland commemorates Richmond as "The Birthplace of Recorded Jazz."

The seven-story hotel with 112 rooms was built in Spanish Colonial Revival Style. The top floor of the hotel features Lionel Hampton and Woody Herman suites. The popular main floor restaurant is Ellington's, which specializes in steaks and chicken piccata.

Queen Anne furnishings, popular during the reign of King George I and Queen Anne in the early 1700s are throughout the hotel. The Leland Hotel was added to the National Register of Historic Places in 1986.

And it's for sale.

"It's a challenge to be successful in an off-the-highway property," says Robert B. Nelson, senior consultant at Professional Planning Consultants Inc., during a recent interview in the hotel lobby. The Clarion-franchised hotel is owned by the Columbus, Ohio-based consulting firm. Nelson, 62, spent 18 years with Red Roof Inn.

The Hotel Leland is about 15 minutes south of I-70. The hotel has been down this road before. The Raddison chain owned the hotel between 1985 and 1990 (when I stayed at the Leland for the first time). The Raddison closed in bankruptcy in October, 1990. It sat empty until Professional Planning Consultants bought it in April, 1993. The new company got the building without its

Photo by Lisa Day.

The remains of a Gennett Record Music Co. building in a
Richmond, Indiana, railroad gorge near the Whitewater River.

millions of debts.

"This is a gem of an old property," Nelson says. "Our rates
start at $52 and that's not a lot of money to pay for a classic old
hotel. But it's difficult to find people who appreciate fine old
hotels. The average overnight guest is someone who wants to stay
near the interstate . . . and stay in a place they've stayed before
with lots of retail around them.

"And a significant part of the traveling public has never stayed
in a 'hotel,' only stay in motels. So they think 'hotel,' and they're
going to have to pay to park their cars, there will be a bellman
who will want to carry their bags and expect a tip and it adds on
and on. Well, that isn't the case for us."

The Hotel Leland has free parking adjacent to the property and
bell service is provided if needed.

Nodding toward the front lobby Nelson says, "In the height of
the motel concept, you could drive your car in here. I have
difficulty visualizing that."

Indeed, in 1963, the original lobby was ripped out and turned
into a drive-in area when the hotel became the Leland Motor Inn.
The change was remodeled for a "functional modern trend,"

according to local newspapers.

In addition to being a jazz mecca, Richmond is where Harley Henley invented the roller skate, home to a pioneer in greenhouse rose growing and the place where Singing Sam the Barbosol Man once lived.

Nelson said, "Richmond is a unique town in that it has its own symphony orchestra, an art gallery, a player's theater—and all those groups have functions at this hotel. It's a special place."

May 24, 1998

POSTSCRIPT:

The Hotel Leland closed in February, 2000. Music pilgrims can still inspect the original site of the Gennett Record Music Co., nestled in a gorge just south of the Main Street Bridge on the edge of downtown. The Richmond-Wayne County Chamber of Commerce is hoping to develop a jazz museum on the site and is also working to reopen the hotel.

VEHICLE

a. p.

1F 99

OHIO

STEUBENVILLE ◉
DINO

COLUMBUS ◉
WHITE CASTLE
-
KAHIKI
-
EYES & DRAINS

Map by Lisa Day.

Chomping on the White Castle legacy

COLUMBUS, Ohio—In a way, it's the mecca of meat.

A mysterious way.

The historic White Castle headquarters have been just north of downtown Columbus since 1934. It's worth a stop if you're quickly passing through—just like the popular burger goes through your system.

You know how it goes down. For decades, the slider has been the butt of jokes: "Ex-Lax on a Bun," "Beef Cookies," "The Meat That Boogies." Columbus is the birthplace of Wendy's, Bob Evans Farm restaurants and good ol' Arthur Treacher's Fish & Chips. But there's nothing like a White Castle.

And it all comes from Columbus. Inside the lobby of the blue and white porcelain and steel White Castle complex at 555 W. Goodale St. (614-228-5781) there's a permanent exhibit of White Castle coffee mugs, matchbooks and diner headgear. Archival photos include a member of the Air Force Reserve who took a sack of White Castles to the South Pole and ardent fans who have held their wedding receptions at White Castle.

But my favorite item is a "petrified" hamburger that slider fans brought to a 1957 garden party for Queen Elizabeth II. There's also an archival exhibit of White Castle's relationship with Chicago in the lobby of the White Castle, 9501 S. Cicero, Oak Lawn (708-636-7377).

White Castle cultists range from cabbies and construction workers to The Smithereens, who wrote a song called "White Castle Blues," and Frank Sinatra. Whenever the Chairman was toddlin' around Chicago, he would call the now defunct 1-800-White Castle and request several sacks of sliders, according to Kim Bartley, director of Marketing/Keeper of the Crave at White Castle.

One of the most unique things about the White Castle cult is the annual recipe contest the company conducts every summer. I've been a judge at a couple of these wing-dings.

When lined up next to each other, the servings in the 7th Annual White Castle Recipe Contest looked like the swirling cars of a wild roller coaster.

There was Castle Breakfast Quiche, Awesome White Castle

Italian Style Pizza Burgers, Castle Stuffed Potatoes (the winner), Lasagne Royale, Stubby's 3 Cheese White Castle Spinach Quiche, Breakfast Enchiladas.

And: Castle Parmigiana, White Castle Taco Fondue, White Castle South of the Border, Fit for a King White Castle Ring and White Castle Italiano.

Nearly 200 White Castle fans from 12 States entered the contest. The final 11 recipes were prepared in the White Castle test kitchen and awaited a verdict from eight judges.

I had a hearty sample from every entry.

In fact, my samples were so hearty, I was the last judge to turn in my ballot. Yes, I guess I was full. The last time I felt so queasy was when I was a kid riding the Bobs at Riverview.

I sat across from Bill Ingram, the chairman of the board and CEO, president of White Castle System Inc. Bill is a wise man.

As I was ripping into the Awesome White Castle Italian Style Pizza Burgers (created with mozzarella and provolone cheese and green peppers by Jocelyn Williams of Park Forest), I saw Bill merely nibbling at his food. You'd have thought we were dining at a Parisian bistro.

Bill also found ample time to talk, time that would otherwise have been consumed by Stubby's Cheese White Castle Spinach Quiche (10 sliders, 16 ounces of spinach, 10 slices of cheddar, American and Swiss cheese, a pound of bacon, chopped green pepper, a dozen eggs in a 9-inch pie shell—I think I'm going to be sick.)

"You know," Bill said slowly. "We have an employee contest like this, where we get entries from India and Pakistan, where they use a lot of curry."

Wonderful.

I'm trying to get through White Castle South of the Border (10 sliders, 2 packages of cream cheese, a can of chili peppers and a can of chili con carne, fortunately without beans) and I'm thinking about beef cookies with curry.

The finalists were judged on best use of a hamburger, originality and taste. We rated each entry on its "crave" factor. Other intrepid judges included Bill's wife Marci; Andrea Bilotti, manager of foodservice marketing of the Chicago-based National Cattlemen's Beef Association, and Bedelia Woods, owner of the legendary Sylvia's soul food restaurant in the Harlem neighborhood of New York City. The finalists will be featured in the 7th Annual White Castle Recipe Booklet, available later this month at White Castle locations.

"I've been a fan of White Castle since I was a child," Woods said in an interview before the winner was announced. "My mom [Sylvia Woods] was a waitress. Mondays were a treat for us because that was her day off. We lived in Harlem, and White Castle was in the Bronx. We would pack all my friends in the car and drive up to White Castle. It was around 1956. At that time White Castle had outdoor service. We looked forward to experiencing that."

Woods also looked forward to being a White Castle recipe judge for the first time. "I really liked the White Castle Italiano [10 sliders, a medium-sized jar of spaghetti sauce, a green pepper, ½ cup of Parmesan cheese]. I love Italian. The sauce made it work for me. The Castle Stuffed Potato? Fabulous."

Winner Joy Bandemer's Castle Stuffed Potatoes also received good marks from Bilotti. "We're always looking for interesting hamburger ideas, and this takes the White Castle to a new level," Bilotti said. "Joy showed a lot of imagination. Most of the recipes were Italian or breakfast. The stuffed potato was a very unique and tasty option. I'm going to make it for the office."

I found the Castle Stuffed Potatoes a little too spuddy, but Bandemer's recipe came near the end of the line. The Castle Stuffed Potatoes were the eighth of 11 tastings and by that time I was staggering.

I gave good marks to the Fit for a King White Castle Ring, kind of a Tex-Mex thing with 10 sliders, burrito seasoning mix, four-cheese Mexican shredded cheese, minced garlic, dried cilantro leaves and two packages of crescent dinner rolls. Brown bun pieces were served in the center of the ring.

The regal recipe underscored the theme of the day. If a man's home is his White Castle, then after eating 11 scrumptious slider recipes, home must be where the heartburn is.

March 29, 1998

Regal Spuds
White Castle's winner is really full of itself

There is only so much you can do with a spud.

Mash it. Bake it. French fry it. Buy him a drink.

But Joy Bandemer cut five baked potatoes in half, stuffed them with small pieces from 10 White Castle hamburgers, threw on some cheese and baked them.

And now, the Bolingbrook homemaker will receive a sack of 10 sliders a week for 52 weeks as the winner of the 7th Annual White Castle Recipe Contest held last month at the company headquarters in Columbus, Ohio.

Bandemer's Castle Stuffed Potatoes beat a fueled-up field from across America that included White Castle Taco Fondue, Awesome White Castle Italian Style Pizza Burgers and Stubby's 3 Cheese White Castle Spinach Quiche. *Belch!*

Bandemer is an old pro at this. Last year her Castle Stuffed Pork Chops was the contest runner-up. Bandemer is to beef cookies what Wolfgang Puck is to cheeseless pizza.

It's funny; Bandemer doesn't look like the type of person who would do weird things with White Castle hamburgers. She wears June Cleaver pearls and her eyes have the kind look that might offer a cup o' coffee—instead of a spud o' sliders. When a visitor gets lost on the way to her ranch house, Bandemer will stand out and wait in the driveway.

Bandemer, 62, has lived with her husband, Fred, for the past 23 years in southwest suburban Bolingbrook. He also likes White Castles; he has no choice. And they have a daughter, Karen, who is a schoolteacher in Minneapolis.

The Bandemers have a black and white cat, Osirus, and a miniature Dachshund named Heidi. And wouldn't you know it, Heidi adores White Castles.

"When we come home with White Castles, she sits and barks," Bandemer said during a conversation at her kitchen table. "Then we give it to her and she shuts up. She won't eat McDonald's, though."

This year Bandemer entered three recipes. She liked her White Castle Oriental with rice, cream of mushroom soup, celery,

Joy Bandemer's Castle stuffed potatoes

Makes 10 Potato Halves

5 large baking potatoes, baked

1 teaspoon salt

1 teaspoon pepper

8 ounces sour cream

10 White Castle hamburgers

1 medium green pepper, finely chopped

1 medium onion, finely chopped

1 tablespoon margarine

1½ cups Cheddar cheese, grated

4 tablespoons chives

1. Slice baked potatoes lengthwise. Scoop out most of potato and place in a large bowl. Coarsely chop and mash potatoes. Add salt, pepper and sour cream.

2. Remove pickles from hamburgers; cut burgers into small pieces—bun included—and place in bowl.

3. Lightly sauté pepper and onion in margarine, then add to potato mixture. Mix well. Put potato/hamburger mixture into potato skins. Fill them over the top until all the filling is used.

4. Sprinkle grated cheese and chives on top. Bake in a preheated, 325-degree oven until cheese melts and potatoes are thoroughly warm, 35 to 45 minutes. Can be used as a meal with a tossed salad or soup.

NUTRITIONAL INFORMATION (per serving)

Calories: 485

From Fat: 186

Percentages of daily value based on 2,000-calorie diet:

Total Fat	21g	32%	Sugars	6 g	
Saturated Fat	12 g	59%	Protein	20 g	
Cholesterol	65 mg	22%	Vitamin A	17%	
Sodium	834 mg	35%	Vitamin C	76%	
Carbohydrate	54 g	18%	Calcium	27%	
Dietary Fiber	3 g	11%	Iron	26%	

onions and soy sauce, but it did not make the final cut. Fortunately, she was hip to the hot baked potato craze. "Everybody loves baked potatoes stuffed with everything," she said. "So why not White Castle?"

I got misty-eyed. I thought I heard Robert Goulet singing "The Impossible Dream" from the Bandemer living room.

"The green pepper and onions give it flavor," Bandemer said, building to a crescendo. "I mix the potato that I scoop out of the baked potato shell with the sour cream and mix everything together at once. I make little mounds and put them back in and bake them. They come out pretty good. Ten White Castles are just enough. You can still taste them, but I also like the taste of the potato and sour cream. Twenty White Castles would be overwhelming.

"They could be a whole meal, you could also cut them into sections for hors d'oeuvres. But I never thought that I would win. I was just trying to think what I could mix White Castle with. Noodles? Turkey? Last year lasagna won [The Ultimate White Castle Stuffed Pasta Shells With Italian Sausage and mozzarella cheese], but I would never mix White Castle, bread and lasagna."

Bandemer is an avid cookbook collector and enters recipe contests for fun. As much as she loves White Castles, she has no idea what she is going to do with 520 White Castle hamburgers over the next year. One thing is for sure: Heidi will no longer be a *miniature* Dachshund.

Ironically, the Bandemers live less than a mile from the nearest White Castle. No, it's not that bad. The Bandemers came first. Bandemer explained, "We were here and [in 1983] two boys went around Bolingbrook with a wagon and got enough signatures to send to headquarters that they wanted a White Castle here. When it opened [in 1984] for the first couple weeks, people came from all over."

Bandemer was born and reared on the South Side of Chicago. A White Castle stand was always in the neighborhood. She attended Calumet High School and there was a White Castle at 79th and Loomis. As a teenager, she'd go to the beautiful Southtown Theatre and after the movies, Bandemer and her friends would stop at the White Castle at 63rd and Halsted.

"It's good to have a White Castle nearby," Bandemer said. "I don't care for breakfast much. Sometimes we hit the road at two or three in the morning for our cabin in Minnesota. We get a sack of White Castles and two or three cups of coffee and take off."

Between 1953 and 1965 Bandemer worked in the Chicago stockyards. She was a secretary to the president of the Pfaelzer Brothers Co. when she met her husband, who was operations supervisor. Bandemer knows meat makes the meal.

"There's only a small amount of meat on each [White Castle] patty," Bandemer said. "But it is good meat. There is no filler, even though it is less than an ounce.

Bandemer remains eligible to enter future contests. She is ready, willing and able to explore future trends such as Cajun White Castle, White Castle Cuban or Pierogi-A-Go-Go.

"Oh, my," Bandemer said. "Can you picture blackened White Castles on Creole rice? Or how 'bout if you battered them in deep-fried squares and put sweet and sour sauce for Chinese White Castle?"

Bandemer seemed dizzy with all the possibilities. That's OK.

Time slides by when you're having a good time with White Castles.

September 9, 1998

That's Amore
Dean Martin's hometown celebrates its love with a truly American festival

STEUBENVILLE, Ohio—Everybody loves somebody sometime.

In this Rust Belt city, they love Dean Martin all the time.

The son of an immigrant barber, Dino Crochetti was born in 1917 in this hilly village on the west bank of the Ohio River. Reborn as Dean Martin, his final visit was in 1950 when he and partner Jerry Lewis performed at a Steubenville High School fund-raiser.

Dean passed on to the "Big Casino" (as Sinatra called it) in 1995.

Dean was away for 45 years, but that doesn't stop his local fans from hosting a Dean Martin Festival. If Graceland is for the King, then Deanland is for the swing. This year's third annual affair runs Friday and Saturday throughout Steubenville. Dean would have turned 81 on June 7.

As any fan of Dean knows, he rarely walked a straight line. So there was no reason for him to turn back. Once Dean became a film and television star, he moved his family away from Steubenville to Southern California.

Steubenville's always been a tough town where residents worked hard and played hard. Dean's first job was in the steel mills along the Ohio River; he fought as a welterweight under the name Kid Crochet and at 16 delivered bootleg liquor around town. During Prohibition Steubenville was known as "Little Chicago" for its diversions into gambling and crime.

Dean was part of the scene. He rolled craps at a gambling room behind the now-defunct Rex Cigar Store on Market Street and began singing in clubs. The economy was hurting worse than a three-martini hangover. Still is.

Dean was not alone in saying, *"Arrivederci, baby."*

According to the Ohio Public Expenditure Council, more than a quarter of the Steubenville residents left town between 1970 and 1990, slicing the population from 30,495 to 22,125. Nearly two-thirds of the residents live on welfare or Social Security payments.

That's why the Dean Martin Festival is so important. It pumps

THE STEUBENVILLE STUMPER

As I wandered through Dean Martin's hometown, I would ask locals the big question, "When the moon hits your eye, like a big pizza pie . . .

. . . What happens?"

Here are a few of the answers:

"I don't know," replied a 24-year-old female clerk at the Steubenville News, 426 Market St. (740-282-5842), where you can buy gobs of Dean memorabilia. She seemed bothered by my query. I was more bothered by the hundreds of X-rated videos in the back of the store.

"That's Amore!" laughed Mike Serafini. (Correct answer: "That's Love!," Dean's song from the 1953 Dean Martin-Jerry Lewis flick "The Caddy.") Serafini in the 25-year-old night clerk at the Twi-Lite Motel, 1201 University Blvd. adjacent to the Twi-Lite Lounge. I stayed here. Nice single rooms are $35 a night. Good cable. (740-282-9725).

"You get drunk," from a guy who said he had been drinking all day at the Colonial Terrace Supper Club, 169 N. Fourth St., a wicked nocturnal taste of old downtown. I bought him a can of Stroh's beer commemorating the Hockey Hall of Fame induction of Pittsburgh Penguin Mario Lemieux. The guy yelled at me because it wasn't Budweiser.

passion back into a tired town.

And whatever you do, don't miss Dean's mural. Featuring 27 outdoor murals, Steubenville is now known as the "City of Murals."

The two-story Dean mural is on the wall of a new Kroger's in the Hollywood Plaza mall on Sunset Boulevard, a mile west of downtown. The mural was painted by Robert Dever, who last week landed a job designing Rugrat characters for Nickelodeon in Los Angeles. Dever, 28, is from Toronto, Ohio, about seven miles north of Steubenville.

The mural depicts four corners of Dean's life, underscoring the fact that he was hardly a square. There are Dean and Frank Sinatra and Sammy Davis Jr. As I viewed the piece the day after Frank's passing, the tears tumbled like dice into my bottle of Asti

Here's some more Dean Martin trivia:

- Elvis Presley's favorite singer was Dean Martin. Who was Dean's favorite singer?

  A. Elvis

  B. Frank Sinatra

  C. Bing Crosby

- What was Dean's favorite food, besides Italian?

  A. Spanish

  B. Chinese

  C. Cajun

- Dean had two favorite pastimes. One was watching old Westerns. What was the other?

  A. Eating

  B. Drinking

  C. Playing golf

- On Aug. 15, 1964, Dean Martin knocked a famous group out of No. 1 on the pop charts with his song "Everybody Loves Somebody." Who were they?

  A. The Rolling Stones

  B. The Bay City Rollers

  C. The Beatles

Correct answers: C, A, C, C ("A Hard Day's Night")

Questions courtesy of the Dean Martin Committee, 300 Market St., Steubenville, Ohio 43952. To access the Dean Martin Web site, punch up www.ridgefieldgroup.com/ deanmartin/.

Spumante.

Beneath the dearly departed Rat Pack, there are Dean and Jerry Lewis in a convertible on their 1950 visit to Steubenville. The left side of the mural features Martin and Lewis in concert as well as Dean with his long-time accompanist, Kenny Lane, who wrote Dean's 1964 hit "Everybody Loves Somebody." The centerpiece of the mural is Dean alone in an elegant tuxedo, standing in front of a blue sky and no doubt singing:

"When the moon hits your eye

Like a big pizza pie"

Wait a minute. Dean doesn't have a cigarette. Or a drink in his hand.

That's amoral.

That's like painting Michael Jordan without a basketball.

"Kroger wouldn't allow it," festival co-chairwoman Rose Angelica says.

Rose, festival co-chairwoman Carol Weber, Mitzi Camerlengo and her husband, Mario, were among those gathered at the cozy Naples Spaghetti House to talk about Steubenville's favorite son. Mario, 80, was born two weeks before Dean on the same South 6th Street block where Dean was born. Dean's homestead is a vacant lot, but late sports announcer Jimmy "The Greek" Snyder's birthplace still stands a block east.

The Antonio Delatore family opened Naples 75 years ago at 329 N. Street (740-283-3405) on the north side of town. It's still in the family. Dean would drop into Naples from Wells High School, across the

Photo by Dave Hoekstra.

Native son, Dean Martin, in one corner of the two-story mural devoted to him on a wall of Steubenville's Kroger.

street.

"Even in high school he'd get chased out of class for making us laugh," Mario says over a bowl of homemade spaghetti. "Dean played drums for the Boy Scouts and he was in the school band. Mario Mancinelli ran a music studio and he taught intermediate students. In 1928 he formed a concert orchestra and Dean and I joined. We'd practice every Sunday at the old K and P Hall. Dean played the drums, I played the violin."

In 1935 Mario Camerlengo, his older sister Helen (on accordion) and Dean formed a trio called the Gondoliers.

In the late 1930s Dean began singing with Steubenville bandleader Ernie McKay. A Cleveland, Ohio, bandleader named Sammy Watkins hired Dean in 1939 and changed his name to Dean Martini. By 1943 Dean was singing at the Riobamba Club in New York City. Frank Sinatra was the opening act.

Some locals say that Dean turned his back on Steubenville. Judy Manfred owns a popular biker bar called Manfred's, 4152 Sunset Blvd. (740-264-2710), down the road from Dean's mural. Dean's greatest hits occupies number 78 on the CD jukebox. It's the closest you'll get to finding a nightspot where you can hear Dean.

Judy, 38, says, "My grandmother Rose talks about going to the old Hi Hat night club and Dean never had a nickel to his name.

"I believe in my city," says Judy, who last September opened Mickey's, a downtown sandwich shop, with her husband, Michael. "My Dad, 'Toots' Manfred, always said, 'You live in the community, you give to the community.' But it's hard." Judy then gave me a souvenir Manfred's T-shirt.

Steubenville was spelled "Stuebenville."

Dean eerily looked down at Judy from a television set above the bar. Dean's black and white concert footage was being aired in a tribute to Frank Sinatra.

Almost every year after Dean left town, he sent $100 to his high school—from which he never graduated—for an advertisement in the student yearbook. "It says, 'Congratulations Class of whatever from Your pal, Dino,' " Rose says. "He bought band uniforms for both high schools [Steubenville High and Catholic Central High]. In 1974, both he and Frank Sinatra bought band uniforms. Dean donated a lot of money to hospitals."

The 25-member volunteer Dean Martin Committee has kept

Dean's philanthropy a priority. They distribute Christmas presents to needy children, they have contributed to the MDA Dean Martin Neuromuscular Clinic at St. Elizabeth's Hospital in Youngstown, Ohio, and they've presented Dean Martin Music Scholarships to area high school students. The committee also monitored the painting of the $12,000 Dean mural, which was paid for by Dean's fans across America and Europe.

The Committee's proceeds come solely from the sale of Dean memorabilia. This year's souvenirs include glass paperweights featuring an etched picture of Dean, T-shirts and baseball caps. I was fortunate enough to pick up a couple of commemorative bottles of Dean Martin 80th birthday wine from last year's festival. It still can be found around town, especially at Testa's Grocery Store, 529 South St. (740-282-5191), in Dean's old neighborhood. A bottle of wine and a cassette tape of Dean's greatest hits sells for $10.

Testa's is a proud reminder of how Dean's neighborhood used to be. "Mr. Testa was in business for 44 years," says 39-year-old Wesley Jacobsen, who, with his wife, is buying the corner grocery on the fading block. "His father-in-law had it for 20 something years across the street."

Before the Testa family changed locations, the current grocery store was a pool hall where Dean learned how to hustle pool. "When his friends from Vegas come back they tell me stories how he'd come in here when he was six years old. He'd bend over to rack the balls, and if a guy wasn't watching, Dean would slip the quarter in his sock," Wesley says. "When he'd walk out of here, he'd do a little dance shuffle so you couldn't hear the change in his sock."

The grocery store still has its original front mahogany counter. A clerk would crack open a box of bulk spaghetti and customers would buy loose spaghetti, four or five ounces at a time.

Today, Steubenville is the home of Wheeling-Pittsburgh Steel Corp. Wheeling-Nisshin is a five-year-old steel mill three miles southeast of Steubenville in Folansbee, W. Va., and Weirton Steel is across the river in Weirton, W. Va. When Dean was in the Gondoliers he performed at the weekly Weirton Steel amateur show at Grant School in Steubenville.

"There's no jobs here for lawyers, people in the medical field and so on," Rose says. "Everything here is steel. That's the biggest industry we have. We're all looking at things like this for tourism. They rebuilt Clark Gable's boyhood home in Cadiz [Ohio]. That's just 20 miles east from here." Someday soon the committee hopes to establish a Dean Martin Museum in Steubenville. The group has the blessing of Dean's family.

Rose, 43, is a music teacher. She is deeply devoted to her committee work. "We're all big Dean Martin fans," she says. "He's the biggest thing to come out of here. He's the everyday person like us that made it. He's the American Dream, whose father was an Italian immigrant and came here with nothing."

Dean Martin was something.

And something stands for a lot in Steubenville, Ohio.

May 31, 1998

Singing Dean's praises

STEUBENVILLE, Ohio—Singing barbers have been around forever. But there's only one trumpet-playing barber who cut the hair of Dean Martin.

And that's Dorman Panebianco, 83, who is sure to be one of the highlights of the third annual Dean Martin Festival, which runs next weekend here.

"Dean's father was a barber," Panebianco says during a Saturday morning interview in Panebianco's Barbershop, a block north of where Dino was born. "He was also a *green cloth* man. Like a craps man. Dean came in here with his father. I'd cut Dean's hair. He had

Photo by Dave Hoekstra.

Dorman Panebianco.

nice hair. It was beautiful. He never wanted a lot off. He always wanted it *touched,* that's what you call a shaved haircut. It would feel like a haircut, but it didn't look like one."

Panebianco's Barbershop has been in the same locations at 245 S. 6th St. since 1931. Haircuts range from $7 to $10. Many times Panebianco will have his trumpet or English horn behind one of his chairs and he'll play a song during a break.

"There were fortune-tellers around here," says Panebianco, who was in a local symphony band with Dino (on drums, of course). "One day Dean told me, 'You know, my mother went to this fortune-teller. She told her I was going to be an actor and hit fame.' I thought he was dreamin'.

"The fortune teller was right."

May 31, 1998

Polynesia, Ohio-style
Tiki bar re-creates island mystique

COLUMBUS, Ohio—The Sunday brunch was winding down at the Kahiki Supper Club, a surreal compound of Polynesian food, drink, and high jinks on the east side of this otherwise normal city.

A 7-year-old boy had fallen behind the sophisticated stride of his parents. He stood alone at the front of the canoelike structure, watching a tall smoking fountain emit Gardner McRays. The kid was full of wonder.

That kid was me.

When I was his age my parents also took me to the Kahiki, not for the mahi-mahi almondine, but for the cascading waterfalls framed by glorious tiki gods, the falling rainfall every half hour and war chants and steel drum rhythms that spin through intimate bamboo huts.

I'm 42. And I'm still impressed.

On my recent visit to the Kahiki, it was amazing to see how kids remain in awe of the restaurant, which in December was placed on the National Register of Historic Places. The federal government agency cited the Kahiki's "rich Polynesian culture, architectural design and influence on national and local restaurant history."

The Kahiki (which means "Sail to Tahiti") was built in 1961. It has maintained a steady and colorful course despite the onslaught of music videos, video games and Dennis Rodman (which means "Macadamia nut").

"There's a mystique in Polynesian culture," says Kahiki President Michael Tsao, who has owned the restaurant for 20 years. "It's atmosphere, food and fun. But the main thing is the fun.

"You find a paradise in Columbus."

Before coming to the Kahiki, Tsao was general manager of Trader Vic's in Beverly Hills, Calif. Tsao, 48, points out, "The main thing is the fun. And this [tiki bar] fun is not achievable in any other place because today everyone is into high-tech, computerized fun. This is natural, cultural fun."

I love tiki bars. I have a fun tiki bar in my basement. The

Kahiki's tiny Polynesian server with a grass skirt and a black eye even sold me the gift shop's *Aloha!* banner for an unbelievable $5.

The Hala Kahiki, 2834 N. River Rd. in west suburban River Grove, is the Chicago area's best tiki tavern. And it's tough to beat the Tonga Restaurant & Hurricane Bar in the basement of the Fairmont Hotel, 950 Mason in San Francisco, where the live tiki trio plays Top 40 music on a pool of water, accompanied by falling rain, thunder and lightening.

But there's nothing like the Kahiki.

The Kahiki's menu features a map and directions on how to get around the 20,000-square-foot restaurant: "Starting counter-clockwise in the entrance is the Grand Foyer, the Cloak Room, the Beachcomber [gift] shop, the Outrigger Bar, entrance to the Village Dining Room, Maui Lounge, access to the Rest Rooms and stairway to the basement party rooms. . . .

"Going into the Village Dining Room [with more than 1,000 tropical fish living in an aquarium that lines the east wall], the Music Bar to your left, Kalakua Street, the Molokai Hut, the Kauai Garden Booth, around to the Niihau Hut, Rain Forest Booths and back to the Music Bar." Whew. The boatlike building is a regular Noah's Ark for party animals.

And that doesn't include Sam, a 16-year-old blue and gold

Postcard reprinted courtesy of Michael Tsao, President of Kahiki Foods, Inc.

The Kahiki at night.

macaw that watches over the Outrigger Bar from his expansive cage. It's tempting to lean back from the bar, stick the tip of your index finger inside the cage and wiggle it at Sam. "Watch out," says the bartender in a Hawaiian shirt and orange lei. "Sam's got *chirpies . . .* and *canarial disease.*" And the bartender hasn't even been drinking.

Back in 1995, a customer hid in the Kahiki compound after the restaurant closed. He stole Sam. The macaw knows only a few words: "Hello," "What, no tip?" and "Help." The birdnapper was caught only after he sold Sam to a local pet store. Sam learned the word "Dumb." Sam now has a microchip in his chest with pertinent identification information.

The Kahiki, 3583 E. Broad (614-237-5425), was designed by the late Coburn Morgan, a painter, decorator and sculptor with degrees in electrical engineering and architecture. The place is rich in Polynesian detail, right down to the bathroom faucets, which are made from armadillo shells. The bathroom basins are giant Tridacara clam shells.

The restaurant's inverse curved roof, which peaks at 60 feet in height, celebrates the design found on many New Guinea war canoes that purportedly repels evil spirits.

You can even taste a kick of the Kahiki without traveling to Columbus. In 1993 a public offering of the Kahiki's common stock was made through Diversified Capital Markets. Proceeds from the stock issue were used to expand the company's wholesale distribution business, and last year the Kahiki struck a deal with Dominick's that allows them to service all Asian food in the food store's kitchens throughout the Chicago area.

When I was a kid in Columbus, celebrities such as Raymond Burr, Gig Young and Arthur Godfrey hung out at the Kahiki. An autographed picture of late comic Paul Lynde used to hang in the Outrigger Bar.

These days a new generation sips from the Kahiki charms. The popular lounge band Combustible Edison loves the Kahiki so much that members are planning a May residency in the restaurant's Maui Lounge. On Saturday nights, Ohio State students fill the Outrigger Bar. And every weekend the Hawaiian Tropic Band steel drum, guitar and bass trio performs while strolling though the Kahiki's bars and dining rooms.

"We took the celebrity pictures down," says restaurant manager Theang Ngo. "They're in our office upstairs. Sometimes a bartender would make a drink, the stuff would splash up and get the pictures dirty. We replaced them [with a tropical wall mural]. But if a customer requests to see the pictures, we'll take them to the office."

Ngo, 25, is from Phnom Penh, Kampuchea (known as Cambodia before 1976). At age 14 he moved to Columbus from a Cambodian refugee camp. Ngo lost his parents, a brother and a sister in the Vietnam War. A friend brought Ngo to the Kahiki, and in five years he had worked his way through the ranks from busboy to waiter to restaurant manager.

Photo by Dave Hoekstra.

The Kahiki's inverse curved roof recalls the design on many New Guinea war canoes said to repel evil spritis.

Ngo peers out into the foyer at a huge tiki god with a fiery red mouth, glaring green eyes and water bubbling from the top of its head. "The tiki god is a symbol for all the tribes to respect and worship," says Ngo, as a "Mystery Girl" walks by, carrying a birthday cake, pounding a drum and singing "Happy Birthday" in Hawaiian.

"There is also a 'Mystery Drink' on the menu," he says. When someone orders it, the Mystery Girl bows to the drink at the command of a gong. Then they deliver the drink to the customer. It's fun."

After some serious questioning, Ngo discloses the "Mystery Drink" consists of rum, vodka and tropical juice.

More than 120 people work at the Kahiki, including natives of China, the Dominican Republic, Germany, Italy, Korea, Nicaragua, the Philippines, Russia and Venezuela. "It is a melting pot," Tsao says. "A diversity of culture. They all end up at the Kahiki because of our uniqueness."

March 15, 1998

POSTSCRIPT:

It was "Aloha" to the Kahiki when the restaurant closed its doors on Aug. 26, 2000. More than 400 tiki fans from America, Canada, and even Australia attended a private Bon Voyage party that featured the live music of Don Tiki (direct from Honolulu) and DJ Brother Cleve, better known as the organist for the now-defunct Combustible Edison lounge band.

The Kahiki will be torn down and replaced by a Walgreen's pharmacy. Kahiki President Michael Tsao decided to sell the site because of declining business and a deteriorating building. Tsao plans to open a new Kahiki by 2002 along the Scioto River in downtown Columbus.

Ohio State's focus is down to earth
University takes look at drains, eyeglasses

COLUMBUS, Ohio—If you don't watch where you're going, you can fall into a rut. That was my mantra during a twin spin through the Celebrity Eyewear Collection AND the Drainage Hall of Fame, located on the campus of Ohio State University.

Gee, where does one begin?

I suppose from the ground up.

Ohio State associate professor and agricultural engineer Larry C. Brown is used to the jokes. He is the curator of the Drainage Hall of Fame, 590 Woody Hayes Dr. He digs his job. He does not drain in vain. Hardee-har-har.

"I know it just looks like a bunch of pictures of a bunch of drainage people," says Brown, standing in front of a glass case with, well, a bunch of pictures of men who have made inroads in agricultural engineering. "But there's a lot of history behind it. We have 19 people in the Hall of Fame.

"All these guys have done international work, like working in developing countries to help them address drainage problems. And with a lot of the technology now used in the U.S. the early research was done in Ohio. We wouldn't be eating as much food as we are in the Midwest if we weren't able to drain the farmland."

The hall honors men who have brought the drainage industry forward. Starting in 1979, an annual Hall of Fame award has been given to a person who has made "significant contributions to the development and use of drainage in agricultural production for an extended period of time," according to a plaque in the glass case.

There's even an annual Drainage Hall of Fame dinner and award presentation at the Ramada Hotel and Conference Center in Columbus. The hall of fame is dedicated to Virgil Overholt (1889-1978), who spent 42 years researching drainage as a professor of agricultural engineering at Ohio State.

Overholt's specialty was agricultural drainage and related soil and water conservation problems. He was a leader in his field. In Ohio, Overholt commonly was referred to as "Mr. Drainage." He was beloved by his students, colleagues and farmers throughout the state.

But there is no "Ms. Drainage" in the hall of fame.

"There have not been a lot of women in the drainage area," Brown admits. "Most of the women in the drainage field are outside of the U.S. There haven't been prominent women engineers in any field of engineering here for a long time. But things are growing here as well."

With proper drainage, of course.

Illinois is represented with the 1997 induction of Carroll J.W. Drablos, a professor of agricultural engineering at the University of Illinois at Urbana-Champaign. He has 32 service years in the drainage industry. His picture hangs near that of Jans Wesseling (a 1987 inductee, the most important drainage scientist in the Netherlands). Translated, Netherlands means *lowlands*.

Then, over by a piece of revolutionary corrugated plastic tubing (that replaced the old pipe 'n' tile drainage method), there's a picture of Fred Galehouse, the only person in the hall who actually has rolled up his sleeves and done real drainage work. The Ohio contractor was inducted in 1982 for teaching other contractors to do better drainage.

I've seen Babe Ruth's locker at the Baseball Hall of Fame. And was touched by the remnants of Otis Redding's airplane at the Rock and Roll Hall of Fame. This ranks right up there. Or down there.

Hall of Fame inductees are carefully screened.

It's no easy pipeline to immortality.

"Nominations have to come from people outside of our department and program," says Brown, a Nashville, Tenn., native who began managing the hall in 1988. "We have a submission policy where people provide enough information to justify that the person is worthy of the award. We also have a jury where we select three to five people from around the U.S. and an international person. Once a year, they review the documents and select one person from that pool."

Brown, 47, is full of drainage trivia.

As I gather my background stuff, like the newsletter "Understanding Agricultural Drainage" and the pamphlet "Wetland Reservoir Subirrigation Systems," Brown tells me to be safe driving home. I tell Brown to check out the work of Oxford, Miss., author Larry Brown (no relation to him).

"And you know that wooden pipeline that was in Chicago

Photos by Lisa Day.

Glasses on display in Ohio State's Celebrity Eyewear Collection include the distinctive specs of Bob "down on the farm" Evans, Col. Harlan "Kentucky Fried" Sanders *(above)*, cosmetic business dynamo Mary Kay Ash *(left)*, and popcorn man Orville Redenbacher *(below)*.

before the Great Fire?" he asks. "That kind of technology was used for drainage, as well. I did a tour of the Water Tower. It's something I'll always remember."

Well. Memories are in the eye of the beholder.

Ohio State Professor of clinical optometry Dr. Robert D. Newcomb oversees the university's Celebrity Eyewear Collection, 338 W. 10th Ave. on campus. Featuring donations from more than 200 celebrities, the collection includes eyeglasses once worn by author Stephen King, a $7,000 pair of sunglasses from Elvis Presley and pink heart-shaped glasses donated by Miss Piggy. Newcomb declines to put a price on the late Harry Caray's glasses, which will be auctioned off for charity.

"It's like collecting art," Newcomb says. "They would be worth thousands to a fan of his and they'd be worth nothing to people who didn't listen to him. There's no objective way to determine a value. It's like you father's glasses. It means everything to you."

It might be, it could be, it's pretty sure Harry wore some of the biggest eyeglasses known. The lenses alone were the size of flying saucers. "There probably wasn't any optical reason for their size," Newcomb explains. "It was just his trademark. There are certain people who choose bold-looking frames to make a statement of authority. Since he was in the media, he didn't want to downplay the importance of good vision and that he was seeing everything on the field."

The celebrity eyeglasses collection began several years ago, when a number of Ohio State optometry professors were having lunch. Original curator Dr. Aron Augsburger wrote more than 100 letters to celebrities requesting that they donate some old glasses. The late popcorn guru Orville Redenbacher was the first to donate. Former President Gerald Ford was second.

"We have a lot of people from Ohio," Newcomb says, standing in front of a glass case of notable eyeglasses. "Bob Hope. Phyllis Diller. But that's not a requirement. It's anybody who's famous."

College of Optometry Media Coordinator Wendy Clark adds, "The original concept was to feature people who achieved great things who also wear glasses. The ones we got from George Bush are interesting. They're all warped because he used to wear them to read while he was in the sauna. Plus, one temple [the piece that goes around the ear] was badly chewed."

Some people could not part with their glasses. Talk show host

Phil Donahue only owned one pair of glasses because he backed over his spare pair with his car. Sen. John Glenn of Ohio declined because he thought his eyeglasses would not fit his public persona.

Clark points to a pair of shattered glasses. "Those belong to [race driver] Bobby Rahal. The lenses won't stay in them anymore. They're in pieces because he said they went to the wall a few times too often."

Newcomb and Clark are always looking ahead.

For example, their dream catch would be a pair of Elton John's glasses. Clark says, "We've tried. He sold his glasses when he sold his wardrobe. All that went for billions of dollars, but we weren't able to pay for them."

No matter. A road trip to the Drainage Hall of Fame and the Celebrity Eyewear Collection is full of riches. Sometimes much can be learned with a narrow focus.

March 8, 1998

a.p.   V E H I C L E   7F 99

WISCONSIN

SEYMOUR ⊚
HAMBURGER HALL OF FAME

APPLETON ⊚
CHRISTMAS AT CLEO'S

MT. HOREB
MUSTARD MUSEUM
MUSCODA ⊚
END OF THE WORLD ⊚ ⊚ MILWAUKEE ⊚
BOOKS-TO-GO
DODGEVILLE ⊚
DON Q INN
KENOSHA ⊚
RAY RADIGAN'S

Map by Lisa Day.

Milwaukee's well-traveled books

MILWAUKEE, Wis.—A good book is a memorable journey. And there are more than 60,000 daily departures at the Renaissance Bookshop, a used bookstore with at least that many volumes, at Mitchell International Airport here.

You thought Milwaukee was only about brats and beer.

Well, there's more than one way to ferment your mind.

I discovered Renaissance last summer when I made the hassle-free decision to fly to New York City from Milwaukee. I had to get to Hoboken, N.J., in time to attend the wedding of Jill Richmond, a friend and former lead guitarist of the Aquanettas rock band. [I love that name, and Renaissance's rock titles include *Piece of My Heart (A Portrait of Janis Joplin)* by David Dalton and *Bossmen*, a book that connects Bill Monroe and Muddy Waters, written by Nashville producer-musician Jim Rooney.]

"Particularly in the last year we've seen more people from the North Side of Chicago who prefer to fly out of here instead of O'Hare," said clerk James Karon, who has worked at the airport bookstore since 1990. "In some cases the airfare price structure is so strange that even if they have to fly back *through* O'Hare en route to their destination, they get a better break. Some people

Photo by Lisa Day.

enjoy flying on Midwest Express, which is based here. And a lot of people like the smallness of this airport. Even if you're going from one extreme end to gates on the opposite concourse, you can easily walk it in 10 minutes without a strain."

Karon is a typically excellent bookstore clerk. That was way more than I needed to know.

But Renaissance is worth checking out for bookworms who are crawling north to see the Smashing Pumpkins and the Jayhawks at Sunday's final day of SummerFest or for the legions of Cubs fans who are driving (or flying?) to Milwaukee for the Cubs-Brewers series that begins at 7:05 p.m. Thursday and runs through next Sunday at County Stadium. Besides, you'll need a good book to get through the horrible I-94 construction at the Deerfield Toll Plaza and at the Wisconsin border.

Considering the bookstore is in an airport, it's pretty accessible. Customers should head for short term (30 minutes) parking and bring in their parking stubs—and Karon says that even a copy of this column will do—and they will be validated for the first two hours.

Renaissance Bookshop owner Robert John has a larger store with 300,000 used books at 834 N. Plankinton Ave. in downtown Milwaukee. In 1979 he opened a used bookstore at Mitchell International, about 20 minutes south of downtown.

"There had been a regular bookshop in the airport prior to that," said John, 52. "They threw in the towel. The convention bureau sent out a letter to bookstores in town saying how the space was vacant and we could bid on it. My initial reaction was 'Huh?' But the more I thought about it, the more I liked the idea. It's been great."

The high-flying Renaissance has since grown by leaps and bounds. One expansion took over some storage space and the most recent addition became available when the airport's video arcade shut down. Over the years the Renaissance/Airport grew from 500 square feet to the 3,000 square feet it occupies today.

I landed in the Sports section, which was better than the average used bookstore. For $9, I picked up a hardback copy of *Willie's Time*, a 1973 sociological baseball memoir about Willie Mays by Charles Einstein. I also saw *Stealing First in a Two Team Town—The White Sox From Comiskey to Reinsdorf* by Richard Lindberg and biographies of Casey Stengel, Dizzy Dean and even *Hondo—The John Havlicek Story*, a vintage 1960s basketball bio written by Havlicek and Boston newspaperman Bob Ryan.

The Renaissance/Airport has an average Travel section, but during a recent tour of the shop, Karon said Travel isn't the bookstore's specialty. A resident of suburban Fox Point, Wis., Karon explained, "It's a growing area, but we're known by our regular customers for our American history as well as world history [and] World War II. And the pilots and other people interested in aviation like our aviation section. Out here, there's a much bigger section of that than in the downtown store."

A colossal black and white July 14, 1938, picture of Howard Hughes' plane at the start of his flight around the world in less than four days hung on the wall above Karon as he talked. One of the bookshop's seven staffers owns the poster. Other clerks have built the World War I and B-29 model airplanes that float in the bookshop's hurried airport breeze.

The bookshop is immaculately organized by interests: Military, Drama, Erotica, Antiques, Journalism, and even a Wisconsin section that featured way too many books about Appleton's favorite son, Sen. Joe McCarthy. The shop also stocks more than 5,000 periodicals and comic books, including an impressive collection of vintage Life magazines.

The Renaissance/Airport has unusual items like a re-bound series of French plays that were printed in the 1790s and 12 volumes of the works of Russian novelist Dostoevsky, $650 for the set, published in 1922.

"A place for everything," Karon said, "and every thing in its place. There's some authors or categories of books where it's a toss-up as to where you're going to put it. Like, do you put it in 'Philosophy' or 'Essays and Criticism' or do you put it in 'Travel and Adventure' or 'Nature' or the more academic 'Biology' or 'Zoology' areas?"

Any metropolitan airport is full of those kind of questions, and Mitchell International is no exception. It's certainly the only airport in the world with a used bookstore down the way from a Harley-Davidson gift shop, so Koran has seen his share of characters.

"We get media people, some actors, athletes and politicians," Karon said. "Occasionally people miss their planes because they've been browsing. We try to remind people of their flights and connections."

With a bookmark, no doubt.

Renaissance Bookshop is at Mitchell International Airport, 5300 S. Howell Ave., Milwaukee. Hours are 7:30 a.m-10 p.m. Call (800) 672-6657.

July 5, 1998

Love, Wisconsin style
A wonderland of cheese vats, ceiling mirrors

DODGEVILLE, Wis.—Bathing in a 300-gallon copper cheese vat was just the first wave of a strangely romantic gateway to the Don Q Inn, a southwest Wisconsin fantasy motel with a 1970s disco feel.

The vat was perched on a ceramic basin, creating a bird bath effect. You could be all you want to be. I was a golden-winged warbler. A wren-thrush. A horned lark! Enough.

We [and I stress *we*, I would never do this alone] were in Don's Den, a basement "suite" with golden brown shag carpeting on the floor—as well as above the bathroom mirror and below the sink. My lust was illuminated by a fake fireplace and mirrors above the bed.

My girlfriend was reviewing escape routes.

The weird weekend also included the sleepy acoustic music of "The Bob and Rod Show" in the Don Q Supper Club, car trouble that took us to downtown Dodgeville and a rescue from a car salesman named Dean Martin. Now I see why Land's End clothing is headquartered in Dodgeville (pop. 4,200), about 45 miles south of Madison. We felt like we were at the end of the world.

The Don Q Inn was built by the late Don C. Quinn (*get it?*), a former World War II fighter pilot. After the war, Quinn was a pilot for United Airlines before becoming corporate pilot for John Christopher Doyle, the multimillionaire owner of Javelin LTD, a Canadian mining company.

Quinn died of cancer in the summer of 1988. He was 64. He bought the 280-acre plot of Don Q land on Highway 23 just north of downtown Dodgeville in the mid-1960s. In 1968 he opened a classic Wisconsin supper club in a barn that had been built in 1914. The supper club's beams are from the old Douglas Aircraft plant, which stood where O'Hare Field is today.

Quinn moved his family into a home in the dandy Don Q compound, but that wasn't enough. He also installed a 3,000-foot gravel runway where he parked his plane. Today, a Boeing C-97 is on display on the runway. It was once—back in the 1940s—the largest plane in existence. Why a Boeing C-97? It was used in

Lincoln-Mercury television commercials which featured Farrah Fawcett-Majors. Her autograph appears on the side of the plane, which is appropriate.

This place spells *Farrah*.

Work on the 45-room Don Q Inn began around 1972 and the motel opened in 1974. Quinn's idea was to replicate the supper club as much as possible, using heavy timbers to create a barn-like feel. Quinn was a resourceful guy.

Postcard courtesy of the Don Q Inn.

"Northern Lights" and "Sherwood Forest"—two of the Don Q Inn's romantic room options.

The supper club's "Pump Room" once featured a shag carpet that covered the pre-stress concrete ceiling. The carpet had to be suspended by shooting nails through the carpet and into the concrete with a nail gun.

"Each nail required a washer to keep the nail head from pulling through the carpet," said Ron Dentinger, Quinn's best friend, who was the hotel's entertainment director and general manager between 1974 and 1985. "Each washer cost one and a quarter cents, so he decided not to use the washers. Don shot the nails through pennies. The pennies worked as good as the washers, and Don saved a quarter of a cent with every shot."

The motel's rooms include lamps made from old fire extinguishers, and classic Singer foot treadle-type sewing machines have been transformed into television stands. The

Swiss cheese vats/bathtubs were imported from cheese factories throughout southwest Wisconsin. All these features are part of the motel. Once you begin to understand Don Q, you understand the inn.

And Quinn loved his ceiling mirrors. Dentinger—whose 59th birthday is on Valentine's Day—said, "He often joked, 'It looks like a naked skydiver is coming right at you.' "

But these days the Don Q Inn looks as if it has seen better days. The motel is owned and operated by Royal Hospitality in Burnsville, Minn., a suburb of Minneapolis. "Don's Den" was dank and dusty, although the mirrors worked fine.

"Don's Den" is one of nine "Theme Suites" that also include "The Float" (a queen waterbed set in a Viking ship surrounded by mirrored walls) and "Shotgun" (a queen-sized bed complemented by a deer hunting theme, vintage shotguns on the wall and a 300-gallon copper cheese vat tub). Theme suites are $85 a night, $95 on Fridays and $110 on Saturday nights.

The Don Q cleaning ladies allowed us to take a peek into the "Tranquility Base" two-story suite down the hall from "Don's Den." Guests sleep in a re-creation of a Gemini Space Capsule propped up by iron stilts. A moon crater hot tub sits underneath the space capsule, which is filled by a waterfall flowing from "moon rocks." The room includes AM/FM stereo and a Super Nintendo video game. And just in case you get *really* lonely, the room features a life-sized mannequin dressed as an astronaut. The "Tranquility Base" ranges from $164 to $224 (on a Saturday night).

Finally, the "FantaSuite" Suites (which range from $139 to $199) include "Cupid's Corner," a Valentine's Day dream anchored with a heart-shaped bed with mirrored ceiling and black marble whirlpool, as well as the "Jungle Safari," done as a thatched jungle hut with a whirlpool.

If Elvis is indeed alive and well, he's at the Don Q Inn.

We checked into Don's Den and checked out the room service menu. You can't order breakfast in bed, but there's a full-tilt wine-service menu, which includes California Corbett Canyon Chardonnay ($12.50 a bottle) and the deep berry-flavored product of the Wollersheim Winery in Sauk City, Wis. ($16.50 a bottle). Although wine and cheese vat sounded tempting, we passed in favor of a visit to the supper club lounge.

Even that was weird.

We walked through a dimly lit 325-foot winding tunnel that connected the tunnel with twists and turns in order to add to its mystique. He installed old miners' picks and animal bones in the ceiling. Quinn even did his own blasting for the tunnel, putting ripples in lakes more than 50 miles away.

Once we emerged from the tunnel, we made our way into the lounge. Middle-aged folk singers Bob and Rod were singing ballads to a half dozen regulars who looked like miners at the end of a long workday. Bob and Rod sang covers like Jimmy Buffett's "Changes in Latitudes" and Van Morrison's "Brown Eyed Girl" with all the force of a down pillow.

Bob's smoky, laid-back vocals reminded me of the late Charlie Rich. I shouted across the quiet bar to ask Bob and Rod if they knew any Charlie Rich songs. His mid-1970s bedroom classics like "Behind Closed Doors" and "The Most Beautiful Girl in the World" are fine foreplay tunes. Neither Bob or Rod had heard of Charlie Rich. I then asked, "How about Buddy Rich?" referencing the late maniac jazz drummer. Rod laughed before launching into "Summertime."

After a few Leinenkugel Reds ($2.75 a bottle), we struck up a conversation with Joann Jewell, a 31-year-old supper club waitress. In a warm and friendly manner, she gave us more information about the history of the Don Q than anyone at the front desk. Her father is Ron Dentinger. It's that kind of connection that makes small town visits fun.

Besides being former general manager at the Don Q Inn, Dentinger is an ex-Milwaukee cop. He delivered 17 babies in a five-year stint as a patrolman. These days he writes jokes for Rodney Dangerfield and Reader's Digest. He even does local humor: "A dummy tried to rob the local bank in Dodgeville with a sawed-off shotgun," Dentinger said in a Dangerfield accent. "But he had sawed off the wrong end." *Rim shot* with that gun, please.

"I used to describe Dodgeville as a place with history so vivid you can touch it," Dentinger said. "It's alive. You wouldn't want a world full of people like Don, but thank God there's a few.

"In 1978 he had some matchbooks printed up. In big silver letters they said 'Thym's House of Fine Foods.' [Thym's Supper Club is across Highway 23 from the motel.] And in small letters, 'Across the street from the Don Q Inn.' He cleared it with the owner before he had them printed."

The next morning we awoke in Don's Den, ready to meet our friend Marty in the neighboring town of New Glarus, a.k.a. "America's Little Switzerland." But we were in for big trouble when my car wouldn't start. Apparently it had been on Don Q's frozen tundra for too long. We never left the hotel once we checked in around dinner time on a Friday night.

A jump didn't help and the locals found delight in informing city slickers that no gas stations were open until Monday morning (when the car started fine.) I had it towed to the local General Motors dealer. A friend of the tow truck driver was kind enough to give us a ride to Gordon's Café, a downtown coffeehouse and restaurant where we arranged to meet Marty. Gordon's is across the street from the Land's End Outlet Store, 113 N. Iowa St.

Once Marty showed up, I began telling him about our tribulations. Carla Lind, the owner of Thistle Hill Tabletop Company, was sitting at the next table at Gordon's. She overheard our conversation and asked if she could help.

Linda called the home of Dean Martin, the salesman at the dealership where my car had been towed. Dean was in the shower, but he agreed to meet us at the dealership to get us a loaner. He was on his way to an appointment. He didn't have to help me out, but he did.

As Dean was filling out paperwork, I wondered aloud how difficult it is to go through life being Dean Martin. "I don't get sick of it," said Dean, 45. "I have a good time with it." He added that Dodgeville doesn't have any residents named Jerry Lewis.

Several minutes later we pulled out of the parking lot in our loaner. It was a silver '94 Lumina, clocking in at 148,000 miles. The car was the size of the plane in the front yard of the Don Q Inn. I felt like it was 1973 and I was in high school again. My girlfriend scooted a little closer on the split bench seats and a Charlie Rich song played across my mind. The riches of travel pay off in the most peculiar moments.

To get to the Don Q Inn, take Interstate 90 north to Madison, Wis. Take the Highway 12/18 Beltway west to 18/151 (Dodgeville exit). Head south on 18/151 to Dodgeville, exit Highway 18. Go southwest two miles to a four-way stoplight, which is Route 23. Turn right. You can't miss it. It's got that big plane on the left hand side of the road. For reservations, call (800) 666-7848.

February 13, 2000

Sketches of tradition
Artist brings celebrity to Kenosha

KENOSHA, Wis.—I'm guessing that traditions begin as a way to stay grounded in an ever-changing world. For the last couple of years I've celebrated Valentine's weekend in surprise road trips with Lisa, my favorite traveling companion.

Last year I took Lisa to the Edgewater Hotel, built in 1948 on Lake Mendota in Madison, Wis. Boy, was she surprised. She never knew I could waste so much time in the hotel's Cove Lounge looking at autographed pictures of Tony Bennett, Roger Ebert, Cyndi Lauper and more than 200 other celebrity guests.

This year she took me to Ray Radigan's Restaurant, Sheridan and Russell Roads in Kenosha (262-694-0455). Radigan's is one of the most remarkable steakhouses in the Midwest. Kenosha native Orson Welles ate there. I bet he ate a lot. Jack Benny's roots were in nearby Waukegan and he stopped by Radigan's. I bet he didn't tip much.

In 1933 Radigan's opened in a converted farmhouse less than a mile from the Illinois border. It was a true roadhouse restaurant,

Photo by Lisa Day.

Ray Radigan's, one of the most remarkable steakhouses in the Midwest.

as Sheridan Road used to be the main route between Chicago and Milwaukee, prior to the interstates of the 1960s. As diners enter Radigan's from a gravel parking lot, a red neon sign promises, "Wonderful Food." And it is.

The Radigan tradition of wonderful food began when late founder Ray Radigan imported sides of prime-grade beef from the Chicago stockyards. And today his son Mike buys only Minnesota-bred chickens. When Radigan's was profiled in the winter 1998 issue of Doubletake magazine, Mike Radigan told writer Nicholas Dawidoff that Southern hens are fed "fish meal or somethin' and they don't taste as sweet."

Lisa ordered the chopped sirloin steak, three-quarters of a pound of lean certified Angus chuck. The restaurant still dry-ages and grinds the meat daily on the premises, just as Ray Radigan did. I had a zesty 10-ounce boneless, crushed-black-peppercorn pork chop, finished with a pork *au jus* glaze.

Although it was a Friday night, the restaurant was relatively empty during our visit. We drove through one of this winter's rare snowstorms to get to Radigan's. We sat in the dining room, which can best be described as pristine.

I had never been to Radigan's. The first thing I noticed was a wonderfully innocent oil portrait that hung on the west wall of the dining room. The Radigan family portrait was done in shades of blue. It was dated 1954. Mike was a smiling 6-year-old, dressed in a dark green-blue shirt.

Mike was obediently in the shadow of his mother Wilma, who wore a sea blue blouse. On her other side was Mike's 12-year-old sister Tricia, who wore a powder blue sailor top. The stuff was beyond Norman Rockwell. The portrait's soft tones carried the charm of those folks in the Dick & Jane primers. It was the most traditional artwork for a most traditional roadside steakhouse.

"Let me tell you about the artwork," Mike said in a later conversation at the restaurant. He pointed to a detailed charcoal sketch of his parents that hangs in the bar area. "Some 42 years later, he does that by memory. That was done after my parents passed [Ray and Wilma died in 1994]. Our employees and customers commissioned him to do that for the restaurant."

I had to find out who this artist was.

And that was a piece of cake.

Everyone at Radigan's knew of Kenosha artist George Pollard, who had three works hanging in the restaurant, including a dashing portrait of Ray Radigan, and outgoing Irishman.

Pollard was quite a find. He was commissioned to paint President Harry Truman, the first of several Pollard presidential portraits. He's painted Jackie Gleason, Frank Sinatra and Oprah Winfrey. Everyone in Kenosha still talks about the day Muhammad Ali visited Radigan's in December 1977.

Ali was in town to appear at the grand opening of a minority-owned General Motors dealership. Pollard sketched the champ over lunch.

During a conversation in his 44-year-old Kenosha split-level home, Pollard called Ali "one of the most interesting people I have ever drawn." He continued, "Ali says, 'When you're through sketching me, I want to sketch you. People don't know my father was a sign painter and I have artistic ability.' Muhammad was ready to eat his second piece of coconut cream pie. He picks up a Christmas placemat, turns it over, borrows a pen from somebody and starts sketching me. He scratches something off. He moves something around. He makes about five attempts and finally crumples up the placemat and says, 'You white guys are hard to draw. You all look alike.' I saved it. My son's got it framed in his studio."

In 1998, Mike Royko's brother Bob commissioned Pollard to paint the late writer at his beloved Billy Goat Tavern. Just as he did with the Radigan clan, Pollard gives all his subjects a sweet, all-is-right-with-the-world innocence. Even a celebrated curmudgeon like Royko is breaking into a smile.

There are traditional feel-good portraits throughout the Pollard coffee table book *The Journal of a Portrait Painter (and His Family of Artists)* (Whitman Press, $49.95). Pollard's brushes with fame include Vince Lombardi, Mother Teresa and Dan "Bonanza" Blocker. Even Ted Kennedy looks good in this book.

"I do cosmetic surgery on people," Pollard said. "Nobody else does it, so I'm inundated with work. I widen the eyes a little bit. I give them more prominent cheekbones. I give them more hair. I straighten their teeth."

Hey, Detours needs a new logo!

Most of Pollard's subjects come to his home, which he shares with wife Nan, across the street from Lake Michigan. Members of the NBA's Milwaukee Bucks drive to Kenosha if they miss their portrait appointment in Milwaukee. Despite their losing record this season, all the Bucks are smiling in Pollard's portraits in the team program.

Pollard's subjects stand in his living room for up to three hours. They're given a break every half-hour. The living room is so traditional the Pollards keep their artificial 9-foot Christmas tree up all year long. That began four years ago when it became too cumbersome to take the tree down. The family does change decorations according to the season.

A classic 9-foot antique mirror from the Burlington (Iowa) Opera House sits directly next to the Christmas tree. Burlington is Nan's hometown.

"I stand them where they can see themselves in the mirror," Pollard said. "They see the reflection of me painting them in the mirror. Now that's not my idea. Diego Velazquez, a painter from the 1600s, was the first guy to do that."

But Pollard came up with his own technique to make people smile.

"Especially when doing sports portraits, you always run into one guy who is macho and won't smile," Pollard said. "So I walk up to them and plead with them." Pollard stood up from a chair and came this close to me. With the palm of his right hand, he gently slapped me in the face.

"And they do just like you did," he said. "They laugh." Pollard also used that technique on Milwaukee Mayor Henry Maier.

Pollard begins with two charcoal sketches—a detailed sketch of his subject's face, another of the pose. He then uses pastels for his final oil-on-canvas product. "People see everyone coming in and out of here," Pollard said. "Our neighbors call Kenosha 'The Florence of the U.S.A.' "

George Pollard turns 80 on Monday.

He's been married to Nan for 52 years. They have four children between the ages of 40 and 51. In keeping with the family tradition, they are all working artists.

George was attending the now-defunct Layton School of Art in Milwaukee in 1946 when he met Nan, who was also an art student. Together, the young artists worked the Chicago-Milwaukee market.

They collaborated on children's celebrity paper doll books for the now-defunct Samuel Lowe Publishing Co. in Kenosha. Pollard painted the portraits for The Honeymooners, Patti Page and The Bob Cummings Fashion Models cut-out books. Nan designed the celebrity dolls' clothes.

"One day we got in our car and drove," George recalled. "We got as far as Evanston, and we thought that was too close to Chicago. We went to Racine, and that was too close to Milwaukee. So we thought we'd try this town for a few years. And we've lived in Kenosha for 52 years."

In a tradition that hasn't faded with time, Ray Radigan's was the hottest spot in town. The Pollards still eat there up to four times a week. "It was a big deal," George recalled. "Most of their clientele was from Chicago, especially the North Shore. Ray knew I did portraits, so he said, 'How about a portrait of me?' And I did the whole family."

One of Pollard's biggest breaks came on the road.

James Scott Kemper, the head of Chicago-based Kemper Insurance, saw Pollard's portrait of President Kennedy hanging in the Mars Cheese Castle, just off Interstate 94 at 2800 120th Ave. in Kenosha (262-859-2244).

Kemper was so knocked out by Pollard's traditional style, he commissioned the artist to paint the portrait of all 68 members of the Kemper Insurance board of directors. Each portrait paid $1,000. At the time Pollard was making $25 per portrait. He didn't have a checking account.

Pollard laughed and said, "He said he always did two things when he traveled in Wisconsin. He'd buy Danish kringle in Racine and Wisconsin cheese in Kenosha. Kemper was very influential.

"He was the ambassador to Brazil under [President] Eisenhower, so he sent me to Washington to do portraits of Everett Dirksen, Supreme Court Justice William O. Douglas, Pat Nixon and others. That's how my career started. According to the former curator of the Pentagon [Alice Price], I have more portraits in Washington, D.C., than any other artist in the United States. Not bad for a little guy from Kenosha."

I know that traditions start with small intentions.

And just like the portraits by George Pollard, the best traditions stand tall with the test of time. Ray Radigan's Restaurant is a fine place for such a wonderful realization.

A permanent collection of Pollard's portraits is on display at Landmarks Gallery, 231 N. 76th St., Milwaukee (800-352-8892), as well as at Williams' Café, 235 Depot St. in Pollard's home town of Waldo, Wis. (920-528-7252). Where's Waldo? It's 14 miles west of Sheboygan.

March 19, 2000

Hamburger History

Get your buns to Seymour for burger lore

SEYMOUR, Wis.—Well, this is one hall of fame that's well done.

The Hamburger Hall of Fame includes thousands of hamburger-related artifacts, souvenirs and a tender tribute to "Hamburger Charlie" Nagreen, who in 1885 brought the burger to this borough. The hall of fame and museum is at 126 N. Main St. in downtown Seymour, a half-hour southwest of Green Bay.

The non-for-profit hall of fame opened in 1993, celebrating the offbeat spirit of Hamburger Charlie. He debuted his hamburger at the 1885 Seymour Fair (now the Outagamie County Fair). Charlie was 15 years old. He lived in Hortonville, about 25 miles southwest of Seymour.

"He came to Seymour with an ox and a wagon to set up a food booth," says Vivian Treml, hall of fame president, during a tour of the grounds. "He was serving fried meatballs. But that wasn't going well. They were hard to eat while walking around. So he flattened them out and put them between two pieces of bread. And he called them hamburgers."

Treml wears a Green Bay (meat)

Seymour, Wisconsin
"The Home of the Hamburger"

Postcard courtesy of the Hamburger Hall of Fame.

Seasoning the world's (then) largest hamburger.

Packers sweat shirt. She radiates an honest, folksy nature which fits in with her volunteer job. She points out, "The term 'hamburgers' was not new. That came from Europe." As early as the 14th century, German merchants from Hamburg were introduced to tough, shredded meat as they traded in the Baltic provinces.

Charlie served hamburgers at the fair until he died in 1951. He had a flair for the fair. He would play guitar and harmonica and chant, "*Hamburger, hamburger, hamburger hot/With an onion in the middle and a pickle on top/Makes your lips go flippity-flop/Come on in, try one order/Fried in butter, listen to it spudder.*"

Charlie's 100-year-old Gibson guitar is in the museum along with his hand-crafted spatula and red teapot. "When kids come through I say, 'What do you think Charlie did with a teapot in a hamburger stand?' " Treml notes. "They guess all kinds of things. But he kept butter in it. Nowadays everyone is so cholesterol-conscious, but he made 'em good." Charlie would fry his hamburgers in butter and liberally smother them with onions. He reasoned that the smell of the onions drew the crowds.

A few cities have had a beef with Seymour's claim as the birthplace of the hamburger. Treml cites Hamburg, N.Y.; Athens, Texas (southeast of Dallas), and St. Louis for its 1904 World's Fair. Merchant Fletcher Davis served ground-up beef patties in Athens before bringing his sandwiches to the St. Louis fair. "But nobody else has come up with a date earlier than ours," Treml says with pride. And nobody else has come up with all the dressing.

Much of the museum features diner placemats, hamburger-shaped Avon lipgloss coasters, hamburger underwear from Frederick's of Hollywood, a 1984 "Where's the Beef?" beach towel and a 45 of Jimmy Buffett's song "Cheeseburger in Paradise." Visitors can even have their pictures taken next to an authentic fiberglass Big Boy roadside figure.

The hall of fame gift shop includes a hamburger-shaped bank, a Hamburger Charlie collector's plate and recordings of the 1996 regional hit "Home of the Hamburger Polka" by Alvin Styczynski, a merry 64-year-old concertina player who lives in nearby Pulaski.

Another portion of the museum contains pictures of 5-foot-tall foam characters such as a bun, a burger with a sesame-seed top and a 6-by-6-foot ketchup bottle. Collectively, they look like the dream that follows too many White Castles.

Hamburger Cookies

Hey, I went to the Hamburger Hall of Fame and all I got was this recipe for Hamburger Cookies. Yum.

2 vanilla wafers   Yellow frosting
Red frosting   Thin mint patty
Green colored coconut

Place a wafer flat side up. Spread a dab of red frosting (ketchup) on top of the wafer. Dip the wafer in the green coconut (that would be the lettuce). Put a dab of yellow frosting (mustard) on the flat side of the other wafer.

Place the thin mint (hamburger) on top of the yellow frosting. Place just a dab of red frosting on top of the mint to adhere it to the coconut.

Put both wafers together, coconut side to red frosted mint.

Bon appetit!

Treml introduces the main characters as "Bunard the Bun" and "Patti Burger." She apologizes for the fact that that Bunard and Patti lived together for years "without the bonds of matrimony."

She explains, "So in 1990, Patti and Bunard were married, and these characters [Oscar Onion, Peter Pickle and Missy Mustard] were part of their wedding party. The next year we had this big announcement that there was 'something in the oven.' The following year we had baby burgers and a contest to name them. We came up with Chucky Weldon and Barbie Q."

The Hamburger Hall of Fame family appeared in small-town parades in the northeast Wisconsin area throughout most of the 1990s. But these days Mr. and Mrs. Bun and their pals are in storage. "Their costumes need to be redone," Treml concedes. "and they're expensive to redo."

The Hamburger Hall of Fame has expensive plans for the future. There's talk about building a new $15 million bronze

Photo courtesy of the Hamburger Hall of Fame.

Models of hamburgers of all kinds at Seymour's burger museum.

cheeseburger-shaped museum. I am not making this up: An orange-colored glass pavilion would look like a stack of french fries. And the outdoor theater would resemble a pickle. Green Bay architect Bob Martens' rendition and mock model of the complex alone is worth the trip to Seymour.

A visit to Seymour should be sandwiched with a trip to Granny's Family Restaurant, 247 S. Main St. (920-833-7273), to chow down the best burger in town. Under new owners Roy and Lola Rottier, Granny's uses only Black Angus beef, they hand-patty their burgers and never freeze their meat. A hamburger is $3, a mushroom Swiss burger is $3.25. French fries are included. But truthfully, there are only three other places in town to get a burger. And the only fast-food franchise is a Dairy Queen on the outskirts of town.

The hall of fame section of the museum is so rarefied that there are just two inductees: Hamburger Charlie and the White Castle hamburger. Treml says most major hamburger chains don't cooperate with the hall of fame. "White Castle has," she says. "They're the only one. We approach them, but the big chains don't need us. McDonald's even thought we were infringing on them with our costumes. I don't see the connection."

But corporate attorneys do.

In 1989 Pat Krohlow was a Hamburger Hall of Fame volunteer who solicited franchises such as McDonald's, Burger King, Wendy's and others to partner with the organization. "The only way they were interested was if they had some ownership in it," said Krohlow, now marketing director at WLUK-TV in Green Bay. "White Castle saw a relationship because they view themselves as the first fast food franchise. We did things on a small basis. They gave us hundreds of dollars of coupons for free hamburgers, but in our wildest dreams one of these franchises would come in and help us build a new hall of fame."

Seymour garnered national attention in 1989 when the community gathered to make the world's largest hamburger as part of the first Burger Fest. (The event is always on the first Saturday of August.) The 5,520-pound burger found its way in to the Guinness Book of Records. More than 10,000 people attended the initial festival, which is more than three times the size of Seymour (pop. 3,000). The extra hamburger was distributed through the area food pantries.

Locals constructed a hamburger grill about the size of a double car garage, 24 feet by 24 feet. A dozen propane torches were installed underneath the grill. It cooked with a curved cover, similar to the principal of a Weber grill. Cooking time clocked in at more than two hours. A crane was installed to lift up the grill cover.

Treml says, "To add a little pizzazz to the whole thing, we took a cable that was hanging down from the crane and had a chef swing across [the grill] to season the meat. The picture went around the world." A fiberglass hamburger still sits on the grill, around the corner from the hall on Depot Street.

In spring, 1999, the small town of Saco, Mont., broke Seymour's record with a 6,040-pound burger. "I guess there's not a whole lot of things happening there," Treml says, as if Seymour was Milwaukee or something.

Seymour also caught the eye of the U.S. Olympic Committee with the World Hamburger Olympics that were part of the first four festivals. The Olympics included a ketchup slide (over gallons of ketchup mixed with water and smeared on gym mats), a stale bun toss and a bun run. But Olympics officials protested the use of the name. The burger borough refused to be bullied.

They changed the name of the competition to The Hamburger Meat. This year's Hamburger Meat promises to include the ketchup slide and a bun stacking contest for kids.

Treml's husband, Joe, is the town plumber. The Tremls have four children, ranging in age between 33 and 38. The entire family has volunteered at the hall of fame and the festival. About 1,200 people annually visit the Hamburger Hall of Fame, according to Treml. The hall of fame and museum operate on donations and funds generated from the annual Burger Fest.

Seymour native Carl Kuehne owns American Foods Group in Green Bay (formerly Green Bay Dressed Beef), and he donates money to keep the museum afloat. "It's a great opportunity for a community to bring itself together around something fun like this," says Kuehne, a 58-year-old resident of nearby DePere. "This is really a tremendous source of pride."

The Hamburger Hall of Fame is open by appointment for individuals and tour groups. The hall is open from 10 a.m. to 4 p.m. Friday, Saturday and Monday and noon to 4 p.m. Sundays Memorial Day through Labor Day.

Take Interstate 94 to I-43, exit Highway 172 around Green Bay and Oneida Bingo & Casino to Highway 54 west into Seymour. Take a right on Main Street. For more information, call the hall at (920) 833-9522.

January 30, 2000

The end of the world tour

MUSCODA, Wis.—The Wisconsin River Valley isn't quite at the end of the world. The remote southwest portion of the state just seems like it.

In fact, the liberating farmland inspires a scene of rebirth.

The 1999 Bruce Springsteen World Tour? Its spirit can't match our End of the World Tour.

The trip begins with a visit to Ellis Nelson's studio at 2nd and East Catherine streets in Muscoda, about 200 miles from Chicago. The 71-year-old self-taught metal sculptor received national attention in 1997 when his metal Grim Reapers welcomed visitors to *The End is Near!* exhibition at the American Visionary Art Museum in Baltimore, Md.

The tour concludes 15 miles west down Highway 60 at the Boscobel Hotel, 1005 Wisconsin Ave. in downtown Boscobel. This 118-year-old hotel is "The Birthplace of the Gideon Bible." Located on the National Register of Historic Places, the hotel, restaurant and bar are being resurrected by owners Beth and Jeff Novinska. They're also building a lot of mettle.

"I've built a few Grim Reapers," Nelson says during a Sunday morning conversation in his studio, a former Phillips 66 gas station he opened in 1948 with his brother Carl, now deceased. "I kept improving on the pattern. You can make them things look pretty hideous. I just like the looks of the Grim Reaper. And I like the story of the Grim Reaper.

"It goes back into the 16th century. The Grim Reaper carried a scythe for cutting grain in bundles during harvest. The Grim Reaper would go around and scythe the old people, put them in a big bundle and send them to heaven. [The scythe for reaping debuted in Europe during the 8th century.] Actually, the Grim Reaper is a good creature.

"He gathered up all the souls." Nelson sits in an old orange dentist chair. He is surrounded by red geraniums, yucca plants and hibiscus. The morning sun cuts through a dusty window, leaving half of Nelson's face in a dark shadow.

"I'm not much worried about anything," says Nelson, who lives behind his studio in a mid-1970s trailer. His parents farmed corn about a mile outside of Muscoda—which is Indian for

"Prairie of Flowers." Nelson is married to Rita and they have a son Tom, 36, and a daughter Barbara, 32.

When Carl died in 1974, his brother quit selling gas and became a full-time car mechanic. He is also a self-taught electrical engineer and electric welder.

Nelson has been doing nothing but art since 1985. His first work was a 10-foot-tall metal dinosaur, based on the classic 1960s Sinclair "Dino" logo. "I had never done any artwork before," he says. "I wanted to make a sign for the shop so I thought I'd make a prehistoric animal out of sheet metal. It took me about two days to make it."

The roadside art-work caught the at-tention of the news media, specifically the Muscoda Pro-gressive and the Boscobel Dial news-papers. Since then, Nelson has appeared on "Good Morning America" and CNN, and he's been visited by prominent Chica-goans such as artist Lynda Barry, who once included him in a comic strip. Nelson's sculptures start at $40. His studio is open seven days a week (608-739-3067).

Photo by Ann Parker. Courtesy of Ellis Nelson.

Ellis Nelson and two of his reapers.

The front yard of Nelson's studio is filled with sculp-tures of flamingos, curved-wing metal bats, the two 6-foot-tall Grim Reapers (not for sale) and the Southwestern inspired Kokopelli, the Indian figure who traveled from camp to camp playing a flute to inspire happiness.

The lean and basic nature of Nelson's work lacks the power

that attracts some collectors of self-taught art. But Nelson's magic is how a tinkerer can create such simple beauty. For example, Nelson's cluttered shop—built in the gas station's former garage—contains a cutting torch, metal press and an intricate furnace that burns sawdust from the sawmills of the Wisconsin River Valley. Nelson invented the contraption in 1979.

Nelson has stubby fingers that have been toughened by more than 30 years of machinery. "My hide is so thick, it's probably near a quarter-inch before it gets down to anything besides muscle," Nelson says as he waves his right hand. "One time I got cut near the palm, about three-sixteenth or a quarter-inch. It was deep. The damn thing wasn't going to heal, so I got some fishline and a bent needle and sewed her up *real nice.* I was just about done sewing when a guy came in and said, 'What are you doing?' And I said, 'I'm sewing up my hand.' "

His visitor was repulsed and wanted to get Nelson to a doctor. Pronto. Minutes later the town doctor stopped by to fetch the car that Nelson had been repairing. "The guy goes, 'Hey Doc, look what he did to himself!' " Nelson says with a proud smile. "And the Doc sees my hand and says, 'Looks good. In a week's time have those stitches out and it should be healed.' "

When the master craftsman holds his hands up to the light, his fingers look like old logs floating down a Wisconsin River.

Sometimes his hands tremble, ever so gently.

"As of January 1, [his son] Tom will be chief artist," says Nelson standing near a chalkboard where he scrawled, "Why does man exist?"

"I'll always be here, but I'll be doing special artwork and that will give me time to do it. I don't want to be the manager anymore."

Nelson's first project for the new year is to finish building his 8-foot-tall and 8-foot-wide metal space probe. He says, "That's very appropriate for the year 2000."

He continues, "I have my own idea of religion and it doesn't involve The Creator, but we won't get into that."

Come on, Ellis. This is the End of the World Tour.

"Well, my theory is that man's soul is part of the universe," he says, carefully choosing his words as if they were nuts and bolts. "And nothing ever is lost in the universe. Scientists and philosophers agree. You can take a piece of paper and touch it to fire and it'll burn. But you are not really destroying the paper. You're just getting it into a different form.

"After death, you transform into something else. If something happens to me, I belong to God. But I prefer using the word 'universe.' I've thought about it my whole life. And my conclusion is the entire universe is alive."

Nelson felt most alive in May 1998, when he was Grand Marshal of the annual Morel Mushroom Festival Parade in Muscoda (pop. 1,200). "I felt like I was Marshal Dillon," he laughs. "The priest down the street is a friend of mine. He promised he'd come to the parade. I was waving at everybody, and he steps out and starts waving at me. And as far down the street as I could turn and look back, he was still standing there waving at me."

★   ★   ★

The universe travels along the driftless, unglaciated area of the Wisconsin River Valley to Boscobel (pop. 2,800), where Prussian immigrant Adam Bobel built the Boscobel Hotel in 1865.

In the winter of 1881, fire gutted the building, leaving only the limestone walls standing. Bobel immediately rebuilt the hotel, and much of the work from this period remains today.

But Boscobel earned a spot on the dashboard of our End of the World Tour on Sept. 14, 1898, when aluminum salesman John Nicholson and paper salesman Samuel E. Hill stayed in Room 19 of the hotel. The room rented for 15 cents.

"This was a booming place for the hotel business," says owner Jeff Novinska, a 38-year-old Boscobel native who bought the hotel with his wife Beth, also 38, two years ago. "With the river and the railroad, there was a lot going on. There was a lumberjack convention that night. All the rooms in town were booked except one. The men were a little leery about sharing a room at first, but when they met, they found out they were both Christians."

Boscobel was once a rowdy, beer-drinking community, and the downtown strip still features wonderfully named watering holes like Dave's Silver Dollar, Fin n' Feather, Double K's and the Pour House Bar.

Once the two traveling salesmen retreated to Room 19, Nicholson asked Hill for permission to leave the light on as he read his devotions. Hill asked that Nicholson read aloud since he also was a Christian.

The Gideon name was conjured up when one of the two men opened his Bible, closed his eyes and placed his finger on a page from the Book of Judges. The passage was about Gideon, the Old Testament military leader.

Their spirituality was formally recognized on July 1, 1889, when Hill, Nicholson, and Wisconsin salesman William J. Knights founded the Gideons International movement at the YMCA in Janesville, Wis. The movement was dedicated to "the mutual help and recognition of Christian travelers."

A night in Boscobel could do that to you.

Today there are more than 800 million Bibles in desk drawers and nightstands in 172 countries from Albania to Zimbabwe. The Gideon International is headquartered in Nashville, Tenn. The organization is not interested in material projects such as museums and restoration, but Gideons International Executive Director Jerry Burden says, "From a nostalgic standpoint, the hotel has historical interest to us."

The hotel had fallen into disrepair in recent years. It was almost razed in 1992 before the Boscobel Area Heritage Museum bought the building to preserve it. A nonprofit affiliate of the Wisconsin State Historical Society, the group remodeled bits and pieces of the historic hotel and leased the bar. (There is no actual museum.)

The bar went out of business in 1996. The Novinskas bought the three-story building and bar in 1997 for $80,000. Jeff is a former high school tech-ed teacher, and Beth still teaches first grade in Boscobel.

They have since renovated the bar and dining room and added a new kitchen. Boscobel High School shop class students built and installed the oak dining room cabinets. The dining room has been repainted forest green, and its oak floor has been beautifully restored.

The bar is simply called the Hotel Tavern.

I told Novinska he should rename it Bible Belters.

"We do get a lot of Gideons that stop by," Novinska says. "But for the most part they're teetotalers. A few have had dinner here."

Dinner is served between 5 and 9:30 p.m. on Thursday through Saturday; lunch is served from 11 a.m. to 2:30 p.m. Wednesday through Saturday. A Sunday brunch is offered from 9 a.m. to 1 p.m. House specialties include the Friday night beer-battered cod

($7.75 for full dinner) and the Saturday night prime rib, a cut of Black Angus ($15.95 for a king cut).

The restaurant is open on the End of the World New Year's Eve, but reservations are recommended since the 40-seat room sells out (608-375-4714). The ambitious bottled beer menu features Hooch, Mississippi Mud, Sam Adams and four versions of Leinenkugel's, including the heavy Doppelbock. Beer prices range from $1.75 to $3.75.

"We're doing the restaurant and bar on the premise it pays for itself," Novinska says. "When we start realizing more income, we'll start working on the upstairs." He estimates it will take another $80,000 to restore the upstairs rooms. The game plan is to turn four rooms into apartments and use the remaining 12 rooms as a bed and breakfast.

The hotel roof is shot, and there's water damage on the second and third floors. There's no heat upstairs, although Room 19 is preserved pretty much in its original state, complete with a Gideon Bible. Novinska is more than happy to take visitors to the Gideon Room for a look-see.

John F. Kennedy also used Room 19 to "freshen up" for several hours during a mid-March presidential campaign trip through Wisconsin. Ralph Goldsmith was publisher of the Boscobel Dial newspaper from 1956 to 1992. He covered the Kennedys during their visit. Now a spry 85 years young, Goldsmith says, "He hadn't seen his wife for a couple weeks. Jackie joined him here."

The rest is history.

John F. Kennedy Jr. was born on Nov. 25, 1960, just under nine months after his parents stopped in Boscobel. Goldsmith smiles and says, "There was something else conceived in that room besides the Gideon Bible." Indeed. Rebirth runs rampant along the Wisconsin River Valley.

December 5, 1999

The Magical Mustard Tour

MOUNT HOREB, Wis.—It's easy to unlock any inhibition in the child-like aura of the Mount Horeb Mustard Museum.

This operation is bold—set right downtown in this Norwegian borough of 4,500 about 20 miles southwest of Madison. And it's energetic and fun-loving: The bright yellow two-room museum features a collection of 2,931 different mustards. More than 400 mustards are for sale, including raspberry, peanut and cranberry mustard, the last being one of the museum's best sellers.

After you are hopped up on the herbs, take Route 151 two hours north to see the handcuffs, leg irons and straitjackets that are part of the (Harry) Houdini Historical Center, 330 E. College Ave. in downtown Appleton (920-735-9370).

You have done the Magical Mustard Tour.

Detours doesn't go in for yellow journalism, but this had a special twist. The minute I hit the storefront mustard museum at 109 E. Main St. (800-438-6878), curator Barry Levenson and his 11-year-old son, Matthew, show me their "Amazing Mustard Dollar Bill Trick." Matthew's dream is to be a magician when he grows up.

Matthew asks me to sit in the front row of the museum's Mustard-Piece Theater, the screening area for a 30-minute video that depicts how mustard is made. Barry asks me for a dollar bill. Fortunately, I had a couple of bills left after purchasing some Habanero-pepper laced "Mustard From Hell" from Glendale, Ariz., ($5.25) and radio personality Spike O'Dell's "Bite Your Butt" mustard (proceeds from the $5 a jar sales go to WGN Radio's Neediest Kids' Fund).

Matthew reads aloud the serial number from my dollar bill. Barry writes the number on an envelope, sticks the bill in the envelope and seals it. He then puts the envelope in a box with a jar of mustard. The box is covered with a black silk. Barry and Matthew say the magic words and open the envelope. The dollar bill is gone. Next, they open the jar of mustard with the tamper-proof seal intact-and inside the jar is the dollar bill in plastic.

The serial number is the same as my bill!

"Mustard and magic do go together," says Barry, who used to practice hoodoo of his own as a former Wisconsin assistant attorney general. Barry and Matthew are perfecting a Houdini-inspired trick where Matthew will escape from a huge, sealed mustard jar.

The mustard museum has a magical reputation. It's been voted Best Small Museum in Wisconsin by readers of *Wisconsin Trails* magazine. On June 13 the museum will host its annual Mustard Family Reunion, inviting people from across America whose last name is Mustard.

Barry has stocked the "Cooperstown of Condiments" with antique mustard pots that go back to the 18th century as well as mustards from more than 60 countries. "India, Germany, Greece," Barry says, waving his arm with gusto as he wanders about the museum. He glances at a new jar of mustard in a front window display. "We just got our 2,931st mustard in today. It's Weber's Hot Garlic Mustard from Buffalo, N.Y. They're known for their horseradish mustard, but this is a new one for them. They're members of the World Mustard Association—headquartered here."

Barry is a walking, talking encyclopedia of mustard. He began collecting mustard on Oct. 27, 1986, the night of the sixth game of baseball's World Series. A 49-year-old native of Worcester, Mass., Barry's beloved Boston Red Sox failed to cut the . . . well, you know the rest. They lost the sixth game of the series when a 10th inning ground ball rolled through Bosox first baseman Bill Buckner's legs, the key moment in the New York Mets two-out, three-run rally.

"I was devastated," Barry says. "They came so close. But I don't blame Buckner. To me, [relief pitcher] Bob Stanley is the goat for throwing a wild pitch [with relish, no doubt]. I was so depressed I went to an all-night supermarket in Madison. I needed a new hobby. As I walked by the mustard aisle, I heard a voice that said, 'If you collect us, they will come.' That was it. I started buying mustard."

Why mustard? Why not ketchup?

"*Pleeeze,*" Barry groans and recoils. "On National Mustard Day [the first Saturday in August] we have free hot dogs here. But people can't put ketchup on them, or it will cost them $10. We have to discourage that sort of anti-social behavior. Ketchup? That's bad stuff."

Our conversation is interrupted by a group of museum visitors. Barry greets them at the door. To the tune of the "On,

MIY catalog cover courtesy of Barry Levenson and the Mount Horeb Mustard Museum.

Wisconsin" fight song, he sings, "*On our hot dogs, on our bratwurst, mustard is so cool!/Never mayo, never ketchup, they're against the rules! Gleaming gold and mellow yellow, smooth, rough, sweet and hot. Fight POUPON U., we'll fight/And eat some lunch.*" Barry explains this is the Poupon University fight song. Accredited museum visitors can receive personalized Poupon U. diplomas.

"This started as a hobby," Barry says. "Then in 1991 I decided I didn't want to practice law anymore. I just wanted to do mustard. I've always liked mustard. I grew up in Fenway Park, where they have that good brown spicy mustard. I've always liked mustard the simple old-fashioned way: mustard seed, vinegar, salt and water. No preservatives or additives."

About three years ago Barry was invited to appear on "The Late Show With David Letterman." His spot never aired because Dave overdosed on mustard. Barry explains, "They asked me to bring a bunch of mustards. One of the ones I brought was this one," and he picks up a small bottle of Royal Bohemian Mustard, made in northern Wisconsin. "It doesn't look like much, but it's very strong. I warned him. But he took a huge gob of it. He was on the floor, thrashing, screaming and swearing. The segment never aired."

Despite Dave's experience, mustard makes people happy. Barry says, "This has caught on because we have fun here. People like to share that. And we're not part of any conglomerate. We're a one-of-a-kind thing."

Just like Harry Houdini.

Houdini was born Ehrich Weiss in Budapest, Hungary, and his family moved to Appleton when he was a child. He later claimed he was born in Appleton. And 72 years after he died of appendicitis on Halloween eve, he still casts a magical spell over the town of 68,000 along the Fox River. This is a good thing. Until the Houdini museum opened in 1989, Appleton was best-known as the hometown of Sen. Joseph McCarthy, who was censured by the Senate in the 1950s.

The Houdini Historical Center, on the second floor of the Outagamie Museum, is the caretaker of the Sidney H. Radner Collection of Houdini memorabilia. With 125 different artifacts and 150 classic photographic images, posters and handbills, it is the world's finest collection of Houdini artifacts.

"Children as young as the first grade know who Houdini is,"

says Nancy Leschke, marketing and publications officer for the Outagamie County Historical Society. "He's become part of popular culture. That's because he did the impossible in a way that's never been captured in the same way by anyone else. People associate him with exceeding the limits of imagination."

The Houdini Historical Center features handcuffs, leg irons and lock picks. One of the highlights of the collection is the Guiteau handcuffs, which held President Garfield's assassin and from which Houdini escaped.

"Everyone likes the [60-gallon] milk can he escaped from," Leschke says. "And we have a full-bodied straitjacket, a corporal punishment suit. He used it a number of times." In the museum gift shop, I picked up a reprint poster from the May, 1918, Ladies Home Journal where Houdini wrote the text to the photo essay, "How I Get Out of a Strait-Jacket." Sometimes it comes in handy during those down days on Detours.

Houdini is buried in Mechpelah Cemetery in Queens, N.Y. He has yet to visit the Historical Center or the mustard museum. "About 10 years ago, there was a séance held in Appleton," says Leschke, a 28-year-old native of Combined Locks, Wis. (and that is not a handcuff joke.) "He was a no show."

More than 40,000 people visit the Houdini Historical Center annually. Actor Harvey Keitel has been corresponding with the museum in preparation for the role as Houdini in a new movie about the master illusionist. And two years ago magicians Penn & Teller went through the museum. After perusing the gift shop, they each shipped a case of Houdini Root Beer to their parents. Made by the Adler Brau brewery in Appleton, the golden brewed root beer is $1.89 for an oversized bottle. Everyone knows that mustard and pretzels go well with root beer. But how does mustard taste with magic?

After Leschke stops laughing, she says, "We can make it work. But that thing about Combined Locks never occurred to me. They're referring to river locks."

No matter. The Magical Mustard Tour will make for unchained memories.

★   ★   ★

"And mustard has a big role in drama," says Barry Levenson, curator of the Mount Horeb Mustard Museum. Shakespeare wrote about mustard in 'Taming of the Shrew,' and Levenson dramatically recites Grumio's line to Katherine, "What say you to a piece of beef and mustard?" Katherine replies, "A dish I love to feed upon!" And from "Henry IV, Part 2," Falstaff says of Poins, "His wit is as thick as Tewkesbury mustard."

Ironically, England's Tewkesbury mustard is the 1997 grand champion of the World Mustard Competition, held in conjunction with the annual Napa Valley Mustard Festival. It's available for $6.25 a jar at the museum.

For more information on Shakespeare and mustard, check out the current issue of the Proper Mustard, Levenson's twice-a-year newsletter, available for $3. To order, write the Mount Horeb Mustard Museum, 109 E. Main St., P.O. Box 468, Mount Horeb, Wis. 53572.

May 10, 1998

The Road Tape

"Too Old To Cut the Mustard"
Rosemary Clooney & Marlena Dietrich

"Do You Believe in Magic?"
The Lovin' Spoonful

"Too Much Mustard"
Teresa Brewer

"Abracadabra"
Steve Miller Band

"Mean Mr. Mustard"
The Beatles

"Astral Weeks"
Van Morrison

"Could It Be Magic?"
Barry Manilow

Christmas all year long
Bar taps into holiday mood

APPLETON, Wis.—A place filled with year-round Christmas lights can only bring out the best in you. There's a surge of warmth, hope and trust. It opens your eyes to possibilities.

The best Midwestern bar for year-round Christmas lights is Cleo's Brown Beam, 203 W. College Ave. in downtown Appleton (920-739-2288). The bar is open every day of the year, all Christmas, all the time.

Owner Cleo Alice Marie Brown began installing Christmas lights when she opened the Beam in 1961 at its former location next door at 205 W. College Ave. She never stopped.

The old place was filled with between 10,000 and 15,000 twinkling lights. The lights used to be left on 24 hours a day because the power surged when they were turned on and off and tended to blow circuits. The new two-year-old, 2,000-square foot tavern has about 5,000 lights—along with Mr. and Mrs. Claus figures, a snowman, nutcrackers, toy soldiers and a partridge in a pear tree.

It's like drinking at an Amling's.

I often read more than I need to into a bar or restaurant with year-round Christmas stuff. The proprietor isn't making any kind of sentimental statement. They're usually just too lazy to take down and put up the lights every year.

"The way I heard it from Cleo is that by April of her first year, she hadn't taken her Christmas decorations down," says bartender Rick Wittmann, who has worked at Cleo's for 10 years. "Everyone was giving her a hard time, so as a joke, she started adding more lights.

"Then a customer from a local retail store told Cleo he had a truckload of display items he was going to throw out. Cleo took them. He sent the truck over with two employees, and they spent the day putting up all this strange stuff—a boat [a 7-foot-long rowboat, to be exact], bathtub, mannequin heads."

Legend has it that Cleo installed the original cedar brown beams on her own. At the old place, who could tell? You couldn't see them. The beams were covered with strings of Christmas lights. The original beams have been reinstalled at the current location.

The tavern is dotted with two dozen bright red barstools. A toy elf sleeps on a shelf. A brown baby grand piano sits near the front door, but the piano hasn't been used for a decade. All the drinks spilled over the keys have made it untunable.

Cleo's is easily identifiable from the street because of a 1960s cursive neon sign. The sign is framed by tassled maroon damask curtains with gold cherubs, making the scene more Moulin Rouge than Midwestern tavern.

"I like the ambiance and warmth of the bar," says Carleton "Cully" Selig, who has been coming to Cleo's since 1970. A retired plumbing inspector for the city of Appleton, the 75-year-old Selig is the "Chairman of the Bored" of the "Four O'Clock" (p.m.) group of 15 regulars who meet Monday through Friday at Cleo's.

Over a Monday afternoon whiskey and water, Selig says, "We talk about the issues in the news. Today the big topic is the Packers," who had just suffered a rare Sunday home loss to Carolina.

Over the years Cleo's has become a favorite hangout for NFL teams who stay in the nearby Paper Valley Hotel when they play the Packers. Up until 1997 Packer quarterback Brett Favre would roll through Cleo's with pallies (center) Frank Winters and (tight end) Mark Chmura as "The Three Amigos."

Surprisingly, Cleo's jukebox only has one Christmas CD, a compilation of classics such as "The Christmas Song" by Nat King Cole and Tony Bennett's "White Christmas." The holiday CD is nestled alongside traditional roadhouse fare such as Brooks and Dunn, Fleetwood Mac and Stevie Ray Vaughan.

A couple of years ago Cleo's was embroiled in a controversy when the tavern's lease ran out. Building owner Joe Draeger wanted to buy Cleo's, but the tavern's attorneys couldn't reach an agreement, according to Draeger. So he opened his own bar, called Cosmo's. "He figured Cleo would move out and he'd have the bar," says Wittmann, 40. "But it didn't work out that way."

Cleo's was forced to pick up all its Christmas lights, brown boat, bathtub and mannequin heads and move one storefront west.

But Cosmo's only had a three-month run. Draeger is vice president of Draeger Oil Co. in Antigo. Former Budweiser sales representative Craig "Fuzzy" Ogden bought Cosmo's and opened

Fuzzy's Sand Trap, 205 W. College (920-831-0245).

Cleo's reopened in November 1997 in a new bar built out of a former NASCAR gift shop. "People thought Cleo got ripped off by having to move," Wittmann says. "A lot of people boycotted that bar, but things are starting to pick up."

Ogden adds, "Things are going real well. I used to be their [Cleo's] sales rep. We share customers, and on nights off we barhop with each other."

It's a warm and Fuzzy story.

Cleo, 80, doesn't come around her bar anymore. The Appleton native broke her left hip last year and then her right hip in September. Her health is so poor that she couldn't be interviewed for this story. An oil portrait of Cleo hangs behind the tavern's cash register.

But Cleo's 85-year-old sister, Lila, still does the bookkeeping.

Embrace these characters while you can.

December 19, 1999

IOWA/

MINNESOTA

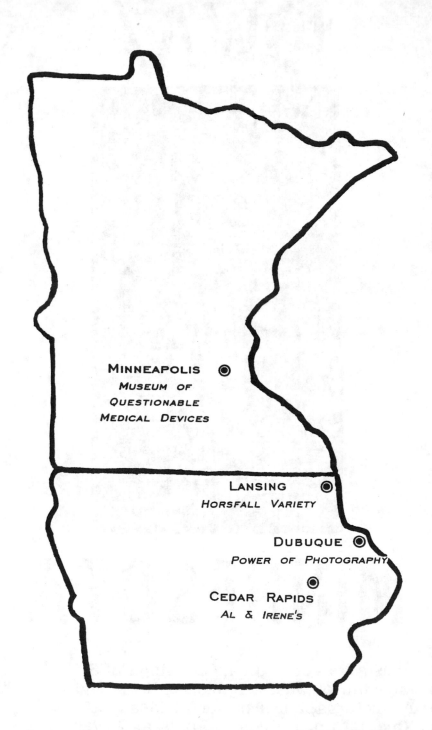

MINNEAPOLIS ◉
MUSEUM OF
QUESTIONABLE
MEDICAL DEVICES

LANSING ◉
HORSFALL VARIETY

DUBUQUE ◉
POWER OF PHOTOGRAPHY

◉
CEDAR RAPIDS
AL & IRENE'S

Map by Lisa Day.

He's got it all
If you want it, Horsfall's will have it

LANSING, Iowa—If variety is the spice of life, then the Horsfall Variety Store is full of eternal bliss. The store contains nearly 1 million items, from rubber jar seals to plastic Rubik's cubes.

And did I mention 100 different spices, including adobo seasoning, fennel seed and turmeric?

Or instant nectar for hummingbirds, available year-round?

Only a hummingbird could comfortably navigate the 30-inch aisles of the store on 300 Main St. in downtown Lansing (pop. 1,200). The store is a block west from the sandstone bluffs of the Mississippi River, about 35 miles southwest of LaCrosse, Wis.

Lansing is in the heart of Allamakee (pronounced *Al-ah-mah-KEE*) County, one of the most dramatic stretches along the river. Horsfall's Variety Store abuts Mount Hosmer, a 104-acre city park located atop a 450-foot bluff from which visitors can see three states—Iowa, Wisconsin and Minnesota.

The store is owned and operated by Paul Horsfall, Jr., who was reared 35 miles west in Decorah. His father managed a department store in Decorah, and he helped out at the store when he was a kid. He just didn't care for the decorum in Decorah.

"We had to wear ties and stuff like that," said Horsfall, 45. "I liked the casual atmosphere, so when this store became available, I went for it." The Horsfall family has had a riverfront summer home in Lansing since 1959. Horsfall bought the store in 1975 from Leo S. Krieger, 81, who had run Krieger's Variety Store for more than 40 years.

The first thing Horsfall did was expand.

"Retail changed where you gotta be a one-stop shop," said Horsfall. "We carry rubber jar rings, sprinkler tops and pop bottles and the old shelf paper with the edge that folds down.

"In a town the size of Lansing, if you sell shoes only, there might be a day where nobody buys a pair of shoes. But if you sell thousands of items, there's going to be something that people need. The big stores don't carry anything in depth because they don't want a high turnover. The key to our success is selection and low turnover. For the most part, if we don't have it, they don't need it."

Like more than 50 types of heavy hairnets.

Or more than 100 metal cookie cutters.

Horsfall runs his business with the acumen of Sam Walton. He pays attention to merchandising trends, such as the need to buy stuff in massive quantities. Wearing a gray flannel shirt and baggy jeans, Horsfall explained, "In the old days you could buy what you needed and you wouldn't get hurt price-wise. Now, to get a decent price, you have to buy a lot at one time. But you only have so much space."

Indeed.

Photo by Lisa Day.

Paul Horsfall's store has got it if you want it.

The variety store encompasses only 3,800 square feet. Horsfall owns another 6,000-square-foot building down the block at 360 Main St. that sells fabrics, clothing, towels, rugs and more than 50 kinds of mini metal cookie cutters (two for $1). But Horsfall's is not as cluttered as Horsfall's Variety Store. "We have such narrow aisles here that when we get a truck shipment, we use the other building as a warehouse," said the 280-pound Horsfall, who negotiates the aisles with ease. "It's what makes us a close community, getting by your friends and neighbors in the aisles."

The jam-packed variety store is open from 9 a.m. to 5 p.m. Monday through Thursday and Saturday; until 6 p.m. on Friday, and noon to 4 p.m. on Sunday.

A customer stood at the counter. She was buying a set of

batteries.

"Enjoy the sunshine," Horsfall said.

And while it was a sunny and balmy 75 degrees outside, you wouldn't know it from inside the store. The light coming through some windows was obscured by stuff; shades covered other windows.

How could Horsfall tell if it was sunny?

"We just had a delivery," he answered. "I saw the light outside. And you barely can see a crack of light coming through." The variety store carries more than 1,000 sunglasses, most of them $3.99.

One of Horsfall's most unusual items is a 1940s metal mend-et ($2.69), which is used to repair holes in pots and pans. Horsfall said, "Mend-ets are basically out of the past.

"Our best seller is stamp needlework to embroider. The big stores just want to carry the fast-selling patterns. We try to go for things people can't get anywhere else. Even though there's a slow turnover, it gives us a monopoly. They have to come to Lansing, Iowa, if they want the big selection of quilt blocks, pillow cases and tablecloths to embroider."

Horsfall has a staff of five, including himself and his wife, Dorothea. He conducts inventories in his mind and he generally remembers where he keeps stuff. "Basically, it's where I put it the last time," he explained. "I keep things in the same place for the most part. Once in a while we shift things around because of seasonal merchandise. Then it gets crazy. There's three levels to most of the shelves and there's two or three items per pegboard hook because of our close quarters."

Horsfall wouldn't admit it, but he began to look faint.

The variety store draws customers from the Chicago area, especially in summer and fall. Longtime Chicago folk singer Bonnie Koloc lives in the area, and I stumbled across the variety store several years back while visiting Chicago club owner Bill FitzGerald, who used to have a summer home in Lansing.

But most customers come from neighboring towns such as Decorah; Sparta, Wis., and LaCrosse, Wis. Nearly 20 people wandered through the store during my Thursday afternoon visit. Horsfall said 16 of them were from out of town. There isn't a Wal-Mart within 35 miles of Lansing. "These days when people go shopping, there's a tendency to go on an *outing*," Horsfall said.

"You get a day off, you want to pile in the car and just go for a ride. Thank goodness the Mississippi River leads to Lansing, Iowa."

November 7, 1999

Rejuvenate at nation's wackiest museum

MINNEAPOLIS, Minn.—I had been ill for a few weeks. Nothing could cure my ailments. I tried cold pills, lemon chills and tequila thrills.

So I grabbed a handful of Replacements tapes, got in my car and drove to the Museum of Questionable Medical Devices in Minneapolis to consult with curator Bob McCoy.

About a year ago the museum relocated to the historic St. Anthony neighborhood on the banks of the Mississippi River. The museum is at 201 Main St. S.E. (612-379-4046) on Minnesota's first cobblestone street.

The museum is also around the corner from the charming Nye's Polonaise, 112 E. Hennepen (612-379-2021), the best retro Polish restaurant since the demise of Chicago's Busy Bee. After you check out the museum, don't miss Lou Snyder, who plays Sinatra, Dean Martin and lots of requests Friday and Saturday nights in Nye's piano lounge. She's been there 33 years.

The museum was formerly a Chinese restaurant. Now it's the dim sum of dubious medical parts from the early 18th century to the present. For example, McCoy walked over to a Calbro Magnowave Radionic set that looked like your granddad's Zenith console radio. This contraption was going to cure my cold.

"What I need you to do is blow your nose in that little opening there," McCoy said as he pointed to a half-dollar size hole near the top of the radio. "It will test your mucus. Look, it goes up almost to the top of the scale!"

Of course, I did not stick my stuffy nose in the radio.

And of course, the device was hardly the real McCoy.

"What do we do?" McCoy asked theoretically. "We turn on a radio and set it for the same frequency as your mucus. Then we turn on this transmitter to send 'healing rays' by radio."

McCoy turned on the machine. "Outer Limits" sounds. He said, "No matter where you are, those waves will get inside your head and cure your cold."

According to a 1920s-era brochure, this bit of quackery was

created in the name of "Radionics," the science of "locating disease in the human body by detecting the abnormal or reflex action manifested when normal tissue cells are being overcome by disease."

The Radionic machine is just one of 240 questionable medical artifacts, part of a collection that Gadfly magazine recently rated as the top wacky museum in America—ahead of the Barney Smith Toilet Seat Art Museum in San Antonio, Texas, and the Spinning Top Exploratory Museum in Burlington, Wis.

Although McCoy has guested with David Letterman and was leaving town the day after my visit for his Conan O'Brien debut, he still gets excited when he's talking about his museum. "I've been on Letterman's show six times," he said. "But I never can get him to sit in the [MacGregor] rejuvenator." The imposing 100-pound tank allegedly reverses aging.

The roots of the museum are seated in another chair, technically called the Phrenology machine. Built in the 1920s, the 1,000-pound machine is run by a continuous motor-driven belt that contains 165 statements about 32 mental faculties, rated one through five, "deficient" to "very superior."

"Someone gave me one of these machines," McCoy said as he stood behind the big chair.

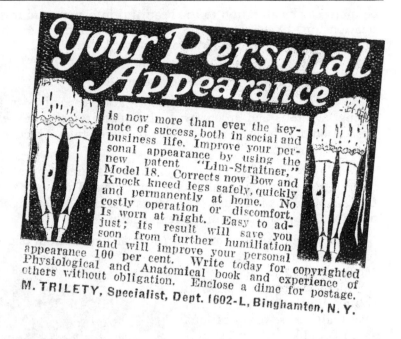

"That's how all this started. My friend's father [Frank White] got on the Hiawatha Train across the river here to go to Milwaukee. That was a steam train that went 100 miles an hour. The inventor [Henry Lavery] sat next to my friend's father. By the time they got to Chicago, he [White] decided to sell all [$28,000] of his 3M stock and invest it in a phrenology. His family never forgave him. Phrenology was the mistaken idea you could tell personality by the bumps on your head."

The subject sat in a chair connected to the machine, and a heavy, Hannibal Lecter headpiece was lowered and adjusted around the forehead. The operator then pulled back a lever that activated the belt-driven motor, which received low-voltage signals from the headpiece and stamped out the appropriate statement on a paper tape for each faculty.

Like any good idea, the machine had its moments.

A booth was set up in the Black Forest Village at the 1934 Century of Progress Exposition in Chicago, and it raked in more than $200,000 from a standing-room-only crowd.

I sat in the machine to have my quirky personality read. Here are some of the readings that I can share:

3, IDEALITY: Average. Appreciation of the cultural in life may be increased by attention to the beautiful in Nature and in social relationship. "You could read more poetry and go to the art museum once in a while," McCoy observed.

5, WIT: Very Superior. Don't let your unusual sense of humor cause you to overlook the seriousness in life.

5, AMATIVENESS: Very superior. Your capacity for being loving, amorous and ardent with the opposite sex is excellent. Discretion may be exercised. "That's way too high," McCoy said with a strait face.

McCoy began carting his Phrenology machine around to the Twin Cities to goof around at civic functions. That's the interactive charm of his museum. Visitors can go through strange magnetic belts or actually sit in the rejuvenator.

"I knew the AMA [American Medical Association] had some of these things in storerooms," McCoy said. "I'd drive to the AMA in Chicago and pick up things like vibrating chairs. Eventually these organizations said I could keep them on permanent loan."

McCoy is a grandfatherly curator, delivering his lines with a straight and gentle face. He is assisted by a paid staff of five people. "They're mostly graduate students," he said. "They like coming here because when they apply for a job they can put down that they've been Associate Curator for the Museum of Questionable Medical Devices."

Antique Phrenology Machine — 1905

You Ought To Have
Your Head Examined

Postcard courtesy of the Museum of Questionable Medical Devices.

McCoy, 71, was born and reared in St. Louis. He was a steel salesman who was transferred to mills in Pittsburgh, Cleveland and finally, in 1960, Minneapolis. His father was Wilson McCoy who sketched and wrote the "Phantom" comic strip for the defunct Chicago American newspaper. When the older McCoy lived in northwest suburban Barrington, Bob would pose as a model for the "Phantom" when he visited from Pittsburgh.

With steely wit, McCoy plugs his place as "A museum that's dedicated to lies, deceptions, and mistruths [Not to be confused with the Nixon Library]." Other popular museum pieces include the Foot-Operated Breast Enlarger, which was advertised on late-night television as recently as the mid-1970s. Nearly 4 million women spent $9.95 on the gadget that promised to enlarge cup sizes threefold.

Then, there was the 1918 Prostate Gland Warmer, which promised to heat up the male sex drive. Step A was to plug it into a wall socket. Step B was to insert it into the patient's rectum. "It was supposed to excite a man's abdominal brain," McCoy said. "Did you know men had abdominal brains? Well, the U.S. Government said we did. The gland warmer got a 1918 patent." It sounds like vibrating Viagra to me.

"It's not like I set out to do this," McCoy said, waddling around his museum of quackery. "My wife [of 34 years, Margaret] is a physician with an HMO here in town. She doesn't have much to say about this. She keeps me in line.

"Some months ago a woman came in here by herself. A frown on her face. She looked uncomfortable. I talked her into having a [phrenology] reading. She still didn't say anything. She turned away and suddenly said, 'You know, mister, I know it's all B.S., but it sure was nice having you tell me those things.' She was right. Where else can a perfect stranger tell you all about yourself?"

Admission to the Museum of Questionable Medical Devices is free. Hours are 5 p.m. to 9 p.m. Tuesday-Friday, 11 a.m. to 10 p.m. Saturday and noon to 5 p.m. Sunday.

June 21, 1998

A photographer's powerful ideas

DUBUQUE, Iowa—Photographer Archie Lieberman has rambled all over the world, but he has found contentment in the picturesque hills of Illinois' Jo Daviess County, east of the Mississippi River.

Lieberman, 73, is one of the premier photographers of our time. He has published 22 books, and his work has been exhibited in the Metropolitan Museum of Art in New York and the Art Institute of Chicago.

A Chicago native, Lieberman moved full time to Scales Mound, Ill. (pop. 750), in 1983 to be closer to the community he chronicled in the 1993 book *Neighbors*. It was a sequel to 1974's *Farm Boy*, which followed the life of a farm family in Scales Mount, near Galena.

Lieberman is a photographer with deep soul. He wonders what makes the Earth move. He pursues the spiritual quality of people and their relation to space. This way things reveal themselves.

Lieberman spends two days a week teaching a class, "Powerful Ideas in Photography," at the University of Dubuque, a private university of 1,200 students affiliated with the Presbyterian Church.

He shows his students videotapes of late 1950s Beat poet-philosopher Alan Watts to help them understand a total view instead of linear view. Watts, a Zen Buddhist, was a compatriot of road warrior Jack Kerouac. The native of Chiselhurst, England, studied at Seabury-Western Theological Seminary in Evanston when he came to America in 1939.

"We want to look for a better way of living," Lieberman told his class a couple of weeks ago. "A more united way of living. Photography helps you see those things."

Lieberman and Esther, his wife of 52 years, live in the scenic northwest corner of the state, where you can see three states (Iowa, Wisconsin and Illinois) from a roadside stop like the Grant Hills Motel, 9372 U.S. Route 20 West (815-777-2116). It sounds like a cliché to call this God's country, but Lieberman is so convincing about the region's attributes you can't help yourself.

On a good day after class, Lieberman will retreat to Mario's, 1298 Main St. (319-556-9424), a down-home Italian family restaurant in downtown Dubuque. On this day Lieberman has shown his class some of his best-known work: *The Israeli Scribe*, an intense 1960 portrait of a scribe handwriting on a parchment Torah; the only known shot of Carl Sandburg with Frank Lloyd Wright, made at the Museum of Science and Industry in 1953, and a terrifically honest "Farm Boy" picture of a 13-year-old Bill Hammer Jr. admiring his rugged father, Bill Sr. I wondered how Lieberman captured these precise, personal moments.

I wondered if he saw a basic goodness in people.

Lieberman paused. He took a bite from a plate of linguine. The old pictures seemed to put him in a reflective place. Lieberman first visited the Galena area in the 1950s at the same time he was doing gritty work in Chicago. In the mid-1950s he spent three months chronicling blacks moving into an all-white housing project in Trumbull Park on the Southwest Side.

And once a month between 1959 and 1962, he visited five men on Death Row at Cook County prison. One man, Vincent Ciucci, was executed in 1962. He was charged with murdering his wife and three children so he could marry another woman. Ciucci lived through a dozen stays of execution.

Lieberman finally answered, "Yes, I thought about that [goodness] of the five men on Death Row. It was the day of the [Ciucci] execution. We were sitting in Warden Johnson's office. Vince asked his mother to be with him on that last day. He's getting worried.

"Vince turns to the warden, who he calls 'Jack,' which is different than what you see in the movies. He says, 'Hey, Jack, what happens if the governor doesn't give me a reprieve?' The warden says they'll have to pull the switch. So he turns to me and says, 'Hey, Arch, make this one last picture of Mom and me.' " Lieberman made the picture. Ciucci was executed later in the evening. The stunning portrait ran in Look magazine, with text by Jack Star.

Lieberman said his faith in the human spirit might have given him an edge over some of his peers, but then he added, "I'm tired of making pictures. I've made a million pictures. [Nobel Peace Prize Winner] Elie Wiesel asked, 'Why did God make man?' He wouldn't let you answer. He said, 'God made man because He loves stories.' And that's how I think. But I'm not that curious anymore."

I was curious.

A master's photo tip

Here's a tip on travel photography from Archie Lieberman:

"Space is a wonderful thing to work with," he says. "Because if you have a little man in a big space, it says something with the language of photography. Space is important.

"There's a picture in [his critically acclaimed book] *Farm Boy* of the boy hauling hay and his father is on the tractor. And all this space is around them. What it does is take away from saying, 'Here's a guy picking up hay.' If I wanted to do that, I'd get close up.

"And I do have pictures of him standing with a hay bale, but the one that I like best put him in his environment."

Why?

"Because God left me," Lieberman answered with a sly smile. "He's not with me anymore. He used to be every place I walked. But now He's gone to watch other people, and that's OK."

Lieberman misses his friends. His longtime book collaborator, Chicago journalist Bob Cromie, died last year. "He was one of the kindest men I ever knew," Lieberman said. And in 1997 Lieberman donated 40 years' worth of tapes, notes, films and prints to the University of Dubuque. He is a close friend of Walter Peterson, chancellor and former university president.

Lieberman and his wife have two sons. Bob lives in Chicago and is a professional photographer. Eric is president of Flint Logic, a computer software company in La Crosse, Wis. The youngest son, Kurt, died of AIDS in 1988. He was 31.

"I photographed him while he was dying," Lieberman said. "That was hard. He was a brilliant writer and a wonderful painter. I started a book right after he died. The title has changed many times. Even the approach has changed. I've got a lot written. I think I'm going to like it. I did a lot of research on AIDS. You want to know where to pick up homosexuals? I've got books on it. But it came down to where this had to be a personal story."

Lieberman was born in Chicago. His father, Sol, was a Jewish barber who immigrated from Europe and gained his citizenship in

Havana, Cuba. Sol's barber shop was at 3602 W. Lawrence at Central Park. "He was a great linguist," Lieberman recalled. "Someone once asked him if he lived in a changing neighborhood. They'd go, 'Hey, Sol, what are you doing here?' He'd say he was learning Greek. A few years later they'd ask, 'Hey, Sol, what are you doing here?' And he'd say he was learning Korean. And it was true."

Lieberman was introduced to photography by at the Albany Park Boy's Club. He was 13 years old and working in the club's workshop when he wised off. "I took a swing at some woodshop people and was literally thrown through the air," he recalled. "They said, 'You think you're tough? We're twice as tough as you.' I thought I was clever, so I said, 'There's twice as many.' I landed on a guy by the name of Bull Drell."

Phillip "Bull" Drell was the club's photography instructor. One of the first things Drell taught his students was not to take swings at photography instructors.

Lieberman moved on to study at the Institute of Design in Chicago, where instructors included Buckminster Fuller. After Lieberman attended the institute, his father allowed him to build a darkroom in the back of his barber shop.

Lieberman got his first major break in 1951 when Modern Photography magazine asked him to do a story on what photographs can be made in Chicago during a 10-hour stop.

"I went all around Chicago, but mostly Skid Row," Lieberman said. "That's not an attractive tourist place. But it ran. It [old West Madison Street] was interesting. It was rich. Full of textures."

At the same time, Lieberman was working for a travel magazine called the Chicago Welcome. Lieberman said, "It was one of those sleazy little magazines. We used to go around to all the West Madison Street strip clubs. Club Aloha. Johnny Merola's. I made pictures and met the owners of these places. I met some of the boys from the mob. That was the way I learned journalism."

Ernest Hemingway wrote most of *The Old Man and the Sea* at Villa Cubero, N.M., one of the driest stretches along Old Route 66. Lieberman found that a country-city counterpoint worked well for him in the 1950s and '60s.

But Jo Daviess County has changed. "It was more rural than it is now," Lieberman said. "When we came out here to live, it was farmland. But a lot of people came out here [from Chicago] and bought second homes. Their culture changed a lot of things. Make no mistake—farmers enrich our culture."

The area hasn't changed so much that it can't host vintage country music revues. Country Music Hall of Famers Porter Wagoner and Kitty Wells appear at 7 and 9 p.m. Thursday at the Meskwaki Casino & Hotel, 1504 305th St. in Tama, Iowa, ($15, 800-847-6330) two hours west of Dubuque.

Like a traditional country song, Lieberman has outlived most of his subjects. Even Bill Hammer Jr., his beloved "Farm Boy," died a few years ago. He was 49. Lieberman shot 2,500 rolls of film between 1954 and 1974 as Hammer grew to manhood. "Heart," Lieberman said without blinking an eye.

He continued, "One of his fields is near where we live. After he died, I went over there and a guy was pulling out his bales of hay. I asked what was happening. He said, 'The old farmer died so we're taking this away.' It was so funny to hear about the 'old farmer' dying. This was the little boy I met."

Lieberman also found meaningful farm ethics in making pictures of the Land's End catalogs between 1984 and 1997. "They're nice people to work with," Lieberman said. "Again, farm communities. They speak the language."

Land's End started in 1963 in a basement along the river in Chicago's old tannery district. The direct merchant clothiers are now headquartered in Dodgeville, Wis., not far from Lieberman's home. He traveled worldwide for Land's End, making portraits of Shetland sheep shearers in Scotland and clothing fashion in Italy and France.

Between the 1950s and the 1970s Lieberman made pictures for Look, Newsweek, the Saturday Evening Post, Collier's, Paris Match and others. How have magazines changed over the years?

"They don't have the immediacy they had," he answered. "The influence is not there. More important is what newspaper photographers do. It may not be glamorous, but boy, those guys and gals call themselves *shooters*, and they make great pictures day in and day out.

"It makes you want to weep because there's no pretense."

Lieberman is considered the godfather of the majestic CITY (Chicago in the Year) 2000 project, coordinated by former Sun-Times photo editor Rich Cahan. More than 100 Chicago photographers are documenting the city throughout the year. Inspired by Gary Comer, the reclusive founder of Land's End, the project is privately funded by the Comer Foundation.

"The *Farm Boy* book is one of the greatest photo stories that's ever been printed," Cahan said. "No question. The quality of it and the determination of him to stick with it makes it unique.

"Like any art, after you learn how to take pictures, you then become yourself. So his pictures reflect who he is as a person. Most great photographers believe in the dignity of mankind, and that's something he's always searching for."

Chicago author Studs Terkel has known Lieberman for 52 years. They met at Stuart Brent's Seven Stairs Book & Record Shop on Rush Street. Lieberman was one of five photographers who collaborated on Terkel's 1986 book *Chicago*.

Lieberman captures a measured working-class spirit in pictures that is similar to what Terkel gets with words. "My gosh, I love Archie's wonderful landscapes," Terkel said. "His farmlands are beautiful."

All of Lieberman's books are out of print, but used copies can be found at Main Street Fine Books & Manuscripts, 206 N. Main (815-777-3749) in downtown Galena. Lieberman's *Neighbors* ranges from $100 to $200 for a first-edition autographed copy. "I'll do anything to keep a bookstore going," Lieberman said.

At this point in the road, you realize Lieberman does not "take" pictures. He "makes" pictures. "It's derogatory," Lieberman said as he tidied up the university's "Dr. Archie Lieberman Darkroom." "I don't allow the class to use the word 'creative,' either. Nobody's creative. The Big Bang was creative, but you diminish the pure meaning of the word. What we do is 'make' pictures. We invent. That's what people do. You make discoveries and put things together in a new fashion."

The well-traveled photographer looked around the small-town restaurant and said, "We build on everything that ever happened in the world."

April 9, 2000

Eating at Al & Irene's
Diners 'cue up in Cedar Rapids

CEDAR RAPIDS, Iowa—Searching for the best soul food in Iowa is like looking for a square dance in Harlem.

Fat Chance is swinging with Slim Pickins.

But professors at the University of Iowa recently told me about Al & Irene's House of Bar-B-Q, tucked away in a strip mall on the northeast side of Cedar Rapids. I smelled road trip.

I love barbecue. I'm intrigued by the revitalization of Cedar Rapids, the second-fastest-growing city in Iowa next to West Des Moines. And my parents are named Al and Irene. For me, this place might as well have been called Mom & Dad's.

Good soul food and barbecue are virtually unheard of in Iowa. There is not mention of Iowa in Rick Browne and Jack Bettridge's fine new book, *Barbecue America: A Pilgrimage in Search of America's Best Barbecue* (Time/Life Books, $24.95). But Al & Irene's is indeed some of the best barbecue I've ever had.

I've gnawed down at the country's hottest spots: Big Nate's Barbecue (owned by ex-Chicago Bull Nate Thurmond) in San Francisco; N. N. Roadhouse in Chicago; Interstate Bar-B-Q and Charlie Vergos' Rendezvous in Memphis, and Gates Bar-B-Q and Arthur Bryant's Barbecue in Kansas City, Mo.

Al & Irene's tender beef back ribs ($7.50) remind me of Arthur Bryant's. Calvin Trillin called Bryant's the best restaurant in the world, and if that's so, then Al & Irene's might rank second or third. Owner Al Quarterman hickory smokes his meat, just like Bryant's. And Al & Irene's sweet, smooth barbecue is accented by a homemade sauce that favors white sugar over brown sugar.

"I put everything but the kitchen sink in it," Quarterman says with a sly smile. "It's made like any other barbecue sauce, except the [12] herbs and spices are different." He does not elaborate. Al & Irene's serves their secret sauce hot and mild—similar to the temperament of the Al and Irene I knew while I was a hyperactive teenager.

"One year an Iowa City radio station ran a contest between my ribs and Carson's out of Chicago," Quarterman says while taking a break from the kitchen. "Everybody said I won. But then Chicago said he won. It was a bunch of fun. I guess everybody won."

Al's & Irene's one-ups Arthur Bryant's because they offer dessert, which includes a killer sweet potato pie. Bryant's does not have desserts. Quarterman also ventures off into soul food with collard greens ($1.05 for a side), black-eyed peas ($1.05) and hot wings and fries ($3.50).

August is a good time to visit Al & Irene's and Iowa.

A couple hours down Interstate 80 in Des Moines, the Iowa State Fair runs between Aug. 10 and 20 at the Iowa State Fairgrounds, East 30th and University (800-545-FAIR).

Western Swing masters Asleep at the Wheel appear at 8 p.m. Aug. 13. And check out this "Rock n' Roll Reunion 21" with headliners the Little River Band and "The Rock n' Roll Army" featuring Gary Lewis & the Playboys, Mitch Ryder, Brian "Itsy Bitsy Teeny Weeny Yellow Polka Dot Bikini" Hyland, Dickey Lee, Mark Lindsay (of Paul Revere & the Raiders), Chris "Let's Dance" Montez and Billy J. Kramer at 7:30 p.m. Aug. 12.

Quarterman, 70, cut his chops back when the Rock n' Roll Army was prime. Between 1972 and 1983 he was a manager at Jim's Rib Haven in Rock Island and East Moline, Ill. Owner Jim Overton is Quarterman's brother-in-law. Singer Pearl Bailey was a regular at Jim's. Quarterman remembers her visiting the restaurant incognito. Guess that Quad Cities paparazzi can get pretty intense.

Quarterman opened his first Al & Irene's in 1983 in Cedar Rapids. Al & Irene moved to their current location at 2020 Northtown Lane N.E. in 1988. "I had relatives here," Quarterman says. "And they said there was no place around that served barbecue. My brother-in-law and I came up from Rock Island, looked around and I decided to open a place here. We're still here, so we must be doing something right."

Cedar Rapids Mayor Lee Clancey is spearheading the rebirth of Cedar Rapids (pop. 115,000). Companies doing business in Cedar Rapids include Quaker Oats, General Mills, U.S. West phone carriers and AEGON, a Dutch life insurance and investment services company. Since Clancey became mayor in 1996, the city has seen the completion of a new downtown police station, the National Czeck & Slovak Museum & Library and an ice arena for a professional hockey team.

On Aug. 15 the city will hold a special election to raise the Veteran's Memorial Stadium levy 30 cents per $1,000 valuation (property tax) to help finance a new $15 million stadium for the Cedar Rapids Kernels baseball team in the Midwest League. Professional baseball has been part of the Cedar Rapids fabric since 1891. (At 2 p.m. Aug. 13 the Kernels host the Chicago White Sox' Burlington Bees affiliate, when a $1,095 men's watch and woman's $1,500 diamond ring will be buried in the infield dirt after the game. Adult fans will be able to dig around for the booty. Call 319-363-3887.)

Clancey is a fan of Al & Irene's. The 51-year-old Winnetka native says, "It is the best barbecue in the state. No holds barred. My kids go there every chance they get, and I've been there a number of times. Don't order anything else but the ribs."

In humble tones Quarterman says, "I can barbecue as well as anybody else. It's just a matter of adjusting to cooking and adjusting the recipes. All hogs are not tender. But you have to be able to tenderize the meat when you cook it. When I left Jim in 1983, I also made the recipes different from his."

Quarterman makes everything from scratch. He cuts the cabbage for his homemade coleslaw ($1.35 a pint), and they cut their own home fries. "We make the baked beans [$1.40 a pint] from scratch," he says. "We don't buy anything pre-made."

Al and Irene have the right recipe for love.

They have been married for 44 years. Al is from Savannah, Ga. His parents, Arthur and Lillian Quarterman, were sharecroppers. Quarterman's father died when he was 9 months old, and his mother remarried Frank Jenkins.

Irene is from the country town of Vandalia, Mo. They met in Newark, N.J., when Quarterman was chef at Perry's Restaurant. Their idea to open Al & Irene's House of Bar-B-Q was a no-brainer.

"Whatever we sit down and talk about what to do is to do it together," says Quarterman, who stands 5 feet 11 inches and weighs a lean 168 pounds. "We've done it together all these years. We've raised three kids. We've been truthful to one another. And when you argue, *always* make up before you go to sleep. Be thankful for the Lord giving you the new day."

Irene, 69, hasn't been around the restaurant for a few weeks. She's recovering nicely from a triple bypass. "Irene helps me make the pies," he says. "Sweet potato. Apple. Cherry. Peach [$7 for a pie, a buck for a slice].

"As soon as the oldest granddaughter gets out of high school in

Moline, Ill., she's coming here, and they're going to take over the restaurant."

"And I'm going fishing."

Pick up Interstate 80 just west of Joliet, take it to Interstate 380 near Iowa City, then head north to Blairs Ferry Road.

Take a right on Blairs Ferry. Go two blocks to the light, turn right on Center Point Road. At the next corner turn right on North-town Lane. Al & Irene's is halfway down the block on the right. Call (319) 393-6242.

July 30, 2000

a.p.   V E H I C L E   7F 99

ROUTE 66

STARTS HERE

1
2
3
4
5
6
7
8
9
10
11
12

─── KEY TO ROUTE 66 DESTINATIONS ───

1	COUNTRYSIDE, IL	*WISHING WELL*
2	WILLOW BROOK, IL	*CHICKEN BASKET*
3	WILMINGTON, IL	*LAUNCHING PAD*
4	GARDNER, IL	*RIVIERA*
5	McLEAN, IL	*TRUCK STOP BARBER*
6	SPRINGFIELD, IL	*COZY DOG*
7	RAYMOND, IL	*OUR LADY OF THE HIGHWAY*
8	MT. OLIVE, IL	*A STATION WITH SOUL*
9	LITCHFIELD, IL	*DRIVE-IN*
10	SPRINGFIELD, MO	*RED'S HAMBURGER - R.I.P.*
11	TULSA, OK	*CAIN'S BALLROOM*
12	VICTORVILLE, CA	*ROY ROGERS MUSEUM*

Map by Lisa Day.

Bobby Troup still gets kicks from his 'Route 66'

The timeless mystique of Route 66 makes it difficult to imagine Bobby Troup retired and playing golf in Southern California.

Troup is the swinging jazzman who in 1946 wrote "(Get Your Kicks On) Route 66." Troup was tooling down the original Route 66 with his first wife, Cynthia, in their migration from Pennsylvania to California.

These days, Troup is 73 years old. He is married to Julie London, who in 1955 recorded the sultry hit "Cry Me a River." They live in a nice home in Encino, nestled in the San Fernando Valley. Troup spoke to me from their kitchen, which they were having remodeled.

At the very least, I expected him to be in the garage, tinkering with the underbelly of a 1941 green Buick convertible. That was the automobile he drove down Route 66. Troup bought the car from his first royalty check from "Daddy," a hit for Sammy Kaye.

Troup is rambling out of retirement to kick off "The 66th Anniversary of Route 66" tour. He will sing "Route 66" backed by the Texas swing band Asleep at the Wheel between 3 and 5 p.m. today in a free party at the Hard Rock Cafe, 63 W. Ontario (312-943-2252). Troup's only other appearance on the tour will be May 17 when the road show closes out at the Greek Theatre in Los Angeles. Besides the live music, Route 66 memorabilia will be on display today. And Troup plans to donate his original "Route 66" sheet music to the Chicago Hard Rock.

Then, the commemorative tour officially revs up at 7:30 p.m. tomorrow when Asleep at the Wheel and country star Ricky Van Shelton play at the Odeum, 1033 N. Villa Ave., in Villa Park (708-941-9292). The live music will be accented by more than 150 vintage slides of "The Mother Road."

In truth, it was Troup's first wife who inspired the classic song. The Troupers were driving the Pennsylvania Turnpike (Route 40) from Harrisburg to Pittsburgh when they stopped for lunch at a Howard Johnson's.

"We were looking at a road map and Cynthia said, 'Why don't you write a song about Route 40?,' " Troup recalled. "I thought it was kind of silly since we were going to pick up Route 66 out of Chicago and take that all the way into Los Angeles. Then, about three days later—she was always hesitant about making suggestions—she leaned over and whispered in my ear, *'Get your kicks on Route 66.'* I said, 'Gee, what a title!' So I wrote the first part of the song in the car as I was driving along. I got the 'more than 2,000 miles' part with a ruler. I measured the map according to scale. Fortunately, I wasn't going too fast."

"Route 66" was only half finished when Troup played it for Nat King Cole, who was the first to popularize it. The Nat King Cole Trio recorded "Route 66" in March, 1946, just after Troup hit Los Angeles.

"I didn't know anybody when I got to California," Troup said. "After five days [Tommy Dorsey sideman] Bullet Sturgell took me over to the King Cole Room. It was a small room in the Trocadero Nightclub on Sunset Strip. Nat had his own room there."

Sturgell told Cole's manager that the hipster who wrote "Daddy" was in the room. He asked if Cole would listen to a couple of Troup's newer·compositions. "Very reluctantly, Nat agreed," Troup said. "I told Nat about a song I wrote on the way to California. I never played 'Route 66' on piano before. But Nat liked it so much, he started playing it, too. He told me to finish 'Route 66' and he would record it." With a road map in hand, Troup went back to his hotel and finished the song.

Looking in the rear view mirror, are there any places Troup regrets he left out? (Legend has it that Cynthia Troup thought he should have included Albuquerque, N.M., in the lyrics.) "But Albuquerque is not a very pleasant word," Troup chuckled. "Get your turkey in Albuquerque? But on the map I saw a little town called Winona, which rhymes with Arizona. The line 'don't forget Winona' turned out to be a classic, because Winona is so small that when you go by, you can miss it."

As any songwriter knows, there is always a demand for a sequel. But Troup has resisted the temptation to pen an updated version of his hit. He isn't even doing a "66th Anniversary of Route 66" song.

"Everyone suggested I write 'Route 40' or 'Route 1' [which runs down the California coast], but I never did," Troup said. "I thought I reached my zenith in 'Route 66.' "

So, the only disappointment Troup encountered in the 46 years since he wrote "Route 66" was when the television series "Route

66" debuted in the fall of 1960. Troup was told his tune would be used as the show's theme. At the last minute, Nelson Riddle was hired to do a new jazzy 'Route 66' instrumental to avoid paying Troup royalties.

"Route 66" has since been recorded three times by Asleep at the Wheel, once by Buckwheat Zydeco, and thankfully only once by Depeche Mode, whose obtuse dark dance version has nothing to do with the open spirit of The Mother Road.

"My kids ask me about Depeche Mode," Troup said. "My comment is, 'At least I can understand the lyrics.' That is the most positive thing I can say. Chuck Berry? The Rolling Stones? I'm glad they did it, but that's not the kind of song I had written. I love the Manhattan Transfer's version. Or the Four Freshmen. But Nat's is still my favorite."

So much attention is paid to the lyrics of "Route 66," people forget that Troup's spacious arrangement is what makes the song swing. "It has what I like in writing and in jazz solos," he said. "Miles Davis always advocated to leave spaces. And 'Route 66' leaves spaces. 'If you ever plan to motor west . . . ' and there's an ol' big space. There's not a lot of notes in that song."

Troup understands he will always be associated with Route 66. In 1984, when Williams, Ariz., became the last Route 66 city to be bypassed by the interstate, Troup was flown in to cut the ribbon.

"I feel like I'm the luckiest guy in the world that I wrote it," Troup said. "My youngest daughter is a costume designer. A few weeks ago she called me from Lawrence, Kan., and said, 'Daddy, I came to eat breakfast at this diner and guess what was playing on the jukebox?' Nat Cole's 'Route 66,' " Troup said in very proud tones.

"I think the song contributed quite a lot to the legend."

May 1, 1992

POSTSCRIPT:

Bobby Troup died of a heart attack on Feb. 7, 1999 in Sherman Oaks, CA. He was survived by wife Julie London, two children from his first marriage, one child from London's marriage to actor Jack Webb and three children from the Troup-London marriage.

A lifetime on Route 66
Neighbors feel like family

The promise of a morning sun peeked through the Arie Crown Woods in west suburban Countryside. A young couple awoke in Room 14 at the Wishing Well Motel, at Joliet Road and Brainard Avenue across the street from the forest preserve.

They got up and walked through the motel's front yard. They walked past old maple trees and through tall grass to a dusty stone and iron wishing well, set back from Joliet Road, old Route 66.

A sailor's knot punctuated the weatherbeaten rope that dropped into the wishing well. Last summer, journeyman piano player Don Younker made the knot in honor of Emil "Mickey" Vidas, a World War II Navy veteran and the late husband of Wishing Well owner Zora Vidas.

Life's twists turned Younker into a Wishing Well resident for the past couple of years. He lives in the motel's courtyard cottage with his wife and two daughters, if you ever want to talk sweet big band music.

The young couple was more familiar with the sting of the blues: Snooks Eaglin, old Buddy Guy and Sunnyland Slim. Maybe that's why they threw new copper pennies into the wishing well.

Dreams converge at this intersection.

They weren't the first to cast a coin into the well, look west and think about the future. The shallow well was built in 1941, the same year the Wishing Well Motor Court went up along U.S. 66.

Just west of the Wishing Well Motel is the Flame of Countryside, 803 Joliet Rd. (708-352-3442), a throwback 1960s supper club where veteran Chicago piano player Johnny Gabor is sure to sing "As Time Goes By."

Across the street from the Flame is Tone's Roadhouse, 10901 W. Joliet Rd. (708-246-3188), a cozy neighborhood bar and restaurant run by Cheryl Tone Herman and inspired by her father , Tone Herman. Until his death in 1990, Tone was the owner-operator of popular restaurants like the Melody Lane in Countryside, the Abbey in Westmont and the Pancake Plantation in Western Springs.

And the Wishing Well, Tone's Roadhouse and the Flame

Historic postcard courtesy of the Wishing Well Motel.

coexist.

"This is one of the most unique corners in the Chicago area," said Nanci Makris, owner of the Flame, "just by the longevity of the three of us being here on such a famous road. There's a lot of history because our families have been here from the get-go. At least 40 years now. My dad [Peter] and Cheryl's dad [Tone] were good friends.

"We're accommodating to each other as if we were family."

Herman has hired Gabor to play parties at her home. Her mother and father would dance at the Flame when they were a young couple. They'd always request "It Had To Be You." Younker will sit in at the Flame in mid-June when Gabor goes on vacation. And Gabor has crashed at the Wishing Well when he's too tired to drive home to Prospect Heights.

The Wishing Well was originally built as five separate, small motor court cottages with a house in the back. The roadside motel had grown to 10 units by 1958 when Zora, Emil and her parents, Charles and Mary, pooled their fortunes and bought the Wishing Well. They paid $55,000. Rooms were $6 a night. (Now the rooms are $45 a night).

"This was all wide-open space back then," said Vidas. She lived in La Grange Park when the family bought the motel. "The Flame was Fernando's Hideaway, an Italian restaurant. The roadhouse was the Bey Lor Tap. An Italian family ran a vegetable farm right behind what became the Flame."

Vidas, 68, is a coal miner's daughter from McKeesport, Pa. A native of Croatia, Charles left Pennsylvania for Chicago to become a tool and die maker. Zora Vidas married Emil Vidas (they already had the same last name) in 1948. She was 18 years old. Vidas will always remember her honeymoon.

She sees it every day.

"Our honeymoon was all the way down Route 66 to Los Angeles," Vidas said. "It was a three-week trip. Even in November, the trees were beautiful in Tucumcari [New Mexico]. It snowed in Arizona that year. We danced to Lawrence Welk at the Palladium Ballroom in Los Angeles. We drove a 1949 Mercury. I'll never forget it. Those were our dreams."

They were a young couple.

"I would have been married a long time," Vidas said as she leaned on a white and green 1960s 7-Up machine that dispenses only bottles. "I was married 35 years when my husband died of kidney cancer. But I would have been married 50."

In 1960 the Vidas clan remodeled the Wishing Well, moving all the cottages together into the 18-unit cedar-sided motel that it is today. During a tour of the motel, Vidas opened the faded brown door of Room 14 and looked inside. The angular room was accented with rust brown shag carpeting, gold and black wallpaper and a water bed.

"This used to be the center of the motel," Vidas said as she looked into the room. "We moved this section to the end. This is new. It's gotta be 37 years ago we did this." Vidas touched the stormy gray ceiling. "Oh, did my dad love the swirl plaster." Her dad would be proud.

The Wishing Well is a working-man's motel.

A sprinkling system repairman from southern Illinois was in Room 3. He stays at the Wishing Well four night a week. A UPS driver was in Room 1. The woman in Room 2 was gathering her thoughts after a divorce. The guy in Room 12 was a cable television installer.

"We cater to small business types just like us," Vidas said. "A lot of ladies here are between apartments. There's three of them here tonight. These are the people who need us. The IBM salesman who is on a $125-a-night expense account would not stay here. We appeal to the little guy."

In 1959, White Sox owner Bill Veeck's public relations man, Coy Poe, dropped into the Wishing Well for a couple of nights and dropped 10 complimentary World Series tickets on the Vidas family. "Coy was wonderful," Vidas recalled. "He [co-] wrote the [Boswell Sisters] ballad 'The Object of My Affection.' "

Other notable Wishing Well guests included the Santa Fe Speedway race car drivers who competed in the since-razed racetrack near La Grange and the rock band Chicago. Vidas groaned and said, "The Styx [rock band] stayed here, too. Oh, my God, I went out there and saw all the long hair."

The Wishing Well is particularly popular with big bands. The Jan Garber Orchestra were regular guests, as was Tex Beneke's Band. "Al Pierson [bandleader of Guy Lombardo's Band] was just here last night," Vidas said.

Younker, 59, added, "One of the reasons the bands stayed here is that it was close to the Willowbrook [Ballroom in Willow Springs]. They might have had a Melody Mill date [in North Riverside]. Or they could hop right on 66 and head out to Dubuque, Omaha, Texas or wherever they were going the next day."

As Younker talked, Vidas looked around the wooded two-acre plot of land that anchors the Wishing Well. She wore a purple blazer and white slacks. There were silver rings on her fingers. She has a heart of gold.

An elderly man was living in Room 11. He became homeless after his grandson accidentally set fire to his apartment. "We help everybody," Vidas said. "We work with the churches in town when someone is in need."

The Brainard Avenue Baptist Church sits just north of the Wishing Well. Last fall, Pastor Jim Johnson and the church's men's club volunteered to repaint the old motel. "I cried when they told me they wanted to do it," Vidas said of the monthlong painting project. "They even wanted to buy the paint, but I wouldn't let them do it. This is such a sharing neighborhood."

Tone Herman bought his neighborhood roadhouse in 1969, and it has remained in the family. Cheryl, 48, remodeled and reopened the restaurant around Thanksgiving. She said, "I wanted to re-assert family control and transform it into a cozy, upscale atmosphere that serves good food."

Tone's Roadhouse seats about 80 people in the dining area and along the square bar. The room is dotted with bright cherry red chairs and nostalgic black and white photographs of Tone. An eclectic CD jukebox includes selections from Tony Bennett, Merle Haggard and jazz great Stan Getz.

The menu is classic roadhouse: a half-pound burger broiled to order ($6.25) and barbecue chicken slow-roasted with fresh herbs and garlic ($8.95). Roadies can wash the grub down with a bottle of Route 66 root beer ($1.50) or Tone's Roadhouse Special Ale, a pale ale custom brewed by Leinenkugel's at $3 a pint.

"To me, a roadhouse is distinct Americana, especially with restaurants and taverns along a country highway," she said. "In its heyday, Route 66 was rich with gems like that. Even though the Mother Road itself and roadhouses have disappeared, Tone's is still on the first leg of historic Route 66."

When Herman and Vidas want to get away from it all, they'll walk across Route 66 to the Flame, a 450-seat restaurant, lounge and banquet hall that looks like it belongs on Fremont Street in Las Vegas instead of suburban Chicago. The Flame opened in May 1958. Johnny Gabor, 57, has been playing in the Flame lounge since 1981. He's there with his trio from 7 p.m. to 12:30 a.m. Tuesday through Thursday and 8 p.m. to 12:30 a.m. Friday and Saturday. No cover. And Gabor is no relation to Zsa Zsa.

But he's got some well-traveled stories of his own.

"In 1983, I was booked on the Stella Oceanis cruise ship," Gabor said. "We were going to go all over the world. We were going to start in the Caribbean and play every island. We were going to make the crossing to the Mediterranean and do Spain, Italy, Greece. But . . . "

Gabor gazed at the lounge's trademark 20-foot tall artificial tree, adorned with twinkling white lights and plastic pink, red and yellow flowers. The tree is based in an actual tree stump. Gabor picked up steam.

"The first day I was on the ship, we were leaving San Juan, Puerto Rico. It's New Year's Eve. I've got my white tux on and I start playing the piano. They raise the anchor and I felt like the ship had gone up about 25 floors. I was holding onto the piano and turning green. *Oooh, my.*"

Gabor was seasick.

He took Dramamine and finished the Caribbean leg of the cruise. But he couldn't continue. He's never played a cruise ship again.

Vidas doesn't know what will happen when her cruise down Route 66 is over. She said she gets weekly offers to buy the Wishing Well, but she will likely leave the future up to her two sons, Michael, 47, and Mark, 41. Michael is an ear-nose-throat doctor in Peoria and Mark is an eye doctor in Bourbonnais. Vidas has five granddaughters, including one set of 16-year-old twins.

Vidas smiled and said, "The twins say, 'Gramma, when you get tired of the motel, we're going to make it into a resort.' I'll keep that in mind."

It's a good idea.

There's a junction in everyone's life where they find a reason to believe that wishes can come true.

May 30, 1999

Fish Heads Go Fine In a Chicken Basket

Some inclinations are too tempting to ignore.

A few months ago I ran into Chicago bluesdude Mark Hannon at the Old Town Ale House, a foreboding place where, truthfully, the strangers are fiction. Hannon told me about a gig he had just played with his band, The Fabulous Fish Heads, at a roadhouse restaurant called Dell Rhea's Chicken Basket on Old Route 66 in Willowbrook.

Fish Heads. Rock and blues. Fried chicken. Old Route 66.

Show me the way.

Readers of this pow-wow are probably weary of repeated mentions of Route 66, but one trip to the Chicken Basket illustrates the innocent splendor of the Mother Road. In order to reach the Chicken Basket you exit off of Route 83 and navigate through a soulless industrial park that includes a Budgetel Motel, a Denny's restaurant and a Holiday Inn.

Then, on a magical turn around a bend, nestled in a shrubby valley, is the Chicken Basket. It is a panorama of the past. The outside consists of light red brick punctuated by large windows and a Coca-Cola sign. An exquisite red, white and blue neon sign that says "Dell Rhea's Chicken Basket" winks at passersby. The sign has stood in the same spot since 1946.

"One day two women from a local farm came along," said Pat Rhea, the present owner. "They saw how the owner [Irv Kolaric] was doing a brisk business because of Route 66. They offered to teach him how to cook fried chicken if he would buy his eggs and chicken from them. That's where our recipe came from."

The golden-brown chicken was a warm complement for the national acts who occasionally appeared at the Chicken Basket in the '40s and '50s. Rhea said, "In the winter, Irv used to flood the flat roof above the main dining room, let it freeze and he'd have professional ice skaters with lights shining on them to draw people in off the highway."

The Fish Heads—Hannon, guitarist Bob Levis and bassist Harlan Terson (each formerly of the Lonni Brooks Band) and drummer Bob Carter—will play rock and jump blues in the Roost dining room this weekend.

"It's fun playing there," Hannon said. "Something about the

name evokes a feeling. You're on Route 66. There's the cool name Dell Rhea's. You can imagine a band out of Texas called the Del Rays. The Chicken Basket is a bluesy thing, and we're partly a blues band. I had never heard of it before until we were booked there." And Hannon has been singing and blowing harp on the Chicago blues scene since the early 1970s when he sat in with Lefty Dizz.

"Not much has changed in the 47 years we've been here." said Rhea, who is 38. "We're not in a lot of the Route 66 books because we've kind of been forgotten. This little section of the road has been passed by." All is not lost. Dell's Rhea's Chicken Basket is a member of the Route 66 Hall of Fame in the lobby of the Dixie Truck Stop in McLean, Ill.

Rhea, who reinstituted live music around Thanksgiving, bought the family business in 1986. His father, Dell, died at age 85 in October. Dell Rhea was an executive director of the

Photo by Lisa Day.

Chicago Convention Bureau and was instrumental in bringing the 1933 World's Exposition to Chicago.

Between 1943 and 1953 he owned the Woodbine Restaurant, which was across the street from the Chicken Basket. When the Chicken Basket became available in 1963, Rhea fowled through (we couldn't resist one horrible pun) on his dream of owning the restaurant and added his name to the historic sign. "The old highway was dead and the restaurant was dying," his son said.

If you prod Rhea a little bit, you can get him going on the way life used to be. A go-kart track once existed where the Budgetel is. As a kid, he played miniature golf down the old road. "This was a perfect place to stop, going into the city or coming out of the city for a Sunday drive," Rhea said. "There used to be an [Hinsdale] airport across the street. That's one of the reasons we have all the windows, so people could watch the airplanes. But you can't stay as a little part of rural America because the city is coming out here.

"My main goal is just to keep this as it always was."

February 26, 1993

Rocket man
A giant nod to Space Age

The food is out of this world at the Launching Pad Drive-In restaurant in Wilmington, about 20 miles west of Joliet.

And so is the maitre d'.

The friendly Gemini Giant roadside figure greets visitors in the parking lot of the Launching Pad, 810 E. Baltimore on old Route 66 in Wilmington. The big man stands 28 feet tall and weights 500 pounds.

Wearing a space helmet and glimmering green body suit that recalls David Bowie's Ziggy Stardust, the giant was erected in 1965 after original diner owners John and Bernice Korelc saw the fiberglass statue at a National Restaurant Association show in Chicago.

Naturally, the Korelcs were ahead of their time.

Only the Gemini Giant combines a Space-Age millennium spin with the outer limits of hype given to Chicago's fiberglass cows. The cows are just truncated roadside art.

"The United States was getting into the space program in 1965," said Sharon Gatties, 55, who owns the Launching Pad with her husband Jerry, 58. She bought the restaurant from her father after his 1986 retirement. "They came up with the Launching Pad idea because of that."

Her parents opened the diner in 1960 as a Dari Delite, selling only hot dogs and ice cream. When the Korelcs decided to expand the menu to include hamburgers, chili and french fries, they also looked to change the name.

"They were looking for something unusual," Sharon understated.

The Korelcs bought the giant for $3,500 and had him shipped on two flatbed trailers from Venice, Calif., to Wilmington. A contest was held among Wilmington schools to come up with a name for the town's biggest resident. Fifth-grader Cathy Thomas came up with the name as a tribute to NASA's Gemini space program.

"Actually, there's several different statues," said Sharon, whose black and white Route 66 earrings dangled from her ears.

"There's an Indian, a lumberjack. They saw the form and had him made into an astronaut." Jerry added, "The arms and body sections can be made into different things." Theoretically, the Gemini Giant could also be a lumberjack astronaut.

This presents all kinds of possibilities for giant Village People figures.

According to Kevin J. Patrick's article in the spring-summer 1995 journal of the Society for Commercial Archaeology, fiberglass figures depicting the likes of steely-eyed Muffler Men, Paul Bunyans and astronauts were produced in the 1960s by an unknown California company that went out of business in the mid-1970s.

The giants were made in three pieces: legs, body and head. They were bolted together using standardized fittings so that parts of different giants could be interchanged. Patrick wrote that the fiberglass figures "were rendered with indistinguishable uniformity, the antithesis of competitive commercialism."

Patrick is a geographer who teaches in the Geography and Regional Planning Department at Indiana University of Pennsylvania in Indiana, Pa., of all spacey places. "I've tried to track down where these things came from," Patrick said last week. "All indications point to Southern California, like Compton and Venice. But the only evidence is from people who have them, and they are second- or third-generation giant owners. Many of them are dead or gone."

John and Bernice Korelc are both 80, and they live in Wilmington. John said he saw the giant at the restaurant show and ordered the helmet and rocket from a now forgotten firm in Venice, Calif.

Patrick, 38, said the Gemini Giant is the only big astronaut roadside figure in America. "That's a vernacular genre of giants that have been modified," he said. "That guy is actually a Paul Bunyan type. It's just that it has a helmet. And instead of holding an ax, he is holding a rocket."

Best of all, the Gemini Giant has stood tall in the winds of change.

"He's become something of an icon and a landmark," Sharon said. "He hasn't changed. He got a new paint job a few years ago, but other than that, it's exactly how he's looked since 1965."

But the Gemini Giant has been the target of Wilmington (pop. 5,000) pranksters over the years. The astronaut originally cradled an 8-foot Styrofoam rocket. That was stolen. It was replaced by a fiberglass rocket, which also was stolen. Last year, a new fiberglass rocket was built to resemble the original one. "We've got security on this one," Sharon warned. "And it's bolted in pretty good."

Launching Pad regulars are locked into house specialties like the broiled Route 66 cheeseburger ($2.75 without fries), hoagie po' boys ($3.25) and the Dirt Worm Sundae (crushed Oreos and gummy worms for $1.50).

"We have a lot of visitors traveling 66," Sharon said over a dining room table that depicted a Route 66 map. "Within the last five years tourism has picked up." Jerry estimated between 2,000 and 3,000 European visitors annually stop for some grub in the diner, which seats 70 people. "And every day there's someone taking pictures of the giant," he said. "Every day."

Photo by Dave Hoekstra.

Sharon and Jerry are thinking of having the Gemini Giant commemorate the millennium in some form. Sharon said, "Last year during the football season, the kids put a huge football jersey on him.

"At the millennium, it will be 40 years we've been here. We've seen people come in as kids and then come in with their kids. And those kids are starting to come in. Then you know you've been here awhile."

The Launching Pad is open Sunday through Thursday from 9 a.m. to 10:30 p.m. and until 11 p.m. Friday and Saturday. Take Interstate 55 south to the River Road exit, head east to Route 53 (also Route 66). Turn right until you land at the Launching Pad. For more information, call (815) 476-6535.

October 10, 1999

Roadhouse reverie
The Krafts' restaurant is a classic

GARDNER, Ill.—When the south side of Chicago got too big for Bob and Peggy Kraft, they bought a little peace of mind on old Route 66 in Gardner, about 30 miles south of Joliet.

In 1972 they purchased the Riviera Restaurant, 5650 E. Route 53. The Riviera is a classic American roadhouse wedged in a two-acre grassy ravine along the Mazon River in Gardner.

The two-story white frame, baby blue-trimmed roadhouse opened in 1928. Over the years it has hosted the likes of Gene Kelly, cowboy Tom Mix and the ubiquitous Al Capone, who was checking out his alcohol stills in nearby Kankakee county.

Bob and Peggy like life along their Riviera just fine.

They can do things their way.

Orders are delivered to an upstairs kitchen on clothespins attached to a clothesline. The downstairs waitress rings an old-fashioned doorbell to let the kitchen know the order is on the way.

Prepared food drops downstairs on a dumbwaiter. The waiter's pulley is counterbalanced by a World War I mortar shell. Peggy makes 32 quarts of her secret spaghetti sauce every week in the kitchen. By hand.

Even the Krafts' black and white spotted mutt Cheyenne, 4, is different. She lovingly stares at customers with one blue eye and one brown eye.

Indeed this is a colorful world.

On a recent Thursday afternoon Peggy, 76, was upstairs prepping the kitchen. Bob, also 76, was tending bar downstairs. Fake white stalactites hung above the bar. Bob wore a black leather bow tie with matching black suspenders. One of his customers hand-crafted the bow tie for Bob. Regulars were buying him hot cinnamon shots. He seemed to be having a good time.

"When I came out here, I looked at the cornfield on one side and the creek on the other side," Bob recalled. "I said, 'Where are the customers going to come from?'" Between 1947 and 1972 Bob owned Club Avalon taverns at 82nd and Dobson, Stony Island and Cottage Grove and also at 79th and Luella.

Gardner (pop. 1,200) is a helluva difference from Luella.

During the 1940s and '50s the Riviera was a popular stop along Route 66. The Riviera compound included a zoo, camping grounds and a watering hole.

James Girot, a businessman from nearby South Wilmington, built the Riviera, and its early days coincided with the Great Depression. Located six miles southwest of Gardner, South Wilmington was a mining community and many men were unemployed. Locals still call South Wilmington *South Willy*. It took me awhile to catch on. I thought *South Willy* was some up-and-coming hip-hopper.

Girot was able to afford the land but he didn't have enough money to build on it. So he purchased a coal company office and dry goods store in South Wilmington and local men moved the

Photo by Dave Hoekstra.

Bob and Peggy Kraft in front of the Riviera.

buildings by trailer to a new foundation on its current location. "That was 1927," Bob said. "The buildings were old before they even got here."

Bob and Peggy are only the second owners in the Riviera's history. The restaurant seats 159 people in three subterranean dining rooms. The restaurant is in the basement because in the pre-air conditioning era, that was the coolest spot in the house. A back dining room is bordered by beady-eyed owl tiki lights and Christmas garland.

During Prohibition the restaurant was located upstairs and the basement was a secret rathskeller. Sipping from a 32-ounce plastic mug of iced decaffeinated coffee, Peggy said, "To get down there to the slot machines and bootleg booze, you had to go through the pantry."

And during Prohibition, about halfway between the Riviera and South Willy, locals knew of the "Hole-in-the-Wall." Peggy described a field that had a cement post with a hole in it. Customers put a $1 in the hole and set an empty bucket on the ground. "You drove around the perimeter of the field," Peggy said with a wry smile, "And when you came back, your bucket was full of beer."

The Krafts have done little to change the Riviera's landscape over the years. Peggy chortled, "Never throw the baby out with the bathwater."

Bob did replace the bar. He imported his bar top from Club Avalon. He reasoned, "The old bar had so many ruts that if somebody ordered a shot and a beer, the shot would tip over before they could drink it." Bob is quite the jokester. Ask him about the square barstools he had at the Club Avalon. "That way there were no hangovers," he said. The Riviera bar uses old soda fountain stools. Peggy re-covered the seats in psychedelic orange.

Bob and Peggy met at his Club Avalon at 79th and Luella.

They've been married 29 years. It was Peggy's idea to leave the city for the country. They have no children. Peggy has a son from a previous marriage. But the family, which includes three grand-children and six great-grandchildren, are not interested in the business.

"We're thinking of selling," Bob said during a tour of the grounds. "But I don't want to sell it. I get to drink six nights a week. When we get outta here I know she's not going to let me drink." The Riviera employs 12 people on the weekend: six in the kitchen, six in the downstairs restaurant.

A native of Valparaiso, Ind., Peggy displayed a playfully sassy exterior that failed to mask her passion for the roadhouse. Her spaghetti sauce is simply the best in the Midwest. A small spaghetti with meat sauce is $3.95; large is $4.95.

After careful prodding she talked about the lively sauce. "I put everything in it," she said. "Beef. Pork. Tomato. Tomato paste. Spices. Onions. Green Peppers. Celery. Yep." Peggy also makes her own cream 'n' Cheddar cheese spreads, secret salad dressing and salads.

The Riviera menu has just about everything: A po' boy beef

sandwich with mushrooms ($3.50), a 16-oz. T-bone steak ($13.95), buttercrumb cod ($7.95), catfish ($6.95) and vegetable lasagna ($7.50) all are sure bets.

A draught of Old Milwaukee beer is 75 cents. Bottled beer is $1.75. The Riviera stocks 18 brands of bottled beer. There's so much bric-a-brac around the bar it is difficult to focus on any one thing. There are wacky signs such as: Free drinks for anyone over 90 who are accompanied by their parents.

But on the north end of the bar is a white birdhouse that was hand-painted in a Route 66 motif by grandson Chuck. It was a Christmas gift for Bob and Peggy. Earlier this year, Peggy affixed two tiny toy birds to the house. One wren is brown with a white chest. The other is brown with a pink chest. After talking to Bob and Peggy for a spell, you know who the birds represent. They are birds of a feather.

They will always flock together.The Riviera Restaurant is open Tuesday through Sunday from 5 to 10 p.m. or whenever the last customer leaves.

Take Interstate 55 south to the Gardner exit. Head east over I-55 to Route 53 and hang a left. The Riviera Restaurant is on the right. Look for the Old Style and Schlitz beer signs. Call (815) 237-2344.

May 14, 2000

Truck stop barber gave his clips on Route 66

McLEAN, Ill.—Some big memories surround Wesley "Shorty" Ruble. In the late 1960s, my parents would pull over at the Dixie Truck Stop on old Route 66 in McLean when we traveled between Chicago and southern Illinois to visit my grandmother during the holidays.

I was a long-haired teenager.

Shorty was the truck stop barber.

Dad enjoyed the possibilities.

In my shaggy eyes, anyone who walked into Shorty's two-chair truck stop barbershop came out looking like George Jones. Shorty's scissors resembled twin machetes. He flat-out, flat-top scared me.

Now follically challenged, I felt it was safe to track down Shorty. The humble 5-foot-4-inch stylist operates the one-chair Shorty's Barber Shop in an old drugstore in a turn-of-the-century brick building on McLean's town square. Next month, he celebrates 50 years of cutting hair.

Shorty, 73, looked exactly as I remembered him. He hadn't aged a bit. He still wore thick black Buddy Holly glasses and the same gentle smile that always made me think about the spider and the fly. His hair was . . . still short. Nevertheless, I was fidgety, expecting him to shout *banzai!* as I peeked through the front door.

Shorty does it the old way. He charges $5 for a haircut. A client like 10-year-old Vincent Smith and his mother bicycled to the shop together. They live "right up the road" on Old Route 66.

As Vincent got his haircut, he sat on an aluminum toolbox that Shorty has used for the past 50 years to elevate his youngest customers. After the haircut, Vincent crawled off the chair and scampered toward a small table. He yanked on a sticky drawer and pulled out a Dum-Dum lollipop, his reward for sitting relatively still. Sometimes we all need some Dum-Dums to slow down.

Shorty was born and reared in rural Waynesville, about six

miles from McLean, population 800. Shorty's uncles George and Allen were barbers, and Shorty is a Dec. 15, 1947, graduate of the Peoria Barber School.

"I was taught the 'theory' and 'practical' way to cut hair," Shorty explained during a break between customers. "Practical was just [cutting] clean hair and shaving. I still use an old lather machine. The theory was in how it would look. You almost had to be a doctor to be a barber at that time."

I asked Shorty how he would celebrate on Dec. 15.

"Probably come to work," he answered.

And that's the shear truth. Haircuts are in Shorty's blood. He operated a barbershop between 1952 and 1968 on the McLean town square, about 15 miles south of Bloomington-Normal. In December, 1968, he was hired as house barber at the Dixie Truck Stop, where he remained until 1989, when the shop was closed as part of a renovation project. Shorty's old shop is now across the way from the Route 66 Hall of Fame, which features more than a hundred Route 66 artifacts, including a vintage street light.

Photo by Dave Hoekstra.

Shorty, April, 2000.

"I made a lot of friends up and down the road," Shorty said. "I'd work 12-, 14-hour days at the truck stop. Lots of my customers were from Chicago. [Radio commentator] Paul Harvey would stop in. [Actor] McLean Stevenson. [Country singer] T.G. Sheppard's drummer got his hair cut late one night." Gee. You know how drummers can be.

Although truckers and road warriors were always buzzing through, Shorty took his time cutting hair. "If they're in that big of a hurry," he said in a matter-of-fact tones, "then they don't have time to get a haircut."

The Rubles have been married 42 years and have two children: Daughter Cathy is a banker near McLean, and son Brian lives in south suburban New Lenox.

Shorty and his wife, Mary Ellen, have lived in McLean since 1955. Shorty said, "I worked the truck stop from noon until midnight because of the traffic. And in my 21 years at Dixie, the owners never once criticized me or questioned me. I have wonderful memories. Everyone really started talking about 66 when they built Interstate 55. That's when the nostalgia kicked in. There's not much here anymore. All these small towns have gone the same way. Died out."

Even styles died out. I no longer look like an over-hormoned Michael Bolton. For that matter, neither does Michael Bolton. "I always stayed with the old styles," Shorty said. "I don't go much for long-haired stuff. The last few years I've just taken care of old friends and I've more or less semi-retired. I fish in the creeks around here. I like to play golf.

"But sometimes I wish I would have kept a big ledger," said the shy barber, in a rare moment where he lets his hair down. "I would have had everyone sign it. I had people from all over the world come see me."

November 30, 1997

Drive-In takes trip down 66
Historic Cozy Dog to get new home on old highway

SPRINGFIELD, Ill.—When it came time to close down the old Cozy Dog Drive-In late last month, the restaurant went away quietly. Its bark was never as good as its bite.

Soon the restaurant will be back in a new building doing what it's been doing since 1950, serving battered deep-fried hot dogs on a stick—a version of the corn dog known as the "cozy dog"—on Old Route 66 south of downtown Springfield. Route 66 historians regard the Cozy Dog as the road's original fast food.

Courtesy of Cozy Dogs.

The original Cozy Dog Drive-In was razed June 25, to be replaced by a Walgreens drugstore. A new Cozy Dog restaurant is being built where the A. Lincoln Motel used to stand, north of the original location. It is scheduled to open later this month.

"We spent our whole life here," said Cozy Dog owner Buz Waldmire, 48, sitting in the old dining room as pickle barrels caught water from a leaky ceiling. "I remember standing on a metal milk crate frying hamburgers as a kid. I met my wife here. It's sad to see the old place go.

"We never wanted to move, but we never owned the whole lot. The developer bought this acre of property and the acre of property the motel sat on. It was either make a deal and move to a new building or close for good."

Buz's late father, Edwin Waldmire Jr., became the father of the Cozy Dog while serving in the Army Air Corps.

"My dad stopped at a roadside restaurant in Amarillo, Texas," Buz said. "They had corn dogs on the menu, but it took 20 minutes to get one because they baked them in an oven. When he got back to his air base, he called his college roommate in Galesburg, Ill., whose father owned a bakery. He asked, 'Can you mix me up some batter that will stick to the side of a hot dog while we fry it in oil?' It worked."

Edwin Waldmire called his creation "Crusty Curs" and began selling them on weekends along Old Route 66 in Texas and Oklahoma. When he was discharged and returned to Springfield in 1946, his wife Ginny didn't think much of the name.

She questioned the appetizing lure of a Crusty Cur and suggested the name "Snuggle Puppies." He wondered who would eat something called a Snuggle Puppy. They compromised on a Cozy Dog. Ginny Waldmire designed a logo of two hot dogs in a blissful embrace, which is still used today.

The elder Waldmire registered his invention as an "inbuilt hot dog" with the Illinois secretary of state. Waldmire was a terminal tinkerer. His inventions such as the electric cozy dog fryer and wood-handled batter-dipping gadgets are being moved to the new restaurant as part of a Cozy Dog/Route 66 museum.

The cozy dog made its official debut 50 years ago at the 1946 Illinois State Fair. Three years later, Edwin Waldmire bought half interest in a single parcel with the owner of an adjacent Dairy Queen. With the help of family and friends and $50,000 that they scraped together, Waldmire built the hardboard-siding restaurant from scratch under the shade of a sycamore tree, which since has toppled in a tornado.

At one time, there were three Cozy Dog restaurants in Springfield.

Tom Teague is past president of the Route 66 Association of Illinois and author of the book *Searching for 66* (Samizdat House, 1208 W. Edwards, Springfield, Ill. 62704). "A lot of people are saying it's a damn shame the old place has gone down," said Teague, a Springfield resident. "But that's very much a character of 66. The road was not of ply and amber. It was always about change and progress."

Buz Waldmire said: "When the interstate went around the east side of Springfield in the latter part of the '60s, night business died. . . . But before that happened, the old road in front was the only thoroughfare between Chicago and St. Louis. You had to go by my dad's place."

Ed Waldmire took some big stands for someone who spent so much time with weenies. He was a member of the World Federalists, an organization that strived for world peace through world law. And during Cozy Dog's early years, Waldmire ignored the segregated seating rules generally applied in Springfield restaurants.

"The Dairy Queen manager would hang a sign that said, 'We Reserve the Right to Seat Our Customers,' " Waldmire recalled. "My dad would always tear the sign down. Blacks were always served here."

One of the Cozy Dog's final visitors was comic Flip Wilson, who was touring Route 66 on a recent Sunday afternoon with 300 Harley-Davidson motorcycle riders. The restaurant was closed. Waldmire, his wife and some friends had begun moving 40-year-old fryer parts and cooking equipment out of the basement. Wilson still took in the roadhouse ambiance and autographed the "Liar's Table," where Cozy Dog regulars tell tall tales on a daily basis.

Waldmire smiled and looked down at the Liar's Table. "So he said, 'If you're closed today and I can't get a Cozy Dog, I'll write: 'Cozy Dogs are great. I had 12 of them!' And then he was gone."

The truth is that in 1974 Buz met his wife at the Cozy Dog. Sue was a 16-year-old Springfield native, working part time in the restaurant's kitchen. They were married in 1975 and have six children, ranging in age from 2 to 24. In 1978, Edwin Waldmire sold the Cozy Dog to Buz, who now hopes that one of his sons will want to inherit the business.

"Closing is kind of like when our parents pass on," said Waldmire, with a broken rotary wall phone in the background. "Nobody lives forever. . . . But now we'll have a new building and maybe it will last for the next 50 years."

On the outside walkway, Waldmire's brother Bob carefully removed a 24-foot coast-to-coast wooden map of Route 66. It was so quiet, you could hear passing trucks from the distant interstate.

July 7, 1996

'Our Lady of the Highway' blesses I-55

RAYMOND, Ill.—A guiding light blesses all who travel Interstate 55 in southern Illinois this holiday season. It comes from a statue of the Virgin Mary at the edge of a wheat farm on a west frontage road. The Our Lady of the Highway Shrine is a life-size marble figurine imported from Carrara, Italy.

Next year marks the 40th anniversary of the shrine.

The inscription reads:

Mary Loving Mother of Jesus/Protect us on the highway.

Retired farmer Francis Marten has maintained the shrine since it was installed in 1959 along old Route 66, between exits 72 and 63. The statue cost $400. A cobblestone walkway and a wooden grotto were built with $600 worth of donations.

Marten has been steadfast in his commitment to this roadside shrine. It is what he does, it is part of what he always will be. Any other reasons for his devotion remain veiled in a certain darkness.

Visitors can't purchase Our Lady of the Highway Shrine postcards, T-shirts or shot glasses. After gentle persuasion, Marten might accept a donation, although he said

Photo by Dave Hoekstra.

he has never received anything more than a $10 bill.

Marten turned 85 on Nov. 8. He is in failing health.

"I don't like people making a big deal out of me," said Marten, as he sat in a recliner in the living room of his home, directly north of the shrine. Wearing faded blue overalls, he looked out the front window at the 1930, 1950 and 1970 stretches of Route 66 and continued, "I was born on a farm, I've lived here all my life and I don't have many years left. I'll die here."

Carl Marten, 44, is the youngest of Francis and Ruth Marten's eight children. Ruth died in 1985. They were married 47 years. Carl helps farm his parents' property with his brother Lee. Carl and his wife, Marlene, will take over operation of the shrine after his father passes over.

"My dad still pays the bills," said Carl, standing in front of the statue on a brisk afternoon, a few days before his father's birthday. "He pays the spotlights that kick on at night, the light bulbs and the electric bill. He had it landscaped six or seven years ago.

"And there's one man from St. Louis who drives to Springfield once a month. He puts fresh flowers on the shrine when he comes by." In the summer, hollyhocks blossom and grow 4 feet high at the base of the shrine.

The shrine was installed by the Litchfield Deanery Catholic Youth Council. Marten's daughter Loretta belonged to the group. Her father gave the CYC permission to install the shrine on his property.

At the same time the shrine was installed Francis put up a dozen Burma-Shave influenced Hail Mary signs along a 1/8 of a mile border of his farm. Traveling south they read: *"Hail Mary"* . . . *"Full of Grace"* . . . *"The Lord is with thee . . ."* When I-55 was built in 1970, the state tried to make him take down the signs. They failed. "It wasn't state property," Francis said. "We even had it surveyed. It was our property. Those signs were in the right place."

Carl has no indication if the Our Lady of the Highway Shrine has actually brought good fortune to travelers. Carl recalled, "There was a guy who said 'Hail Mary' prayers as he drove by. It's just to make somebody think about God. The bishop of Springfield has been by it hundreds of times.

"For several years in May [the month of Mary], we would have a pilgrimage. People would come here on a Sunday. They'd walk down the highway and pray a rosary along the way. They would finish the rosary in front of the shrine and say a few more prayers. Now we get people from other states and nations because of the Route 66 associations." The Martens' guest book has signatures from Los Angeles; Sydney, Australia, and Salt Lake City, Utah.

In January, Pope John Paul will visit St. Louis, an hour away from the Our Lady of the Highway Shrine. Could he? Might he?

"I doubt it," Carl laughed. "It would be great if we could pull that off. Get the Popemobile going down Route 66 . . ." His voice trailed off. His father listened with a satisfied smile. Sometimes the strongest light comes from within.

November 29, 1998

Chicken Little

Robert Hastert Jr. was remembering his father during a recent conversation in the stable-like dining room of the White Fence Farm restaurant on Joliet Road in Lemont when the topic turned to the farm's secret chicken recipe. His father died of cancer on Oct. 22. He was 83. Robert Hastert Sr. purchased the roadside restaurant off old Route 66 in 1954.

We just about got Hastert to disclose the farm's legendary mildly spiced, light crispy crust recipe.

"My dad was in the poultry business in Aurora," said Hastert, 62 "I used to deliver chicken even before I had a driver's license. I drove a chicken truck around, many times to a place called the Chicken Joint, which in the late 1940s was one of the first fast-food operations there ever was.

"I'd see this pressure cooker, like your grandmother had—a round pot with a spigot on the top. When it got hot enough, the steam would come out of the spigot. So I'd watch this kid—and he was a kid—flour the chicken, put it in the pressure cooker, cook it, take it out, put it in the cooler and when somebody ordered it, they'd fry it." In the old days, chicken shacks used fattening lard. Today the White Fence Farm uses a clear canola oil, with no fat and no grease.

Hastert continued, "My dad bought the Harmony House [restaurant in Aurora] and he didn't know what he was going to serve, and I told him about the chicken. He was impressed. I went over and gave the kid $200 and asked if he would work for us for a week. So he came over and taught me and the other cooks how to do the chicken."

November 29, 1998

A station with soul on Route 66

MOUNT OLIVE, Ill.—The Soulsby Shell Station is the oldest gas station still standing on Route 66. It was built in 1926 by Henry Soulsby and his son, Russell, in tiny Mount Olive, about 45 miles south of Springfield.

At 13 by 20 feet, the gas station was never big enough to accommodate a car. Oil changes and repairs were done on a drive-up Model T lubricating ramp directly south of the white, wood-trimmed gas station. The iron ramp remains today. A huge oak tree has grown in the middle of the rusted ramp, making it one of America's most genuine roadside landmarks.

And the uplifting Russell Soulsby turned 88 a couple of weeks ago.

He recently drove over to the station in his 1982 Ford Taurus to talk about efforts to preserve the site as a historic and educational attraction. The not-for-profit Soulsby Station Society has repainted the gas station. A picnic table has been added for a perfect late summer outing. The station was shut down in November, 1991, because it did not meet the standards of the Environmental Protection Agency.

A diminutive man with a playful smile, Russell wore blue overalls and a Route 66 baseball cap with pins proudly denoting his 1990 induction into the Route 66 Hall of Fame of Illinois (at the Dixie Truck Stop in McLean).

As I pulled away from the gas station, Russell smiled and extended his crooked right arm. And he waved goodbye, back and forth, back and forth, his arm gently moving like a pendulum. The connection with the past was strong.

I thought of the thousands of times Russell had sent off a traveler like this.

Russell and his sister, Ola, worked at the station all their lives. They hung around the station to talk to travelers even after the station closed. Ola cleaned windshields and pumped the gas at the station for 64 years.

So what did Russell do?

"Awh, I helped out," he said with a laugh. Russell spoke with the warm whistle of a whippoorwill at dawn. "Of course, after awhile, we went into selling radios and televisions. Did you hear about that?

"When we had tubes, I built a radio that had three tubes in it. I was quite a radio man. We figured we shouldn't waste my knowledge. The whole north end of the gas station was radios and televisions. We also sold 'soady' pop, milk and ice cream."

Ola died in 1996, and Russell sold the station in 1997.

The station was first offered to the State of Illinois on the suggestion of the Historic Preservation Agency that it could be functional again. But state money was not earmarked for it. The station was then offered to Mount Olive as a park or museum, but again, money was not available.

Finally, new owner Mike Dragovich of Mount Olive bought the real estate, including the station for $18,100 and two adjacent lots for $4,000. Dragovich, 33, is working with the society to maintain the station. Dragovich had the picnic table built and primed. The society raises money for items that will not enhance real estate value: things like a new Shell sign and a restored gas pump that will go up next spring.

Springfield, Ill.-based Route 66 historian Tom Teague is a director of the Soulsby Station Society, with members in five states. He said, "Someday I'd like to see a museum inside, but the most important thing we can do is make it a social place. That kind of heritage of 66 is hard to recapture.

"It's a charming building, but without Russell's spirit it won't have the same appeal. We won't have Russell forever, so we're trying to offer a smaller pleasure. That's what Route 66 is these days, a road of smaller pleasures, not a road of Disneyworlds and Las Vegas pyramids."

Henry Soulsby loved the world of Mail Pouch tobacco which he snuffed as he toiled in the Hoosier (coal) Mines in Mount Olive. The family lived in a home directly behind the gas station. They opened the gas station four months before Route 66 was commissioned.

"I remember more people were going south [toward St. Louis] than north [to Chicago]," Russell said during a tour of the station. "We went all the way to Chicago on Route 66 once. Another time we went to Springfield.

"There used to be a stove here," he said, pointing to a corner near the refinished floor. "We used coal for heat. Well, those days are gone. Ah, here was my workbench to fix radios and televisions. . . . I had no idea they were going to fix this place up like this."

The canopied, two-pump service station was affiliated with Shell Oil from the day it opened. But the lubricating ramp quickly became outdated. "Almost every week, we'd have someone come by wanting to buy the rack," Russell said. "No go. The width of the wheels wasn't like the new cars. It's kind of narrow. Kids would come along and start riding the edge [in their cars]. We figured someone was going to get hurt, so we put the tree in to keep them from going up on the ramp. But the tree came along and took over."

When Russell was a young man he played clarinet and alto saxophone in the Melodians, a southern Illinois dance band. "We played on Main Street in Mount Olive, our first engagement was at the Ariston [seven miles north on 66: I recommend the catfish filet] in Litchfield," he said. Russell met his wife, Elizabeth, at a dance in Litchfield. She died in 1970.

The Soulsbys had three sons. One died this spring, and two others live out of state. They also had a stillborn child on Christmas Eve, 1943. Russell is a regular visitor to the Litchfield cemetery up the road, where his wife and infant son are buried.

Photo by Dave Hoekstra.

The late Russell Soulsby.

"These days I have a good dancing partner who lives in Staunton," Russell said. "We do all our ballroom dancing in Pana.

We go to the Crystal Ballroom right down the road in Staunton."

And how did Russell spend his 88th birthday?

"The usual thing," he answered." Go to my lady friend's house, sit and watch television and do some dancing. We don't care to go as a single couple. We like somebody else to go, too."

Russell Soulsby could waltz across Texas with the friends he has made on Route 66. One of America's smallest gas stations has cultivated the road's biggest heart.

August 23, 1998

POSTSCRIPT:

Russell Soulsby died of an aneurysm at his home on Oct. 30, 1999, a little over a year after I met him. His funeral procession of 50 cars passed underneath the old service canopy of the Soulsby Shell Station, where Route 66 friends were on hand to wave farewell.

Illinois artist Bob Waldmire made a two-foot square magnet that resembled a Route 66 sign and Route 66 historian Tom Teague affixed the sign to the hearse before the funeral.

Russell was laid to rest next to his wife and infant son at the Litchfield cemetery down the road.

Drive-in movies live on in Illinois

LITCHFIELD, Ill.—Like an old actor drawing a blank, the white screen of the Sky View Drive-In looks across the corn and soybean fields of southern Illinois. It is springtime. And the Sky View is the last drive-in movie theater on the Illinois stretch of Route 66.

The Sky View opened in June 1950.

And it opens for another season Friday night. Located on 16 acres of neatly manicured grass, the Sky View is directly south of the M & M Service Co., a corn and soybean fertilizer plant on Old Route 66 North in Litchfield (217-324-4451). Only the plant's five 200-foot corn and soybean silos distort the view of the starry springtime night.

Litchfield is about a 45-minute drive south of Springfield on Interstate 55.

The Sky View is all about 1955.

Admission is $1 per person; kids 5 and under get in free. There are wooden park benches in front of the snack shop so people can leave their cars and watch a movie under the moonlight. Many locals drive their pickup trucks into the Sky View and set up lawn chairs in the back of their trucks. Starting on Memorial Day, the Sky View will be open seven nights a week.

The Sky View is owned by Norman and Del Paul of Carlinville. Norman is 81. The Pauls bought the Sky View in 1980 from the Frisina family, who operated southern Illinois movie theaters from the 1950s through the 1980s. The Pauls also own the twin-indoor Marvel Theater in Carlinville and the Orpheum Theater in Hillsboro, Ill. And in 1960 the Pauls constructed a 14-lane bowling alley in Carlinville. Norman, Del and his late mother named it Bowlero Lanes.

I love that name.

The Pauls go back to the days when drive-ins ruled the nights in southern Illinois. They also owned the Diane in Carlinville, which they built in October 1951 and closed in the mid-1980s. The Pauls were losing money on the Diane, which was named after their firstborn daughter. There is a happy ending to Diane's story. Today daughter Diane Brunton, 51, is a judge in Springfield. Her sister Denise Ambrose, 47, is an appellate prosecutor for the State of Illinois.

Photo by Dave Hoekstra.

The Diane wasn't the only theater in southern Illinois to hit hard times. The Falcon Drive-In in Collinsville is now part of the Cahokia Mounds site. The 66 Drive-In in Springfield is gone, and the Bel Air Drive-In on Route 66 in Mitchell, Ill., is in ruins.

According to the spring issue of "Route 66 Magazine," 35 of the 42 drive-ins along the 2,448 miles of Route 66 are gone or are in ruins. Appropriately, last June the Sky View was inducted into the Route 66 Hall of Fame at the Dixie Truck Stop in McLean, Ill.

"Drive-ins are few and far between," Paul said last week while waiting for a popcorn delivery at the Sky View. "The advent of daylight-saving time hurt drive-in theaters the most. You can't get started until it's dark enough, and that means around the longest day of the year, you don't start until 9 p.m. Then, there's no question that cable and VCRs have cut into the theater business drastically.

"To be frank with you, my drive-in theater in Litchfield will make more money than either of my indoor theaters. I knew the Sky View had potential. There's a lot of towns around Litchfield, and you're real close to I-55."

Drive-ins still have a parking spot in America's heart. On May 26 the U.S. Postal Service will dedicate a stamp to drive-ins. For each decade of the 20th century, the Postal Service compiled a list of 30 subjects and solicited votes through ballots at post offices and on the Internet. The top 15 choices for each decade will become stamps. The drive-in was the top choice for the 1950s. ("I Love Lucy" was second, Dr. Seuss' *The Cat in the Hat* was third.)

Despite changing times, Paul is proud of his steadfast $1 per person admission policy. That means he operates the drive-in strictly on volume and money he makes from a concession stand stocked with popcorn (which ranges from 65 cents to $2.75), soda (90 cents to $1.40 for a whoozy 32-ouncer), lemonade, nachos, foot-long hot dogs ($1.65) and cheeseburgers. "If the volume drops off, we'd have to increase our admission price," he said. "But attendance keeps increasing every season."

According to Sky View manager Carol Stuttle, the drive-in averages 700 to 1,000 people on a typical good-weather Friday and Saturday night. That translates to about 400 automobiles. Numbers drop to 200 people during the week. And every Thursday is bargain night, $3 for a carload.

The Sky View regularly draws fans from Chicago and Springfield, as well as Route 66 aficionados. "Last week we had people from Texas who came in a motor home," Stuttle said during an interview at the Sky View last fall. "They asked if it was OK to bring a motorhome in a drive-in. We don't care."

A Litchfield native, Stuttle is beginning her 31st season working at the Sky View. She's managed the drive-in since 1992, and one of the Sky View's clear charms is how slow it has been in responding to progress. Stuttle, 47, only installed air conditioning in the snack shop in 1995.

"The one major change we've made in the last few years is that we went to the FM radio frequency for audio," said Stuttle, who by day is a lands administrator for the State of Illinois in Springfield. "[Car] speakers are getting harder to come by. You can't get parts for them, and I don't have anybody to work them. We also had to take the playground area out a couple years ago because of insurance reasons, but we still keep a [grassy] area where kids can bring toys and bat balls around."

Going to the Sky View is like an archeological dig for drive-in buffs. In 1982 a tornado blew down the theater's original wooden screen, which was adorned with a bright shooting star. It's been replaced by a plain white steel screen. Near the front of the drive-in, a weatherbeaten red and white wooden sign warns customers, *Danger! Your tires will be blown*, fair warning back in the days when people used to sneak in the drive-in. Paul said, "Sharp prongs would poke a hole in your tire, but there's nothing there to damage your tires anymore. With $1 admission, people don't bother to sneak in."

Although Paul has been in the business for 40 years, he doesn't have a favorite drive-in movie. "I can't answer that," he said with a chuckle, "because I haven't seen a movie at the drive-in for a long, long time. But I don't like films with violence, and I don't go for 'R' movies.

"Like 'Analyze This.' I haven't seen that film, but I was told the language all the way through was terrible. We're finishing three more nights of it at my theater in Carlinville, and in most cases we would move it to my theater in Hillsboro. But I told my booker I didn't want to move it because it wasn't doing any business, and people in small towns don't like R-rated movies. And I know 'Analyze This' was an above-average grosser."

Last season the Sky View showed hit films such as "Titanic," "My Giant" and "The Horse Whisperer" that were on their way out from Paul's theaters in Carlinville and Hillsboro.

April 18, 1999

Red's sails into sunset
Route 66 drive-in fades into landscape

SPRINGFIELD, Mo.—The book has been closed on a classic American tale of big hamburgers, narrow highways and honky-tonk music. It is a Red, white, and blue story. Sheldon "Red" Chaney opened a hamburger stand 50 years ago this summer on old Route 66 in Springfield, the Gateway to the Ozarks. Red's Giant Hamburg was the birthplace of the drive-up order window. It was easily recognized by the 16-foot-tall sign with the word *Giant* running horizontally, and the *Hamburg* running vertically along the post. Red Miscalculated the space for the "er" in *Hamburger.*

In 1982, Lou Whitney and D. Clinton Thompson, then of the Morells and now of the Skeletons, wrote a popular rockabilly song about the hamburger joint. Of course, the song was called "Red's." And the hamburger stand was featured in a 1984 Rolling Stone magazine article on Route 66.

Red was born in Ithaca, N.Y., and reared in west suburban St. Charles. He ran Red's with wife Julia, a native of Downstate Palmyra, from 1947 until they closed it in 1984. The Chaneys lived behind the rickety frame restaurant on the west side of town.

Red died on June 2, 1997. He was 81. The restaurant was torn down exactly two weeks before he died.

"Red had as much fun after he retired as he did when he was working," Whitney said last week. "I don't think that had much to do with his death. Red was out there when they tore it down." Red died of numerous ailments at St. John's Regional Health Center in Springfield. During the demolition, Chaney told the Springfield News-Leader, "The old place had become an eyesore."

But Red has an ear for music.

"You'd go into his place and there'd by hillbilly music blaring out of a crappy eight-track," said Whitney, who last saw Red a few months ago. "Red had this one beat he'd play on the register."

Whitney tapped out a happy dance with the tip of a pencil.

"That was Red's beat," Whitney said. "He'd play that to everything. He'd start beating a couple of spoons like that. Then he had tricks where he'd slide the root beer down to you.

"I took the Del Lords [the defunct New York rock band led by former Dictator Scott Kempner] in there when they were recording here. They wanted to go there two times a day, every day." Red's was a regular stop for anyone who recorded at Whitney's Studio, where more recently he worked with Jonathan Richman and Robbie Fulks, and engineered the song "Why Would You Wanna Live" for Wilco.

Red and Julia always returned the favor, checking out Morells or Skeletons concerts when they could. They met at an Army dance in 1943 while Red was stationed in Denver. After three dates they were married.

Last summer I stopped in to see Red and Julia. They were living in the same home they bought in 1947. Red recalled their first dance together. "It was the same kind of music Lou [Whitney] plays," Red said. "Same type of dance, same kind of good beat. A lot of big bands played it that way."

Julia smiled at her husband. She walked over to a dresser and tugged at a rickety drawer. It contained invitations to their 1993 golden anniversary party, which read, *"After 50 years they're still cookin'!"*

Spiced by Thompson's sizzling guitar licks, Red's went this way:

"Hamburger, cheeseburger, lettuce and tomato

Brown beans root beer, french fried potato

It's a crazy little place on the west side of town

Got a five-five Buick knee deep in the ground. . . ."

Red had planted a 1955 Buick in the parking lot to prevent customers from backing into homemade "Giant Hamburg" sign.

Red was honored that someone wrote a song about his crazy little place. "That really got me," he said. In confessional tones, Julia added, "Every once in a while we still play the song in our car."

On the record, Red's was known for big homemade burgers, blended with water and kidney suet. The hard fat that once enclosed the beef kidney enhanced the flavor. Off the record, Red would share a couple of snorts of mead with regulars like Whitney.

"His mead was whiskey made from fermenting honey," Whitney said. "Or something like that. If you were hanging around at closing time, he'd shut the door and give you a little of that mead.

We'd perk ourselves up."

Red was always perky. He was known to dance behind the counter. In the days before his red hair turned white, he'd slide up to tables on his knees, arms loaded with platters of burgers. Red played pre-industrial rock on his refrigerator door. "I always played fast music," he told me. "And I played it loud, so people couldn't sit there and read the paper. I wanted to get people in and out."

Red said that after World War II, his father sold his restaurant-tavern near St. Charles. He took a year off to go on the road. "Dad came through this town, backed up and looked at it again," Red recalled. "He said he was going to buy right here. It was just a two-lane highway, but it was packed all the time."

Photo by Dave Hoekstra.

Julia and Red.

Red's father recruited his son and new daughter-in-law to run the operation. Red was a resourceful restaurateur, which is how the drive-in window was born. Old Route 66 was so busy with automobile traffic, the supply couldn't keep up with the demand.

"Down 66 here, I had a buddy who had one of those intercoms we'd use in the Army," Red explained. "With a speaker on one end of a line. Before I saw that, I was thinking of putting a roller-conveyer from the lot to the window. But the speakers would work better. Stuff would fall off a conveyer. So I started building it from his intercom. I built it overnight.

"And I had it working the next morning. At first, people were scared. They'd drive up to the speaker, talk to it and say, 'Hey, this is spooky! A box is talking to me; let's get outta here.' I'd say this was around the early 1950s."

Red shut down the restaurant on Oct. 31, 1984, in honor of Julia's 70th birthday. Julia and Red started to laugh. "We both walked out the day we closed it," Red said, grinning, as if he had pulled a fast one.

Julia added, "We never even cleaned it up!"

Last month, Julia buried her dancing partner next to her plot in a hilltop cemetery in Palmyra, southwest of Springfield, Ill. "I miss him," she said last week over the phone. "He wasn't feeling well at all. But it's tough after you've been married to someone for 53 years. I told him to keep going so we could celebrate our 55th. . . ."

Whitney, Thompson, and the rest of the Springfield-based Skeletons appear at 10 p.m. Aug. 23 at FitzGerald's, 6615 W. Roosevelt in Berwyn. Take time to request "Red's." And then dance from the bottom of your heart.

July 27, 1997

Honky-tonk heaven
Country legends raise voices to Cain's 75th

TULSA, Okla.—Country legend Merle Haggard looks down from the stage at Cain's Ballroom, a hop, skip, and a jump from Tulsa's skid row. A capacity crowd of 1,000 people has packed the rustic dance hall on a hot September night.

The room lacks air conditioning. Instead, a soft breeze is stirred by tall industrial fans whose silver blades spin around like old Haggard 45s. Warm beads of condensation trickle down Budweiser tall-boys.

A sweaty Haggard says, "This is one of the last few honky-tonks in the world." He then launches into Bob Wills' 1950 hit "Faded Love," dueting with his ex-wife and background singer Bonnie Owens (also ex-wife of country star Buck Owens). The places goes up for grabs.

Everyone is up for raisin' Cain.

This year marks the 75th anniversary of Cain's Ballroom, 423 N. Main St. (918-584-2309). Haggard and his band are part of the Dust Bowl dance hall's anniversary concert series. Haggard—who

Photo by Dave Hoekstra.

cites Wills as a major influence—also is the first living inductee into the Cain's Ballroom Walk of Fame on the sidewalk outside the ballroom. (Wills was first, but he died in 1975.)

Built from natural limestone, Cain's was the home of Bob Wills and the Texas Playboys who broadcast live from the ballroom from 1934 to the early 1960s on KVOO Radio. Good call. Wills was from Limestone County, Texas.

Western swing music evolved out of this Oklahoma state landmark because Madison W. Cain opened the room in 1933 as Cain's Dancing Academy. On-the-spot teachers would give lessons in all dance forms—foxtrot and waltz as well as Texas two-step.

The springloaded curly maple dance floor is the last one left in America. It is mounted on sets of Dodge truck springs. The building was constructed in 1924 as an auto garage. In the late 1920s, original owner Tate Brady turned the building into the Louvre Ballroom, a dime-a-dance hall, or "taxi dance" ballroom. The original ticket booth is still standing, taking on all-comers.

Locals know Cain's as the connection for bootleg whiskey. Prohibition wasn't repealed in Oklahoma until 1957, and the phone booth at Cain's was filled to the brim with business cards of bootleggers willing to meet clients in the alley. When overserved patrons go too rowdy, Wills would tap the microphone with the bow of his fiddle and launch into a church hymn.

Most of country music's essential artists have appeared at Cain's, including Hank Williams, Patsy Cline, Spade Cooley, Roy Rogers, Ernest Tubb, and Hank Thompson. Their 3-by-4-foot color-tinted photographs surround the dance floor.

Grammy-winning Asleep at the Wheel vocalist Ray Benson has been known to go down the rows of photos and call out dance tunes that correspond with the picture of each legend. Asleep at the Wheel will play Western swing and traditional country Oct. 16 at Cain's. Road trip.

A red neon star flickers from the ceiling over the center of the dance floor, which is filled with folding chairs and tables for the Haggard concert. About half of the audience consists of rugged Tulsa old-timers, who go back to the wildcat 1920s when everyone traveled to Tulsa to strike oil. Today there are only nine oil companies headquartered in town. Most companies left Tulsa for more fertile ground in Houston and Dallas.

Tulsa was built on the working class ethic of oil barons Waite

Phillips (Phillips 66), J. Paul Getty, and William G. Skelly. After working in the oil fields all day, at night Cain's was a popular place to play.

Rosetta Wills, 59, is Bob Wills' oldest daughter. Last year she wrote *The King of Western Swing: Bob Wills Remembered* (Billboard Books, $21.95). In a phone conversation from her home in Austin, Texas, Wills says, "When I go to autograph singings, everyone has a story about Cain's. The most popular one is how they met their wives or husbands there. People remember their parents or grandparents going and taking their kids. They used to have benches that lined the walls. They remember sleeping on the benches while everyone danced.

"Dad played there in the early 1960s, and I used to go there a lot when I was in my 20s, which was great. Not all his children were able to do that. They didn't live there, or they were younger. That room is like a museum."

In the 1970s and 1980s Cain's owner Larry Shaeffer expanded Cain's mystique by featuring non-country acts like Elvis Costello, Patti Smith, Muddy Waters, and the Sex Pistols. Rock 'n' Roll Hall of Famers Jerry Lee Lewis and Little Richard have appeared at Cain's this year as part of the 75th anniversary celebration. Los Lobos plays Cain's at 8 p.m. Oct. 19, and alternative rockers Primus hit the dance hall at 8 p.m. Nov. 26.

"Non-country artists have complete reverence for this place," Shaeffer says before the Haggard concert. "Beck [Hansen] came into this building when the band loaded in at 11 a.m. Usually, the artists go back to the hotel and sleep. Beck stayed here all day. He walked around. He said he wanted to hear stories."

Shaeffer has owned Cain's since 1976. The Tulsa native also uses the ballroom as headquarters for his Little Wing Productions, which books rock, jazz and contemporary Christian concerts in the Tulsa area. During Bob Wills' heyday, Cain's was owned by the Texas Playboys manager O. W. Mayo, which is why most of the portraits are autographed to Mayo. He installed the portraits between 1944 and 1950.

Marie Myers, an 83-year-old widow from nearby Muskogee (as in Haggard's 1969 hit "Okie from Muskogee") who met her husband at a Bob Wills dance, bought the ballroom from Mayo in 1972 but failed to make Cain's click. Shaeffer purchased Cain's from Myers.

Shaeffer's office is a cornucopia of country music lore, ranging from original Ernest Tubb movie posters to love letters from Bob Wills' female fans he found stuck in a wall during a remodeling project. But a stunning highlight is a red vinyl couch—emblazoned with the Cain's logo—that Hank Williams slept on in October 1952 when he was too drunk to play his second show.

"He got someone to run beer to him all day," says Shaeffer, who was handed down the story from Mayo. "So he's toasted. Both shows were sold out. He got through the first show, although it took two people to hold him up. Hank laid down on the couch between shows, and they couldn't wake him up. He was mixing morphine [for a bad back] with liquor. This was 10 weeks before he died."

Mayo, who died in 1994 at age 93, told Shaeffer he didn't know what to do. He finally came clean and told the audience that Hank was too drunk to perform and that his backing band, the Drifting Cowboys, would play without him. Money would be refunded as fans left Cain's.

"Well, someone opened the door to the office and a line formed," Shaeffer says. "People filed past [a blank Hank] like a funeral viewing. The band played on, and not one person asked for their money back."

It's impossible to describe how much Cain's means to a tried and true country traditionalist like Haggard. In 1973 in Dallas, Haggard and his band

Photo by Dave Hoekstra.

Merle Haggard raisin' Cain for the ballroom's 75th in 1999.

played on Wills' final recording session at Wills' request.

"I'll tell you how much it means," Shaeffer says. "In the early 1980s I booked Merle into Knoxville, Tenn., on a Friday and Asheville, N.C., on a Saturday. Merle always does a medley of Bob Wills songs, and the band used to pass around a bottle of whiskey during that.

"At the Asheville sound check, the building manager says, 'Tell that S.O.B. that if he drinks on my stage he's going to jail.' I sugarcoat it and tell Merle, 'The building director says that there's a city ordinance that if you drink in public, you'll get arrested, so please don't.' And Merle says, 'Get me a bottle of Jack Daniel's. I'm going to drink all night!' The show starts and sure enough, he gets arrested."

Shaeffer sprung Haggard out of jail and around 5 a.m. the promoter and the problem repaired to a Denny's across the North Carolina-Tennessee state line. Shaeffer was wearing a Cain's Ballroom softball jersey.

"Merle says, 'Hey, I got a million Cain's stories,' and then he says, 'In a week we end our tour in Ft. Worth. The next day I'm going to come to Tulsa, take my band to Johnnie Lee Wills' [Bob's brother] Western Store, get them all white shirts, string ties, and Stetson hats, and we're going to come to Cain's and do a radio broadcast."

Haggard was not paid for the gig, and Shaeffer did not charge admission. According to Shaeffer, Haggard walked on stage and said, "I'm going to kick the - - - of the first S.O.B. that asks me to play a Merle Haggard song." Haggard and the Strangers proceeded to do Bob Wills music the rest of the night.

But of all the acts Shaeffer has brought into Cain's, the punk-rock Sex Pistols provide everlasting memories. The Sex Pistols played Cain's on Jan 11, 1978. "They were young kids drinking hot Heineken beer all day long," says Shaeffer, 51, as he leans toward the late Sid Vicious' autograph on the office wall. "The Sex Pistols played seven shows in America. Number six was here. They played the night before at Dewey Groom's Longhorn Ballroom in Dallas. I've got a picture of their marquee. It says: 'TONIGHT: THE SEX PISTOLS, TOMORROW: MERLE HAGGARD.' [Pistols manager] Malcolm McLaren was very bright.

"When the Pistols came to America, he knew he could do New York and Chicago. He elected to take a swing through the South because there would be trouble. And with trouble came publicity.

The Pistols were raucous, but they didn't utter one bit of profanity onstage. It was pure, arrogant, aggressive rock 'n' roll. I'd never heard that before. They showed up about 10 a.m. and lingered around all day. Johnny Rotten and Sid Vicious were screaming at each other getting drunker and drunker. My little anemic secretary finally threw [them] out of the ballroom."

Shaeffer is interrupted by one of his employees. There's a problem afoot in the dance hall. It seems that Haggard's fans drank all the beer. And the headliner has yet to hit the stage. "Order cans or bottles, whatever you can get quicker," Shaeffer says with an Oklahoma calm in his voice. "We only lose money when we run out." The help shuffles away.

He smiles.

"If there's a message that I would send you, it's that Bob and the Texas Playboys were a *religion* to blue collar people," Shaeffer says. "When you were from Oklahoma and you traveled abroad, you didn't say, 'I know Will Rogers.' You'd say, 'I know Bob Wills.' That summed it up."

And to know Bob Wills, you must know Cain's Ballroom.

September 19, 1999

Nothing's lost on him
It's a hoard fest at Roy Rogers museum

If a museum pays tribute to a trail of small moments, then Roy Rogers lived mighty large.

I've been to the Louvre, the Liberace Museum, and I've spent several days lost in the Baseball Hall of Fame. These hallowed halls have got nothing on the Roy Rogers-Dale Evans Museum in Victorville, Calif. Built to resemble an 1860s fort, the museum is a mile off of Route 66, north of San Bernardino. I visited the museum during my 1992 journey from Chicago to Los Angeles. I will never forget it. It makes my compulsion for collecting Wheaties boxes seem normal.

After Rogers died earlier this month, fans reminisced about how the King of the Cowboys had his beloved golden palomino, Trigger, stuffed and put on display in the museum after this horse died in 1965 at age 33. That's just the tip of the pistol.

This guy never threw anything away.

The 30,000-square-foot Roy Rogers-Dale Evans Museum features every pocketwatch and wristwatch Rogers ever owned, a set of tools that belonged to Roy's dad and dozens of autographed baseballs. There are shelves with old pocketknives and shelves with old bottlecaps. A trip to the Roy Rogers-Dale Evans Museum is like going to the Kane County Flea Market.

"And don't forget the rock collection," said Roy's 22-year-old grandson Dustin in a phone interview last week. "He was an avid rock collector. He had his own rock cutter and polisher. He really loved life, and the museum shows that. Back in the 1960s, my grandmother [Dale] used to get all over his case. She'd go, 'Why are you saving all that stuff? It's ridiculous!'

"But as a child he went to the Will Rogers Museum [in Claremore, Okla.], and it was such a disappointment to him because there was very little memorabilia from Will. So much of it was destroyed or it just wasn't kept. He always said if he ever made it big, he'd keep everything. And the man absolutely kept everything."

And Trigger's not the only animal standing up for posterity. The horses Buttermilk, Nellybell, and Trigger Jr. are stuffed and an display along with Roy and Dale's dog (?!) Bullet. The museum is easily spotted from the highway because of an extra-large Trigger replica looking towards the heavens.

In *Happy Trails, Our Life Story*, Rogers wrote, "Everything we've ever done is right here for everyone to see. I've always liked to save things. No matter what came my way. . ."

Rogers was born Leonard Slye in Cincinnati. In 1930, the family of modest means migrated to California, where Rogers picked fruit and drove a truck before forming his first band, which evolved into the Sons of the Pioneers.

The band's fans are affectionately known as P-nuts.

Dustin Rogers works at the museum full time and is a part-time firefighter in neighboring Adelanto, Calif. He said his grand-father was a regular visitor to the museum until about a month and a half before his death. He'd drop in and talk to visitors. But he didn't sign autographs.

"He rode a little four-wheel car, appropriately named Trigger III," Rogers said. "He shared stories with people, and people would share stories with him. He'd ride by and say good morning to Trigger every morning and went on about his business the rest of the day." Rogers underwent triple by-pass surgery in 1978 and was hospitalized several times in 1996 and 1997.

Since Rogers died on July 6, business had been booming at the museum. On July 12, the day after Rogers was buried in Sunset Hills Mortuary, 11 miles down the road in Apple Valley, the museum attracted 472 people, according to Rogers. A typical Sunday draws around 120 Rogers devotees.

And business will go on as usual, just as Roy would have wanted it. Rogers said, "The only thing that will change is that we're adding a display case in memory of Roy's life."

Plans are also moving ahead for RogersDale USA, a Western-themed retail entertainment center that will include restaurants, a theater, and a 150-room hotel. The entertainment complex will be up and running in Murietta, Calif., before 2000. Murietta is 1 hour and 15 minutes from Victorville.

RogersDale officials asked the city of Victorville for $15 million in aid that would help build roads and sewers for the $40 million project. They intended to build the complex on 76 acres adjacent to the Roy Rogers-Dale Evans Museum. They were denied and turned to Murietta.

"We'll also have a completely closed arena in the complex, and they're looking to put a minor league hockey team in there," Rogers said. (Did I hear someone say the Murietta Triggers?) "We'll also have concerts and rodeo events in the arena. It will be something."

The Roy Rogers-Dale Evans Museum is at 15650 Seneca Rd., Victorville, Calif. It is open 9 a.m.-5 p.m. daily except Easter, Thanksgiving and Christmas. Admission is $7 for adults, $6 for seniors 65 and older, $5 for children and free for kids 5 and younger. Call (760) 243-4547.

July 26, 1998

Postmarks from the edge
Artist chases dream out on the open road

Ken Turmel had 35 different jobs at the Oklahoma City post office between 1979 and 1994. He was a box clerk. He delivered express mail. During the day Turmel had the world in his hands. But one night he dreamed of how to make his mark in the world.

Turmel saw himself traveling around Oklahoma. He was collecting postmarks on a sheet of paper.

A dream? It sounds more like hazing.

But Turmel's vision has materialized into "Route 66 and More," a majestic 2-by-3-foot print that features more than 250 postmarks from every post office along old Route 66.

The postmarks have been signed, sealed, and delivered on a map of the eight Route 66 states. There are even postmarks from towns that no longer exist, like the dried-up railroad town of Cadiz, Calif. Turmel obtained the postmark from the shacklike post office in Cadiz on Dec. 29, 1995, its last day of business.

Turmel, 41, calls his work *postmarkart*. President Clinton, country singer Reba McEntire, and Moody Blues members Justin Hayward and Mike Pinder are among those who own Turmel's prints.

Isn't life strange?

"I had never collected stamps," Turmel said from Midwest City, the Oklahoma City suburb where he lives with wife Melissa and their six children. "I never collected postmarks. The Cherokee Strip postage stamp for the centennial of the Oklahoma land run had just come out. It was the spring of 1993. Compelled by the dream, I spent 10 months [driving 5,000 miles] obtaining all the centennial postmarks and putting them on one piece of paper.

"I felt this was from the Lord. A lot of people don't like to hear that, but I'm never going to deny it. I was a Christian before the dream. I always like to say grace before I eat."

In the mid-1980s Turmel was songwriter-keyboardist in the Precedents, an Oklahoma City-based Christian pop band. By the spring of '94, word had gotten out about Turmel's Cherokee "Adventure Centennial Document" *postmarkart*. Postmasters, collectors, and museums from across the heartland tracked down Turmel, asking where they could obtain copies of his work.

"I never intended to make prints," he said. "That's what initiated lithograph limited-edition prints."

At the same time, he met Route 66 author-historian Michael Wallis, who lives in Tulsa, Okla. Wallis urged Turmel to *postmarkart* Route 66. "I said, 'Michael, it took me so long to do one state,' " Turmel recalled. "And you want me to do eight?' I wasn't sure I could handle it."

But in the intrepid spirit of Wallis, Woody Guthrie, Will Rogers and other children of the Mother Road, Turmel took off down Route 66. The passage to postmarks began in September, 1995, when the Route 66 Museum opened in Clinton, Okla. "They had a pictorial postmark commemorating Route 66 and the opening of the museum," Turmel said. "I drove there and got the first official postmark from Clinton."

Turmel tooled around the old road in his 1986 Toyota 4-Runner. He listened to cassette tapes by the Beatles, Julian Lennon, the Brian Setzer Orchestra, and Nat King Cole, who covered the song "(Get Your Kicks on) Route 66." It was impossible for Turmel to drive Route 66 in one swoop, since pictorial postmarks are only issued at certain times of the year for specific celebrations.

"I had to jog constantly from state to state to get all the first-day issues I could," he said. "And I drove the 4-Runner for the entire project. It's got 208,000 miles on it." Turmel finally completed the Route 66 *postmarkart* piece last May.

He titled his work "Route 66 and More" because it includes a few non-66 diversions, including postmarks from the Grand Canyon, Disneyland in Anaheim, Calif. and all the state capitals from Route 66 states. That meant Turmel drove all the way to Sacramento, Calif., just to get the politically correct postmark.

Turmel figures the "Route 66 and More" *postmarkart* cost him more than $6,500 for gasoline, oil, tires, phone calls, motels and—last, but not least—postage stamps.

"If it was good weather, I always tried to find a campground," he said. "It was to save some money and actually stay to the idea of being outside. One night I just slept on the side of the Rio Grande River in Texas."

Like the postal service itself, nothing could stop Turmel.

He absolutely had to obtain a postmark at the Supai, Ariz., post office, where mail is still carried by mule. The postmark commemorated the 100th anniversary of Supai, an Indian Reservation town nestled in the Grand Canyon. The old road ends eight miles before the town begins. Supai has no paved streets and no one in town drives a car.

"You have to park and take a horse down a hill," Turmel explained. "Or you can take a helicopter and walk. I wanted to be authentic. I took the horse. It's a four-hour journey. I had a mule pulled behind me for my gear and artwork. I made a wax container for the artwork so it would be watertight. You can't take any chances with this art. One time it gets wet, it's ruined.

"Once down in Supai I asked the postmaster if anyone was crazy enough to bring such a large piece of work in to collect postmarks. Just like all the other 250-plus postmasters, he said, 'No one has ever come in here with something like this.' I stayed in the canyon overnight and transported the artwork back on the helicopter the next day."

Turmel was born just a few blocks from the end of Route 66 in Santa Monica, Calif. (it's never the beginning, since the migratory path went westward from Chicago). "When I was a kid I was a nut about traveling on that road," he said. "It wasn't so much that it was Route 66. It just happened it was the road my mom and dad traveled to go back to New Hampshire every year. The man in me met the child in me during this project. It got more personal than I thought it would. I met a lot of people on the road that reminded me of days gone by.

People like:

• **Steve and Glaida Funk**, who have operated Funks Grove Pure Maple Sirup Farm Since 1946. The seasonal sugar camp is located in a scenic grove full of hickories, oaks and sugar maple trees in Shirley, Ill., south of Bloomington and just north of the Dixie Truck Stop in McLean. (For information, call 309-874-3220.)

"The maple syrup just stuck in my brain all these years," Turmel said, no pun intended. "You just can't buy this stuff in the stores. Their hospitality impressed me. At seven in the morning, when most people would close the door and say, 'Come back later,' they invited me in for breakfast. They reminded me of the old days on the road when the warmth was overwhelming. Sometimes I even think I parked under the same tree my mom and dad parked at, trying to get out of the sun on the hot days driving down Route 66."

• **Hody Porterfield**, who teaches Native American traditions from his home in a canvas teepee next to the Big Texan Steak Ranch in Amarillo, Texas. Porterfield dresses in traditional buckskin and moccasins, and his teepee has no electricity. Porterfield, 50, was born on the Fourth of July.

"He's a very basic gentleman," Turmel said. "Nothing fancy about this guy, but he gets things done. He knows the ways of the Old West. He conducts classes on tomahawks. He'll shoot his bows and arrows in the [Big Texan] restaurant right when people are eating."

President Clinton heard about Turmel's work from Oklahoma Gov. Frank Keating. A friend of the *postmarkartist*, Keating has Turmel's prints hanging in the governor's mansion.

Turmel recalled, "President Clinton came to Oklahoma City to speak at the [Murrah Federal Building] bombing victim ceremony. The governor presented the president with my 'Oklahoma and Friends' print [a 1995 piece featuring historic postmarks from Arizona, Oklahoma, Texas, New Mexico, Colorado, Kansas, and Missouri]. Three weeks later I got a hand-signed thank you in the mail from President Clinton."

Turmel sells limited-editions of his work for $150. Turmel has been offered as much as $10,000 for the original Route 66 artwork, and it's been appraised at $25,000.

He's not into his art to make money, just to sustain his search for postmarks. "Money coming in now from the Route 66 project will help finance my next one, which is the California Gold Rush," Turmel said. "Jan. 24 is the 150th anniversary of the day [carpenter James W.] Marshall discovered gold at Sutter's Mill. I'll be in California on Jan. 24 to get that 150th postmark!"

January 18, 1998

DRIVE SOUTH

VEHICLE

P.

JF 99

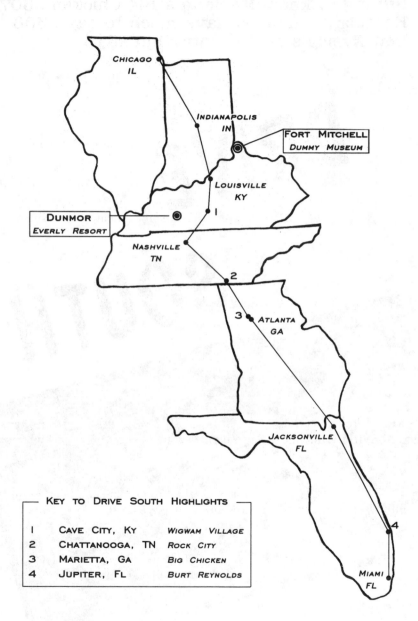

CHICAGO
IL

INDIANAPOLIS
IN

FORT MITCHELL
DUMMY MUSEUM

LOUISVILLE
KY

DUNMOR
EVERLY RESORT

1

NASHVILLE
TN

2

3 ATLANTA
GA

JACKSONVILLE
FL

4

MIAMI
FL

KEY TO DRIVE SOUTH HIGHLIGHTS

1	CAVE CITY, KY	WIGWAM VILLAGE
2	CHATTANOOGA, TN	ROCK CITY
3	MARIETTA, GA	BIG CHICKEN
4	JUPITER, FL	BURT REYNOLDS

Map by Lisa Day.

Whistlin' Dixie on long road south

CHATTANOOGA, Tenn.—The Dixie Highway is a red, white and blue ribbon that runs from Sault Ste. Marie, Mich., to Miami. The highway is nearly 4,000 miles in length, the longest single route in America.

The Dixie Highway—a.k.a. Route 1—is not as rugged as the 3,389 miles of the Lincoln Highway from New York to San Francisco, and it is not as quaint as the 2,448 miles of the world-famous Route 66.

Here, you wind down and start whistlin' "Dixie."

Route 66 and the Lincoln Highway were built as migratory paths for the promise of a better life. People relocated to California. The Dixie was all about the need for escapism. Get out of Dodge, get on the Dixie and enjoy the warmth of the South. And people came home again.

The Dixie turns through Chicago's south suburbs, swings by the Louisville Slugger Museum in Kentucky and rolls by the Wigwam Village, a roadside motel of 15 tepees in Cave City, Ky.

The Dixie sees Rock City in Lookout Mountain, Ga., incorporates the Big Chicken in Marietta, Ga., and takes respite at the Stephen Foster Memorial Park in White Springs, Fla.

And all through Florida, the Dixie is a tantalizing come-on-inn of classic roadside motels and flickering neon signs. The Suwanee River Motel in White Springs. The Happy Time Motel outside Jacksonville. The Sun n' Sand Hotel Court—recommended by late road food critic Duncan Hines. And the Hawaii Motel in—where else—Daytona Beach? (All Rooms $25, Remote TV!)

This year, the Society for Commercial Archeology's annual conference will explore automobile tourism and its impact on the commercial-built environment in the South, emphasizing the Dixie Highway. The conference begins Wednesday and runs through Saturday in and around Chattanooga. (For information, call Jeff Durbin, conference chairman, at 404-651-6546.)

"The Dixie brought Midwesterners South for the first time," said Durbin, a 37-year-old environmental review coordinator in the Historic Preservation Division of the Georgia Department of Natural Resources in Atlanta. "Trains had been doing that. But with the automobile, more middle-class people got the opportunity to head South. For the first time, you're getting automobile tourism that's related to weather."

Miami real estate magnate Carl Fisher is the father of the Dixie Highway. Fisher was a native of Greensburg, Ind. In 1913 he began buying real estate around Miami Beach, which was then nothing more than swamps, mangroves, and sawgrass. Fisher understood that a north-south highway was essential in promoting Florida tourism. He was also an early figure in the formation of the Lincoln Highway Association.

A former race car driver, Fisher held the world's two-mile record in 1904. (Two miles in 2:02 minutes.) He organized the Indianapolis motor speedway as an American proving ground. Fisher amassed a $100 million fortune before he was knocked out by the one-two punch of the Great Depression and the Labor Day, 1935, hurricane that also blew away Henry Flagler's overseas railroad through the Florida Keys. Fisher died in 1939 at the age of 65.

The Dixie Highway was christened in April, 1915, at the Governors Convention in Chattanooga. Attended by more than 5,000 people, the gathering adopted a resolution creating an organization "for the purpose of constructing a permanent highway from a point on the Lincoln Highway, near Chicago, Ill., via Chattanooga, Tenn., to Miami, Fla.," according to the 1994-95 fall/winter edition of the SCA Journal. The group intended to call the high-quality highway the Cotton States Route, but shortened the thought to the Dixie Highway.

The Chicago area became one of only three places in the United States where the Dixie intersected with the Lincoln Highway. A commemorative crossroads fountain is across the street from St. James Hospital in south suburban Chicago Heights. The 10-foot-tall fountain was dedicated on Oct. 13, 1916, to tie the North and South two transcontinental highways and help heal the wounds of the Civil War.

"We are also keen in recognizing the Dixie," said James Wright, a 39-year village trustee in Homewood, just north of Chicago Heights. "We take it for granted; we don't really know historically what it means. We want to start a heritage committee which will promote the Dixie in Homewood."

After the Dixie leaves Homewood, it zigzags south through Chicago Heights—where it becomes better known as Route 1—through Steger, Crete, Beecher, and out of the Chicago area.

Technically, the Dixie has two major divisions The Eastern Branch went from Michigan and hugged Florida's Atlantic coast to Miami. The Western Branch began in Michigan and went through the South to central Florida before winding down at Marco, Fla., at the Gulf of Mexico.

Durbin said, "In terms of tourism value, the Dixie also lent itself to important historic sites. The battlefields of the Civil War. The homes of prominent Southerners. And Northerners really picked up on some of those things because when the Dixie was built, this was only two or three generations after the Civil War was fought."

★ ★ ★

It seems like the Chicago Cubs last won the World Series during the Civil War. Nevertheless, when the Cubs began their magical 1998 season in Miami, I drove the Dixie from Chicago to Florida for opening day. Merely by following Highway 1 signage, I was able to trail the Dixie through south suburban Chicago, Danville, Indianapolis, Ind., and Kentucky.

Adhering to my baseball theme, a logical early stop was the Collectors Corner, Dixie Highway and Indiana Avenue in Beecher (708-946-2177). Collectors Corner owner Patrick Masino has some precious finds. I picked up some cashed 1970s paychecks from former Cubs Bill Bonham and Gene Clines. On Aug. 24, 1978, reserve outfielder Clines was paid $1,832. I paid $20 for this piece of paper. I save stuff like this. I guess that's why I like driving the Dixie Highway.

The above-average sports memorabilia shop and 1950s and 1960s collectibles store (with an emphasis on wacky 1960s board games) is located at the only stoplight in town, across the street from the Princess Cafe.

The Princess Cafe, 502 Dixie Hwy. (708-946-3141), is known around these parts of the Dixie for its medium-rare pepper steaks and porterhouse steaks and seafood selection. The wood-frame restaurant is housed in a former stage-coach stop that was built in 1863.

Heading out of Illinois and Indiana, I completed the baseball double play with a look-see at the Louisville Slugger Museum, the corner of 8th and Main in downtown Louisville (502-588-7228; closed on Sundays). It's a latter-day Dixie attraction that's easy to spot. A 120-foot-high Louisville Slugger baseball bat has been installed near the museum's front door.

The interactive museum includes a pitching exhibit where a visitor can stand in against a present-day pitcher on a 35-foot video screen. A replica press box features legendary calls from the likes of Red Barber, Harry Caray and Vin Scully. "Baseball's Revolutionary—Louisville Slugger Remembers Babe Ruth" is a collection of photographs and memorabilia reviewing and Hillerich & Bradsby Co.'s relationship with the Sultan of Swat. It is up through Oct. 31. The museum doesn't get much into new home run king Mark McGwire since he uses a bat from a competing company.

But you will never strike out at the Wigwam Village, farther on down the road at 601 N. Dixie Hwy. in scenic Cave City, Ky., about 90 miles north of Nashville. Should you elect do do bits and pieces of the Dixie, the hilly, mostly two-lane stretch from Cave City to Chattanooga, Tenn., is one of the most authentic drives because of the way it embraces the past.

The Wigwam Village was one of seven motel complexes built across America during the 1930s. Today only two remain: the Cave City location and on on Route 66, in Holbrok, Ariz. (A third Wigwam Village is in a fleabag state of disrepair in San Bernardino, Calif.)

The 15 steel and concrete wigwams were built in 1937. One- and two-bedroom wigwams encircle a well-manicured lawn, featuring a slide, swing set and picnic tables. The tepee ceilings are flat and low, and standing 6 feet 2 inches, I had to crouch in the shower in the sloped bathroom. A huge gift shop features postcards, Wigwam Village pennants and homemade miniature plaster-of-paris tepees, each one replication a motel room.

Ontario, Canada, native Ivan John bought the entire village three years ago. "This is something you must take pride in," he said during a conversation in his house, adjacent to the tepees. "It's an architectural wonder. The stretch of highway in front of the motel has been designated as a historic route. I'm still not sure in terms of income, but I'm not here for the money. I'm here to enjoy the people who enjoy it."

John is divorced. His cat, Boots, eased up on a sofa. Cars and trucks hummed by on Interstate 65, the big bypass just a few miles west of the Dixie. "You miss something like this on the interstates," he said. "America was built on small businesses like this. On the interstate, when you're gone, you're done. You don't know what America is about. And this is Americana. This is the only Wigwam Village left, with original furniture and artifacts. The one in Arizona is now a Super 8 and they put all their own things in there."

The Wigwam Village has been discovered by the Nashville music community. The site has been used for several video shoots, and CMT (Country Music Television) based a special around the roadside motel. Rooms are $30 for one bed, $40 two beds. (502-773-3381). The motel closes for the season Nov. 15 and will reopen March 1.

It's best to get a good night's rest in order to tackle Rock City Gardens, 1400 Patten Rd., Lookout Mountain, Ga., outside of Chattanooga, Tenn. (706-820-2531). Not much more than a freak of geology, Rock City personifies the 1920s and 1930s tourism charm of the Dixie.

Rock City is known throughout the South for its homespun promotions, which once included more than 900 barn paintings that announced "See Rock City" and roadside motels that featured ashtrays and doormats with the black and white Rock City logo. Some motels even stocked bars of soap with "See Rock City" imprinted on the wrappers.

Open year-round, Rock City lets visitors walk through strange rock formations and interact with wacky fairy tale characters and ol' Mother Goose (Martha Bell Miller, a retired elementary school teacher who was born and reared on Lookout Mountain). This is not a visit to do alone. Like I did.

On Saturday, Dixie Highway conference members will participate in a daylong bus tour of Chattanooga and its roadside environs, which include a 1924 monument erected by the Dixie Highway Association. The tour will conclude at Rock City, where participants will spend the afternoon.

After seeing Rock City, I followed the old highway through Georgia, cut across to Jacksonville, Fla., and began the best retro part of the drive, which are Florida's roadside motels and diners along Highway 1. This stretch of the Dixie incorporates towns like St. Augustine, Daytona Beach, Fort Pierce, West Palm Beach and Fort Lauderdale. If you love what landmark preservations term "ghost signs" and 1960s architecture, allow four or five days just for this historic stretch of the Dixie.

And for the weary traveler who needs to pull off the road for a rest, there may be no better place on the historic Dixie than the Burt Reynolds Park, 805 U.S. Highway 1, in Jupiter, Fla. (561-747-

6639).

The rest stop also includes the Florida History Center & Museum, housed in a Florida cracker-style building. Burt's cowboy boots and fellow Jupiter resident Perry Como's golf clubs are included in the museum. Burt visited his park once, when it first opened in 1988.

"Why is history important to anybody?" asked Wright, past president of the Homewood Historical Society, which doesn't have any Burt booty. "It's important to have a better understanding of where you come from. And it's important to have an understanding of what the Dixie Highway meant to people in the 1920s. People finally had the ability to go out and see more than what they could see in the simple environs of their own communities."

October 18, 1998

Photo by Dave Hoekstra.

Marietta's "Big Chicken."

And getting to know 'The Big Chicken'

MARIETTA, Ga.—No sooner did the Dixie Highway take me into northern Georgia than I began hearing about "The Big Chicken."

Turns out the Big Chicken was the coolest thing I saw on my road trip from Chicago to Miami. It is a 56-foot-tall red, white and yellow sheet metal chicken perched out in front of the Kentucky Fried Chicken, 12 N. Cobb Parkway on the old Dixie Highway (770-422-4716).

The Big Chicken was designed by Hubert L. Puckett, a 1957 Georgia Tech architecture graduate. The Big Chicken was originally installed in 1963 to advertise Johnny Reb's Chick, Chuck, and Shake drive-in restaurant. After Chick, Chuck, and Shake rattled and rolled out of business in 1966, Kentucky Fried Chicken took over.

A storm damaged the old bird in 1993. That spawned a national Save the Chicken campaign during which KFC was swamped with more than 10,000 calls and letters demanding the fowl be rebuilt. The roadside attraction was renovated at a cost of $1 million by KFC and its parent company, Pepsico. Engineers on the project discovered that acidic pigeon droppings had corroded the Big Chicken's infrastructure. Yuck!

But the best part of the renovation was that the chicken's off-yellow beak now opens and closes. The original hydraulic system had been shut down for more than 30 years.

These days the Big Chicken has its own gift shop and Web site (*www.bigchicken.com*). The gift shop includes shot glasses, pins, T-shirts, Christmas ornaments, postcards, birdhouses and, yes, even Big Chicken bean-bag toys. The gift shop is open from 10:30 a.m. to 2 p.m. daily.

During my visit, sales manager Bambi Palmer was working the gift shop. For grins, she had a replica costumed chicken's head that she claimed she only rents around April Fool's Day.

"The Big Chicken is a landmark around here," said the 45-year-old Palmer. "One time a retired pilot came in and told me they still make turns into Dobbins Air Force Base [in Marietta] by looking for the Big Chicken."

October 18, 1998

So much to say
Kentucky museum tells dummies' stories

FORT MITCHELL, Ky.—The Vent Haven Museum is nestled within three cottages on a quiet residential street lined with old sweet gum trees.

Still, the place calls out to you.

Vent Haven is the only museum in America dedicated to ventriloquism. It houses nearly 600 dummies or dolls that represent 20 countries. The oldest figure dates from 1860. There's also a library of 800 books on ventriloquism, sheet music, films, props and 80-year-old oil paintings with moveable mouths. Vent Haven, 33 W. Maple Ave., is one of the coolest museums in America. It is about a 20-minute drive from Cincinnati.

I walked into Vent Haven's main building (vent is a shortened term for entertainers who appear to make their voices come from other objects) and felt nearly 600 pairs of wide-eyed dummy pupils ᴗ.aring at me.

Vent Haven is open only during the summer. Its season begins tomorrow and runs through Sept. 30. The figures tell the story of an important piece of Americana. The museum can be enjoyed from an entertainment perspective and/or from the angle of folk art.

"Ventriloquism doesn't have the national exposure it once had," said curator Annie Roberts during a spring tour of the "camp" grounds. "There's no television venues for performers anymore. Johnny Carson was good about having vents on. [Carson began his career as a vent.] Professionals tell me that Jay Leno doesn't like variety acts so he's not open to vents very much."

That's Roberts' pun, not mine.

The woody community was assembled by Cincinnati businessman William "W.S." Berger, who fell in love with show business as a child after his actor father entertained him with hand puppets. Berger, who died in 1972 at age 94, lived on the grounds.

Berger worked for the Cambridge Title Co. of Cincinnati. He started as a teenage clerk in the mail room and eventually became company president. Vents were always his hobby, but he didn't become serious about collecting vent memorabilia until his retirement in 1947. That's about the time his wife gently persuaded him to get all the dummies out of the house and into the cottages. And most wives think that old baseball cards take up space.

"He had collected over 500 figures," said Roberts, 29. "However, he outlived his entire family. He had a son who fought in World War I who passed away. He had a grandson who died in a car accident."

Berger asked his attorneys to turn the collection into a private museum. They absorbed the money from Berger's estate and put it into a trust. The museum operates off the interest from the trust.

Photo by Lisa Day.

Charlie McCarthy.

Roberts is the museum's only employee. During the winter months she is an eighth-grade English teacher in nearby Erlanger, Ky. She is married to Jon, a home-builder. "When we started dating, I said, 'I have to tell you something' . . ." Roberts said with a long laugh. ". . .I'm involved with this museum. . ."

The museum annually attracts between 600 and 1,000 tourists. Roberts' aunt, Dorothy Millure, was the previous curator. The curator takes care of the grounds and the buildings and maintains the dummies. Roberts never gets the urge to goof around with members of the collection. "One of W.S.'s stipulations was that the curator *not* be a ventriloquist," Roberts said. "He thought vents would feel more comfortable donating their figure if they didn't think someone might give it a different personality."

Museum highlights include a Vent's Hall of Fame that features Shari Lewis (1991), Senor Wences (1989), Jimmy Nelson (1987), Paul Winchell (1986), Edgar Bergen (1988) and others.

The museum has a detailed 1981 replica of Bergen's Charlie McCarthy. The replica was made for Vent Haven with the permission of Frances Bergen, Edgar's widow and the mother of actress Candice Bergen. The original Charlie is in the Smithsonian Institution in Washington, D.C. (David Copperfield bought the second

McCarthy for $112,500 in a 1995 auction.] Bergen and McCarthy made their debut in 1925 at a Chicago amateur tryout that paid $5 a night.

Some Vent Heads can get pretty intense. Roberts said, "Collectors of McCarthy memorabilia will come in and say [she whispers], 'This is an excellent replica, because on the original Charlie the left nostril is slightly smaller than the right nostril.' They are really into it."

Vent Haven also has an entire cabinet of Edgar Bergen memorabilia, including silver spoons featuring McCarthy's head on the handle, Mortimer Snerd's teeth and a 1941 windup toy of McCarthy as a drummer boy.

In other worlds, George, Nettie, Happy, and Old Maid are papier-mache figures (circa 1910) from the Jules Vernon act. Vernon was a vaudeville ventriloquist who lost his eyesight as an adult. In fear of pity, he kept his blindness a secret from the audience. All the figures were connected and seated on a bench. A long black thread was attached between the bench and a spot in the wings. Vernon would use the string to get on and off the stage. Vernon's wife traveled with him and always set up the act. Vernon died in a 1931 hit and run accident.

Chicago figure maker Frank Marshall is recognized at the museum. He made Farfel, the long-snouted dog puppet, for Jimmy Nelson, a Chicago-born ventriloquist, and he carved Max, Turkey and Elmer who were in dozens of western movies in the 1930s and '40s. Known for predominant brown eyeliner and orange paint, these Marshall pieces are on display at Vent Haven.

But I was partial to Kenny Talk, Willie Talk and Deputy Diddy Talk, life-size troopers used in the 1940s and '50s by Kentucky State Patrolman Lee Allen Estes. Fully dressed in cop garb, the figures traveled around the state with Estes as he presented ventriloquism shows on safety. Kenny Talk was the star of the show. He had smoking and spitting mechanisms, and when he got real upset, smoke shot out of his ears.

There are also life-size dummies of Presidents Jimmy Carter and Ronald Reagan and an early 1900s "Sailor Boy," who smoked real cigarettes in a vaudeville act. A head rack features hand-carved wood and papier-mache noggins representing 29 countries. One early-1900s Swedish dummy head was made by a dentist, who used two pearl teeth capped with real gold for his sound bytes.

Photo by Lisa Day.

Dummies on display at Fort Mitchell's VentHaven Museum.

"Figure-making is a separate art from ventriloquism," Roberts explained. "Figure-making is a form of woodcarving. The hardest part of figure-making is the head. The body is basically a box they put clothes on." In a group, the smiling dummies radiate a warm and friendly vibe. They're not as scary as a group of clowns.

Every summer Vent Haven hosts an international ventriloquist ConVENTion at the Drawbridge Estate near the museum. This year's event is July 27-29. Previous guests have included Jay Johnson, star of the television sitcom "Soap," and Willie Tyler and Lester.

One section of the museum tells the story of Louisville, Ky., vent Cecil Carpenter and his little buddy Alex, who made their last stand at the ConVENTion.

"Cecil had a heart attack a month before he came to the convention," Roberts recalled. "His doctors told him not to come. But it was the highlight of his year. He had a great amateur act for open mike. He would tell 'Fractured Fairy Tales.' Alex would say, 'I'm going to tell you about Bleeping Seauty!' And Cecil would say, 'Don't you mean Sleeping Beauty?' They'd go back and forth off-kilter like that. He got up and did the act for open mic and went back to his room and suffered another [fatal] heart attack."

Cecil and Alex were buried together in a Goshen (Ind.) cemetery.

After spending a few hours at the museum—which I did—you begin to wonder how Berger accumulated all the stuff. Ebay wasn't even around. "He wrote letters," Roberts said. "He started the International Brotherhood of Ventriloquists. After he retired, this became his career."

Ventriloquism is an illusion, a trick of the ear.

Roberts picked up "Monkey," a "soft" figure that resembled, well, a chimp. "This is the way ventriloquism is headed," said Roberts, cradling the foam, terry cloth and fake fur "Monkey" in her arm. "Lots of ventriloquists have abandoned wooden figures. The soft figures are light and durable. And they look like Muppets, which gives the general public a connection."

Just like Detours, the human ear has an errant sense of direction. Roberts explained good vents take advantage of that. "The vents tell me the first thing you need to practice is where the dummy's eyes look," she said. "The dummy needs to make eye contact. Practice expressions. And the voice, of course, has to different than your own."

That's why Berger had such a rich life. He lived two lives in one.

He spent his last days in a local nursing home. The first day after Berger checked in, his attorney received a call from a nurse. The attorney figured Berger was despondent because he was apart from his beloved collection.

Instead, she reported he was in the day room entertaining fellow residents with his amateur vent act. Berger loved a captive audience. And he would be happy to know that the show still rolls on in the hills of northern Kentucky.

Vent Haven Museum is open by appointment only, Monday through Friday. The museum is closed on holidays. Admission donation is $2 for adults, $1 for children under 12. To get to Vent Haven from Cincinnati, take Interstate 75 South to the Dixie Highway exit. Turn right on Dixie Highway, make an immediate left on Maple. The museum is the fourth residence on the left. For more information, call Vent Haven at (859) 341-0461.

April 30, 2000

A real country inn

Don Everly's Kentucky resort
showcases music memorabilia

DUNMOR, Ky.—Everly's Lake Malone Inn is surrounded by intrigue, innocence and the beauty of southwestern Kentucky. The 55-room resort was purchased in 1997 by Don Everly of the Everly Brothers.

The inn is about 90 miles north of Nashville near Lake Malone State Park. The rustic stone and wood inn was built in 1974 by Evansville, Ind., oil baron Ray Ryan, who envisioned a private hunting lodge and Hollywood hideaway for his pallies Frank Sinatra, Dean Martin and William Holden.

Ryan didn't live long enough to see his dream played out. He met a mysterious demise in October 1977, when someone rigged a bomb to his Lincoln Continental parked at a health club in Evansville. Ryan had testified against Chicago hoodlum Marshall Caifano at his 1964 extortion trial.

At least there was no boom at the inn.

Everly's Lake Malone Inn is down the road from Brownie, the coal-mining town where Don was born in 1937 (Phil was born in Chicago in 1939). Don and Phil were paying guests at the inn for years. It served as their home base during the annual Everly Brothers Homecoming concerts held each Labor Day weekend in Central City, 15 miles north of Lake Malone.

"The inn is a semi-hobby," Don Everly said in a rare interview from his Nashville home. "The place has a lot of historic value. No one told me about Ray Ryan at first. He was obviously involved in some funny dealings."

Ryan had joint ownership in the Mt. Kenya Safari Club in Africa with film actor William Holden. Ryan wanted to build a private airstrip for his Hollywood cronies, but the locals nixed the idea. That's when Ryan decided to open the Lake Malone Inn to the public.

"It's a fun place," Everly said. "When we bought it, there were tusks everywhere, elephant's feet in the lobby. That's really not my taste. So we've changed it to a country-rock 'n' roll motif. And it's a place for all my *stuff.* I've got things I haven't taken out of storage in 20 years."

Photo courtesy of Everly's Lake Malone Inn.

The Everly Brothers, Phil *(left)* and Don *(right)*, were paying guests at the Lake Malone Inn for years before Don bought the place in 1997 as a "semi-hobby."

Between 1957 and 1967 the Everly Brothers landed 26 top 40 Billboard hit singles, 15 of which cracked the top 10: harmony-filled ballads like "Bye Bye Love," "Cathy's Clown," "Devoted to You," "All I Have To Do Is Dream," "When Will I Be Loved," and others.

The Everly Brothers inspired Simon & Garfunkel, Emmylou Harris, The Byrds, Gram Parsons, and the Beatles. The inn's colonial country restaurant is lined with autographed pictures of friends such as Chet Atkins, actor/singer Harry Dean Stanton and Paul and Linda McCartney.

"You gotta like country cookin' to eat there," Everly said. "I grew up on beans and cornbread. That's all our family could afford." Everly's father Ike was a coal miner and on weekends Ike and wife Margaret performed throughout the Midwest as country singers and musicians. Ike taught flat-picking guitar to Merle Travis—playing the bass strings with the thumb while using a flat pick on the upper strings. Travis' choked style was passed on to country guitar virtuosos such as Chet Atkins and Doc Watson.

"The catfish [$8.59 for the platter] and fried chicken [lemon-peppered chicken is $7.49] is good," Everly continued. "And Ellie May [Steinbrink, cook-dishwasher] has been making coleslaw in the place since it opened. It's Kentucky coleslaw. It doesn't have mayonnaise in it. It's a sweet, vinegar coleslaw." And don't miss the Lake Malone Old Kentucky Favorite Breakfast ($8) with sugar-cured ham and red-eye gravy.

The walls of the lodge-like lobby are lined with Everly Brothers memorabilia, including gold records, a certificate commemorating the Everly Brothers' 1986 induction into the Rock and Roll Hall of Fame and a Decca 45 of Kitty Wells' 1954 hit "Thou Shalt Not Steal," which was written by Don Everly and was one of the Everlys' first successes.

"I'm still working on that lobby," said Everly, who stays at the inn every couple of weekends. "I want to put a guitar chandelier in there. I'm trying to get Gibson [guitar company] to put together something. I hate to use guitars that are still viable, but I gotta figure out how to do it. And I have some old guitars I want to put in there, but again, I hate to put a rare instrument that should be displayed behind glass. But I'll do it."

Rooms range from $47 to $57 a night. Our spacious room included a working fireplace, Gideon Bible and a partial view of the small Lake Adela, named after Everly's wife of two years. Her twin sister inspired the George Strait song "Adalida." "Getting married changed my life," Everly said of his fourth marriage. "I was a real scoundrel. It was like getting religion."

The inn's lobby has a modest selection of biographies of the Everly Brothers, Bo Diddley and others for guests unable to get to sleep at night.

Lake Malone State Park encompasses a 788-acre lake and 338-acre forest filled with hardwood trees, mountain laurel, holly and wildflowers. The park's recreational facilities include a boat dock with 72 rental slips, fishing, camping, hiking and a sand beach that is open from Memorial Day through Labor Day.

Lake Malone is part of Muhlenberg County, which is dry. The inn has a members-only 50-seat private club called Phil's Place. [Local members can sponsor guests for a visit.] Phil's Place consists of an antique bar that Phil Everly was given during a tour of England, Everly's Lake Malone wine ($12 a bottle), a jukebox filled with George Jones, Righteous Brothers and Everly Brothers CDs and a small stage where Don Everly sometimes performs with his Dead Cowboys. His band includes guitarist Albert Lee and Nashville steel guitar legend Buddy Emmons.

"We play country, rock, whatever we feel like," Everly said. "Sometimes we'll play Blondie songs. There's nothing really new with the Everly Brothers. Phil is on the West Coast, and I'm down here. It's been like that for the past 20 years. Our musical tastes have changed to where we can enjoy the Everly Brothers, but I'm at the roots of country music now. Give me a Brother Oswald album, Grandpa Jones or early Roy Acuff. It amuses me and amazes me at the same time. That's where my heart is now."

Everly said more and more musicians are discovering Everly's Lake Malone Inn, and he hopes eventually to have regular live shows and songwriter-in-the-round sessions. "A lot of music came out of that county," Everly said. "Merle Travis' songs like '16 Tons' and 'Dark as a Dungeon' were about the coal mines in Muhlenberg County. And they did haul away most of the coal."

Chicagoan John Prine popularized Muhlenberg County in his 1971 hit "Paradise": *". . . And daddy won't you take me back to Muhlenberg County/Down by the Green River where Paradise lay/Well I'm sorry my son, but you're too late in asking/Mr. Peabody's coal train has hauled it away. . . ."* Prine is a regular at the Everly Brothers Homecoming concerts.

Everly said, "When I was a kid, all the mines were underground. They didn't have the strip mines yet. Those started in the early '50s. It's changed the look of that place. They didn't strip-mine the part of Kentucky around Lake Malone because the limestone was too close to the ground.

"When they strip-mined the rest of the area, they left little strips of trees alongside the road. But you walk through those trees, it looks like a moonscape. It really devastated that part of the world. John [Prine] has always said that, too."

Everly remembered the world's largest steam shovel, which Prine also wrote about in "Paradise": *". . . Then the coal company came with the world's largest shovel/And they tortured the timber and stripped all the land/Well, they dug for their coal till the land was forsaken/Then they wrote it all down as the progress of man. . . ."*

Everly said, "They had two of those steam shovels out there, and I was hoping they would turn them into a museum. It was an extraordinary piece of equipment. And they buried them. They dug a hole deep enough for it because they couldn't move it. It was like 10, 20 stories tall. My cousin over there, who is a

Photo courtesy of Everly's Lake Malone Inn.

Don Everly's Lake Malone Inn.

preacher, often thought about starting a thing called 'Coal Town' that would show what the mines were like.

"You just don't expect to find a place like this in Muhlenberg County," Everly said with a laugh. "I tell people I've got this little hotel in Muhlenberg County, Ky., and they think it's a little motel with a gravel driveway. I invited my science teacher from junior high school. They drove in from Des Moines, Iowa. They thought it was going to be a cabin in the woods.

"When you get here, it's a pleasant surprise."

To get to Everly's Lake Malone Inn, take Interstate 65 south through Louisville, Ky. At Elizabethtown, take the Western Kentucky Parkway west to Exit 68. Head south on 431 to Dunmor. For reservations, call (800) 264-3602.

May 2, 1999

Index

Lake Claremont Press Books in Print

A Native's Guide to Chicago, 3rd Edition
by Sharon Woodhouse, with South Side coverage by Mary McNulty

Literary Chicago: A Book Lover's Tour of the Windy City
by Greg Holden

Hollywood on Lake Michigan: 100 Years of Chicago and the Movies
by Arnie Bernstein. with foreword by *Soul Food*
writer/director, George Tillman, Jr.

"The Movies Are": Carl Sandburg's Film Reviews and Essays, 1920-1928
edited and with historical commentary by Arnie Bernstein,
introduction by Roger Ebert

The Chicago River: A Natural and Unnatural History
by Libby Hill

Graveyards of Chicago:
The People, History, Art, and Lore of Cook County Cemeteries
by Matt Hucke and Ursula Bielski

Chicago Haunts: Ghostlore of the Windy City
by Ursula Bielski

More Chicago Haunts: Scenes from Myth and Memory
by Ursula Bielski

Haunted Michigan: Recent Encounters with Active Spirits
by Rev. Gerald S. Hunter

Forthcoming Titles

A Native's Guide to Northwest Indiana
by Mark Skertic (Spring 2001)

Great Chicago Fires
by David Cowan (Spring 2001)

Lake Claremont Press is . . .

Regional History

The Chicago River: A Natural and Unnatural History
by Libby Hill

When French explorers Jolliet and Marquette used the Chicago portage on their return trip from the Mississippi River, the Chicago River was but a humble, even sluggish, stream in the right place at the right time. That's the story of the making of Chicago. This is the *other* story—the story of the making and perpetual re-making of a river by everything from geological forces to the interventions of an emerging and mighty city. Author Libby Hill brings together years of original research and the contributions of dozens of experts to tell the Chicago River's epic tale—and intimate biography—from its conception in prehistoric glaciers to the glorious rejuvenation it's undergoing today, and every exciting episode in between. As seen in the *Chicago Tribune*, *Chicago Sun-Times*, Chicago *Reader*, and Lerner newspapers, and heard on WGN radio.
1-893121-02-X, August 2000, softcover, 302 pages, 78 maps and photos, $16.95

"The Movies Are":
Carl Sandburg's Film Reviews and Essays, 1920-1928
edited and with historical commentary by Arnie Bernstein
introduction by Roger Ebert

During the 1920s, a time when movies were still considered light entertainment by most newspapers, the *Chicago Daily News* gave Sandburg a unique forum to express his views on the burgeoning film arts. *"The Movies Are"* compiles hundreds of Sandburg's writings on film including reviews, interviews, and his earliest published essays of Abraham Lincoln—which he wrote for his film column. Take a new look at one of Hollywood's most exciting periods through the critical perspective of one of America's great writers. A passionate film advocate, Sandburg early on grasped and delighted in the many possibilities for the new motion picture medium, be they creative, humanitarian, or technological; intellectual, low-brow, or merely novel. In doing so, he began defining the scope and sophistication of future film criticism.
1-893121-05-4, October 2000, softcover, 397 pages, 72 photos, $17.95

Hollywood on Lake Michigan:
100 Years of Chicago and the Movies
by Arnie Bernstein
with foreword by *Soul Food* writer/director George Tillman, Jr.
This engaging history and street guide finally gives Chicago and Chicagoans due credit for their prominent role in moviemaking history, from the silent era to the present. With trivia, special articles, historic and contemporary photos, film profiles, anecdotes, and exclusive interviews with dozens of personalities, including Studs Terkel, Roger Ebert, Gene Siskel, Dennis Franz, Harold Ramis, Joe Mantegna, Bill Kurtis, Irma Hall, and Tim Kazurinsky. Winner of an American Regional History Publishing Award: 1st Place—Midwest!
0-9642426-2-1, December 1998, softcover, 364 pages, 80 photos, $15

Literary Chicago
by Greg Holden, with foreword by Harry Mark Petrakis
Chicago has attracted and nurtured writers, editors, publishers, and book lovers for more than a century and continues to be one of the nation's liveliest literary cities. Join Holden as he journeys through the streets, people, ideas, events, and culture of Chicagoland's historic and contemporary literary world! Includes 11 detailed walking tours.
1-893121-01-1, November 2000, softcover, maps, photos, $15.95

Ghosts and Graveyards

Chicago Haunts: Ghostlore of the Windy City
by Ursula Bielski
From ruthless gangsters to restless mail order kings, from the Fort Dearborn Massacre to the St. Valentine's Day Massacre, the phantom remains of the passionate people and volatile events of Chicago history have made the Second City second to none in the annals of American ghostlore. Bielski captures over 160 years of this haunted history with her unique blend of lively storytelling, in-depth historical research, exclusive interviews, and insights from parapsychology. Called "a masterpiece of the genre," "a must-read," and "an absolutely first-rate-book" by reviewers, *Chicago Haunts* continues to earn the praise of critics and readers alike.
0-9642426-7-2, October 1998, softcover, 277 pages, 29 photos, $15

More Chicago Haunts: Scenes from Myth and Memory
by Ursula Bielski

Chicago. A town with a past. A people haunted by its history in more ways than one. A "windy city" with tales to tell . . . Bielski is back with more history, more legends, and more hauntings, including the personal scary stories of *Chicago Haunts* readers. Read about the Ovaltine factory haunts, the Monster of 63rd Street's castle of terror, phantom blueberry muffins, Wrigley Field ghosts, Al Capone's yacht, and 45 other glimpses into the haunted myths and memories of Chicagoland.

1-893121-04-6, October 2000, 312 pages, 50 photos, $15

Haunted Michigan: Recent Encounters with Active Spirits
by Rev. Gerald S. Hunter

Within these pages you will not find ancient ghost stories or legendary accounts of spooky events of long ago. Instead, Rev. Hunter shares his investigations into modern ghost stories— active hauntings that continue to this day. *Haunted Michigan* uncovers a chilling array of local spirits in its tour of the two peninsulas. Wherever you may dwell, these tales of Michigan's ethereal residents are sure to make you think about the possibility, as Hunter suggests, that we are not always alone within the confines of our happy homes. So wait until the shadows of night have cast a pall over the serenity of your peaceful abode. Then snuggle into your favorite overstuffed chair, pour yourself a bracing bolt of 80-proof courage, and open your mind to the presence of the paranormal which surrounds us all.

1-893121-10-0, October 2000, 207 pages, 20 photos, $12.95

Graveyards of Chicago:
The People, History, Art, and Lore of Cook County Cemeteries
by Matt Hucke and Ursula Bielski

Like the livelier neighborhoods that surround them, Chicago's cemeteries are often crowded, sometimes weary, ever-sophisti-cated, and full of secrets. They are home not only to thousands of individuals who fashioned the city's singular culture and character, but also to impressive displays of art and architecture, landscaping and limestone, egoism and ethnic pride, and the constant reminder that although physical life must end for us all, personal note—and notoriety—last forever.

0-9642426-4-8, November 1999, softcover, 228 pages, 168 photos, $15

Guidebooks by Locals

A Native's Guide to Chicago, 3rd Edition
by Sharon Woodhouse,
with expanded South Side coverage by Mary McNulty
Venture into the nooks and crannies of everyday Chicago with this unique, comprehensive budget guide. Over 400 pages of free, inexpensive, and unusual things to do in the Windy City make this the perfect resource for tourists, business travelers, visiting suburbanites, and resident Chicagoans. Called the "best guidebook for locals" in *New City*'s 1999 "Best of Chicago" issue!
0-9642426-0-5, January 1999, softcover, 438 pages, photos, maps, $12.95

A Native's Guide to Chicago's Northern Suburbs
by Jason Fargo
0-9642426-8-0, June 1999, softcover, 207 pages, photos, maps, $12.95

A Native's Guide to Chicago's Northwest Suburbs
by Martin A. Bartels
1-893121-00-3, August 1999, softcover, 315 pages, photos, maps, $12.95

A Native's Guide to Chicago's Western Suburbs
by Laura Mazzuca Toops and John W. Toops, Jr.
0-9642426-6-4, August 1999, softcover, 210 pages, photos, maps, $12.95

A Native's Guide to Chicago's South Suburbs
by Christina Bultinck and Christy Johnston-Czarnecki
0-9642426-1-3, June 1999, softcover, 242 pages, photos, maps, $12.95

A Native's Guide to Northwest Indiana
by Mark Skertic
1-893121-08-9, Spring 2001, softcover

Full of the fascinating sights, places, stories, and facts that sometimes even locals don't know about, the *Native's Guide* series equips you with everything you need to enjoy and navigate Chicago and its suburbs like a true insider.

Order directly from Lake Claremont Press...

Ticket to Everywhere _____ @ $15.95 = _____
The Chicago River _____ @ $16.95 = _____
"The Movies Are" _____ @ $17.95 = _____
Hollywood on Lake Michigan _____ @ $15.00 = _____
Graveyards of Chicago _____ @ $15.00 = _____
Chicago Haunts _____ @ $15.00 = _____
More Chicago Haunts _____ @ $15.00 = _____
Haunted Michigan _____ @ $12.95 = _____
A Native's Guide to Chicago _____ @ $12.95 = _____
_____ _____ @ $ _____ = _____
_____ _____ @ $ _____ = _____

Subtotal: _____
Less Discount: _____
New Subtotal: _____
8.75% Sales Tax for Illinois Residents: _____
Shipping: _____
TOTAL: _____

Name_____

Address_____

City_____**State**_____**Zip**_____

Please enclose check, money order, or credit card information.

Visa/Mastercard#_____**Exp.** _____.

Signature_____

Discounts when you order multiple copies!
2 books—10% off total, 3-4 books—20% off,
5-9 books—25% off, 10+ books—40% off

—Low shipping fees—
$2 for the first book and $.50 for each additional book, with a maximum charge of $5.

Order by mail, phone, fax, or e-mail.
All of our books have a no-hassle, 100% money back guarantee.

LAKE CLAREMONT PRESS

4650 N. Rockwell St.
Chicago, IL 60625
773/583-7800
773/583-7877 (fax)
lcp@lakeclaremont.com
www.lakeclaremont.com

About the Author

Photo by Lisa Day.

Dave Hoekstra at Rockford, Michigan's The Corner Bar,
home to the Hot Dog Hall of Fame.

DAVE HOEKSTRA has been a *Chicago Sun-Times* staff writer since
1985. He is also a contributing writer for *Playboy* magazine and
the Chicago *Reader*, and has been a contributing editor for
Chicago magazine. He won a 1987 Chicago Newspaper Guild
Stick-O-Type Award for Column Writing. His landscape photography was awarded entry in the "Route 66 Revisited" multi-
media exhibition, 1992, at the Red Mesa Arts Center, Gallup,
N.M. and Near Northwest Arts Council Gallery, Chicago, Ill.

He has traveled Route 66 extensively, driving the entire road
(by himself) in 1992. He also has boated down the Mississippi
River from Illinois to New Orleans, La., and follows the gosh-dang
Chicago Cubs all over the country. Hoekstra lives in Chicago.